Surviving Evil

CIA Mind Control Experiments in Vermont

Karen Wetmore

Manitou Communications, Inc.

1701 Gateway, Suite 349
Richardson, TX 75080
Phone: 1-800-572-9588, FAX: 972-918-9069
rossinst@rossinst.com, www.rossinst.com, www.manitoucommunications.com

---

Library of Congress Cataloging-in-Publication Data: 2014930477

Wetmore, Karen
Surviving Evil: CIA Mind Control Experiments in Vermont

ISBN 10: 0-9815376-3-4
ISBN-13: 978-0-9815376-3-4

1.Mind Control 2. Central Intelligence Agency 3. Vermont State Hospital

---

TABLE OF CONTENTS

APPENDICES: THE EVIDENCE

Dedicated To the Memory of

Phillip Harold Cram

1951-1969

"I will miss you forever."

ACKNOWLEDGEMENTS

A special thank you to Kathy Judge: there is no doubt in my mind that without your help, I literally would not have survived. When I lost all hope, you held it for me until I could hold it once again for myself. You believed in me when I could no longer believe in myself. You trusted in me and showed me that I could take the risk to trust again. You showed me how to accept all that has happened in my life and be able to live despite it all. Thank you for being there when I needed you the most and helping me pull my life out of chaos. I will be grateful to you always.

Thank you, Dr. Colin Ross for encouraging me to write this book. Your advice on CIA drug and mind control programs has been invaluable. Thanks for answering my many questions related to MKULTRA. Your support is much appreciated.

Thanks to my father, George Wetmore, I miss you Dad, and my mother Dorothy Wetmore, who encouraged me to write a book, my brother George (Kip) Wetmore, Sue Wetmore, Jeffery Wetmore, Christopher Wetmore and "King." I love you all.

Thanks to Dr. Thomas Fox. I wish you were here.

Thanks to Dr. Judy Nepvue, Dr. Alan Shirks, Copley Hospital, Rutland Regional Medical Center, (RRMC), and the 1981 nursing staff, Copley Hospital, especially Anna Anderson, Carol Leonard and Cheryl.

Thanks to RRMC psychiatric unit nursing staff: Lynne Colville, Mary Patten, Rosemary Johnson, Tammy, Lesa, Susan and Marlene.

Thanks to Karen Esty, Linda Khoury, Sylvia Boyea, Viola Littlejohn, Henry and Joyce LaVanway, Craig and Peggy Angstadt, Jane Quigley, Marianne, Jules and Mary Denis, Gene and Sally Pagano, John Fillioe, Phil Fass, Jane Youngbaer, Rep. Anne Donahue, Rep. Michael Fisher, Deana Weidman, Ezra The Book Finder and Professor Sandra Coyle (for helping me polish my writing skills in your classroom).

Thanks to Senator Bernie Sanders and Burlington office staff, Jim Rader and Gretchen Bailey, Vermont State Trooper Sharon, my former neighbor, Waterbury Center, Vermont (1981), Vermont State Police, Middlesex barracks (1971-1972).

Thanks to, Bob Pratt, Randal Smathers, Editor *Rutland Herald*, Louis Porter, former Chief Vermont Press Bureau, Associated Press, David Moats, *Rutland Herald* Editorial Page Editor, the *Rutland Herald*, the *Barre-Times Argus*, the Vermont Press Bureau, Blink Films, Smithsonian Channel, Counterpoint Newspaper, "Valtin," Jeff Kaye (for posting the November 30, 2008 *Rutland Herald* article).

Thanks to Jimmy Judge and Peter and Sharon Anderson, and June Austin and Pam Greeno Westcott for helping me fill in childhood memories. I miss you Pam.

Special thanks go to the people who spoke with me on a confidential basis. Thank you for your valuable information.

FOREWORD

People contact me by letter and email to describe ongoing harassment with non-lethal weapons, mind control techniques and intimidation. Many of their stories sound plausible and are told coherently, in detail, and with a context that makes sense of them. This may be a prior husband or boyfriend in the military, prior employment in the intelligence community, working for a defense contractor, or something similar. But, no matter how plausible, none of the accounts can be proven or disproven.

Karen Wetmore's story is completely different. I have never met anyone who has worked so hard for so long to obtain solid documentation of her allegations of mind control experimentation. As you will read in these pages, Karen filed numerous Freedom of Information Act requests with the CIA and military, corresponded with numerous officials and politicians, and read a great deal of background material. Piece by piece, she assembled her facts, until she had documented a large network of professional connections, relationships and contacts between her own psychiatrists and the network of CIA and military mind control doctors.

Karen's claim that she was a victim of CIA mind control experimentation is backed up by extensive circumstantial evidence – enough to establish her case in a court of law, in my opinion – but also by direct evidence and documents. As she explains, the starting point was discovering the name of Robert W. Hyde, M.D. in her medical records. I was already aware of Dr. Hyde. He was cleared at TOP SECRET by the CIA as a contractor in its mind control program, MKULTRA. He received $148,515.00 from the CIA in 1955 under MKULTRA Subproject 10 for LSD experiments. He received $5,580.00 in 1961 under MKULTRA Subproject 61, and $24,500.00 in 1956 under MKULTRA Subproject 66.

In 1955, Dr. Hyde published a paper in the *American Journal of Psychiatry*, volume 111, pages 881-895, entitled, “Experimental

Psychiatry II. Clinical and Physio-chemical observations in experimental psychosis." This paper is about LSD experiments. Dr. Hyde's coauthors were Max Rinkel, M.D., Harry Solomon, M.D., and Hudson Hoagland, Ph.D. Dr. Hoagland worked at the Worcester Foundation for Experimental Biology, which was the site for MKULTRA Subproject 8, funded in 1953 for $39,500.00 to support LSD experiments. Dr. Hyde was the contractor on Subproject 8.

Other coauthors of Dr. Hyde's on published papers include J. Sanbourne Bockoven, M.D., Jackson DeShon, M.D., and Harry C. Solomon, M.D. Keep an eye out for these names as you read Karen's story. In 1958, a book was published entitled, *Chemical Concepts of Psychosis*, edited by Max Rinkel and Herman Denber. The book is the Proceedings of the Symposium on Chemical Concepts of Psychosis held at the Second International Congress of Psychiatry in Zurich, Switzerland, September 1-7, 1957.

Participants and contributors to the Symposium include the following documented CIA and military mind control contractors and LSD researchers: Robert Heath, Hudson Hoagland, Paul Hoch, Abraham Hoffer, Albert Hofmann, Amedeo Marrazzi, and Humphrey Osmond. This is the network of doctors who conducted LSD, brain electrode implant and other experiments for the CIA and US military during the time period that Karen Wetmore was being experimented on in hospitals in Vermont. Paul Hoch, M.D. killed tennis pro, Harold Blauer, with an experimental dose of mescaline provided by the US Army at New York State Psychiatric Institute on January 8, 1953. Harold Blauer was never told he was receiving a hallucinogen. His family received an award of $18,000.00 on June 17, 1955 from the New York Court of Claims.

We know for a fact that CIA and military mind control contractors killed at least one person with mescaline in the 1950's. What are the odds that Harold Blauer was the only one who died? Keep this in mind as you read Karen Wetmore's account of the hundreds of deaths at Vermont State Hospital during the time period of MKULTRA, MKSEARCH and other CIA mind control programs.

The involvement of Vermont State Hospital and Vermont School of Medicine in CIA mind control experiments, which was extensive and lasted over a long period of time, has never been documented before. This is original investigative work by Karen Wetmore. Additionally, she is the first person to bring the existence of the CIA's MKCOTTON program to public attention. I filed a Freedom of Information act request about MKCOTTON as a result of Karen's research, but the CIA told me they had no additional information on it.

Karen Wetmore is a courageous survivor and investigator. She has overcome many severe obstacles in order to get her story down on paper. Read it, and pray for those who died.

Colin A. Ross, M.D.
December, 2013

INTRODUCTION

Before I obtained my medical records from the Vermont State Hospital and the Medical Center Hospital of Vermont, I never could have imagined that the information in those records would lead me straight to the CIA drug and mind control research known as MKULTRA.

My medical records contain shocking details of drug and mind control research including methods employed by CIA known as Special Interrogations. The content of the records would lead to a lawsuit filed by me in 1998 and they would give me the name of a famous CIA Technical Services Division employee and MKULTRA researcher, Dr. Robert W. Hyde. Hyde was involved in my treatment in VSH and he was Director of Psychiatric Research at the VSH during the years I was a patient there. I would go on to identify numerous other CIA researchers, CIA sites, cover funding groups and CIA methods, all of which were operational at VSH-UVM in the 1950's, 1960's and 1970's.

Although CIA drug and mind control programs were conducted using names like BLUEBIRD, ARTICHOKE and Project OFTEN, for convenience, the CIA research will be referred to as MKULTRA unless specifically noted.

For fifteen years, I obtained original source documents that prove not only that Vermont institutions conducted CIA experiments but that a massive, coordinated state and federal cover-up is ongoing, decades after the 1977 Senate hearings on MKULTRA were held. The 1977 hearings never mentioned Vermont or Robert Hyde and at the closing of those hearings, Americans were told that the important details of the secret experiments had been told. My investigation shows otherwise.

While I was going through the process of integration for multiple personality disorder with my therapist Kathy Judge, who I began seeing in 1988, I filed a lawsuit against the State of Vermont and the Vermont hospitals after the State of Vermont refused to provide me with copies of my VSH medical records. Even after I obtained a lawyer, the State was not forthcoming with my medical records. When I finally did receive the incomplete copy of the VSH records and read the contents, I learned that not only did I have far more memory loss than I realized but that I had been subjected to experiments without my knowledge or consent. Robert Hyde's name in my records would lead me on a fifteen-year search for the truth about what happened to me and to thousands of other unwitting VSH patients.

An almost unbelievable set of circumstances began to unfold after the filing of the lawsuit. The phone company informed me that my telephone was wiretapped. They would continue to tell me this over the next fifteen years. Mail, including certified mail sent to a United States Senator would be stolen. I had frequent encounters on the street, in stores and in traffic with strangers who appeared to go out of their way to insure that I saw them. One of these strangers was identified as an undercover federal agent and the car license plates of several other strangers led back to the federal government. I would be harassed until finally I vehemently complained to my Senator and to the FBI.

In 2008, I was the subject of a front page *Rutland Herald* article on the Vermont CIA experiments and I participated in a 2009 documentary on the CIA research for the Smithsonian channel.

My story is extreme. The events and circumstances that I was caught up in beginning at the age of thirteen when I was hospitalized the first time would remain a mystery to me for over three decades. The early childhood trauma I was exposed to and that produced the amnesia and the MPD would not be known by me or by any caregiver until the mid-1990's. VSH and Burlington hospital doctors knew my diagnosis in the 1960's but kept the information from me, my family and from subsequent caregivers. The Vermont CIA experiments stole my chances at an early age to live a normal life, but I was not the only VSH patient to have been subjected to unwitting research.

I obtained documents that not only show that thousands of other VSH patients were used and abused in the covert experiments but that during the twenty-year period when Vermont institutions conducted the CIA drug and mind control research, almost 3,000 VSH patients died - as many as 186 a year, year after year for twenty years in a row until the CIA's MKULTRA was shut down in 1973. VSH death rates immediately returned to a more normal level beginning in 1973 and without the federal funds provided by agencies who admitted wittingly funding the secret CIA MKULTRA research in hospitals all across the country, VSH never again conducted active patient research. Were CIA terminal experiments conducted at VSH? Those who know the answer to this question aren't willing to talk. Federal officials, who have the power to investigate, won't.

This book details my search for the truth about what happened to me and to thousands of other VSH patients during the CIA experiments in the 1950's, 1960's and 1970's in Vermont. Anyone who has read my medical records cannot explain how I survived. My therapist was never sure I would survive integration for MPD. I've had two heart attacks. I have three autoimmune diseases, macular degeneration, PTSD, chronic depression, an anxiety disorder, and schizoid tendencies and although an integrated multiple, I remain dissociative for certain stressors. But I survived.

Not only did I survive, I uncovered the dark, secret history of brutal CIA experiments that no one in the CIA, the State of Vermont or the federal government ever dreamed anyone would discover. Even now, fifteen years after finding the CIA in Vermont, it's still hard for me to comprehend.

Vermont, the place I was born and have lived my life. Vermont, the scenic Green Mountain state, with its majestic mountains, its beautiful autumn foliage and its liberal social attitude. Vermont, the very last place anyone would imagine CIA drug and mind control research. It's apparent to me that CIA thought that Vermont was the perfect place to conduct its research without fear and with impunity.

I survived the evil of the Vermont CIA experiments. Many, I fear did not.

1
MEDICAL RECORDS – WETMORE v. STATE OF VERMONT, 1997-2002

Eight years after beginning therapy for multiple personality disorder and beginning the integration process, Kathy suggested that I try to write a narrative of my life. I was struggling in the fall of 1997 after an intense period of integration. I had been multiple for over four decades and I was feeling increasingly overwhelmed by what I tried to explain to Kathy as the intrusion of some other terrible world. It made no sense to me or to her but she hoped that writing the narrative might offer some relief.

I began to write about my life. I had learned prior to integration that I had several violent early childhood traumas. Because of the amnesia I suffered as a four-year old child, I was never able to tell anyone what had happened to me, and the memory loss kept me from having any conscious awareness of the traumas.

When I got to the Vermont State Hospital (VSH) years, the narrative came to a screeching halt. I realized that I didn't have much memory about my experiences while a patient in VSH. I wasn't totally without memory, but the memories I had didn't tell me much at all about my time in the hospital. Kathy and I talked it over and she suggested that I contact the VSH and the Burlington hospitals I was also a patient in as a teenager to request copies of my medical records.

Although doctors had asked me for my permission to obtain my medical records in the past, I always refused to allow them to do so. I believed that the information in the records would show that I had been the terrible monster that I believed myself to have been while a patient in VSH. I thought that anyone who saw the records wouldn't want anything to do with me. But after going through eight years of therapy with Kathy and knowing that no matter what, I really could trust her, I decided to go ahead and obtain my records.

I phoned the Fletcher Allen Hospital in Burlington and asked for copies of my medical records. There was no problem. I then called the VSH to request my records. The woman on the phone was hostile and insulting. I couldn't believe it when she refused to allow me to obtain copies of my medical records. I reminded her that I had a right to obtain my records, but she continued to refuse to send them to me. I was furious.

The spotty memories I had about my time in VSH were memories I tried to keep out of my head. My entire life had been impacted by my feelings about having been locked up as a thirteen-year old child. I felt that I had been treated like an animal in VSH and the behavior of the VSH personnel on the phone triggered feelings of anger.

I phoned the Vermont Commissioner of Mental Health office to complain about the VSH personnel who refused to allow me to obtain my records. Much to my surprise, the response I got from the Commissioner's office staff was the same. I was flatly refused access to my medical records.

It was always difficult for me to explain how my VSH hospitalizations changed my life forever. Nothing was ever the same. As a thirteen-year old child, I was thrust into a strange and frightening world of madness and cruelty. My life after the first hospitalization was filled with shame, fear and the ever-present sting of the stigma I carried for years. I was never able to return to school and I watched my friends continue with their lives while I remained on the sidelines. I was the crazy girl. I was the one who had been in the state mental hospital. I became lonely and isolated.

I never believed that I belonged in VSH. I knew that I was sick, but it appeared that the doctors didn't know any more about what was wrong with me after my months in VSH than before I was a patient. I remembered being treated badly by the doctors in both hospitals but I could never explain exactly why or what had happened to cause them to treat me so harshly. I believed it must have been something about me that caused me to be held in VSH for so long. Because the memories I had were so broken and spotty, I was never really sure what had taken place. I never spoke about my time in VSH and I carried a deep, lingering fear of returning to the hospital. My entire life had been shaped by my experiences in VSH and in 1997 I was determined to not only find the truth about what had happened to me, but I wasn't going to be treated like a second class citizen by the State of Vermont again

I fumed for hours after my phone conversations with the State. Terrible images filled my mind. I recalled the Burlington doctors shouting at me, threatening me and demanding that I stop screaming. No matter how I had tried to stop screaming, I couldn't. I didn't know why. Surely, I must have been crazy.

Images of my father sitting beside me in the ambulance on the way to VSH in 1965 flooded my mind. Dad tried to reassure me that everything would be okay as I lay strapped to a stretcher, sobbing. I drifted in and out of consciousness that night in 1965 but I always remembered seeing my father cry. It was the only time I ever saw my father cry.

Images of lying on the floor of a seclusion room watching disembodied eyes staring at me through a slit in the locked door crept into my mind. People dressed in white suddenly rushed into the seclusion room, grabbed me, threw me face first against the wall and put me in a straightjacket. They never spoke to me. As they tied my arms and legs to the bed, I was terrified. At thirteen my life had become a nightmare from which there was no escape. There was no one to help me.

In the fall of 1997, I was determined to fight back against the State of Vermont. I took out a phone book and began to look for a lawyer. The first few numbers I called, the lawyers were either not there or not available to take another case. The first lawyer who answered the phone and was willing to meet with me was Alan George. I met with him and after talking for a couple of hours, he agreed to help me obtain my medical records.

Alan immediately encountered problems with the State of Vermont. They continued to refuse to relinquish my medical records. Vermont's Attorney General's office offered excuse after excuse as letters and phone calls were traded for weeks. I asked Alan if maybe the court could help, but he indicated that lawyers preferred to work things out between themselves if possible. My lawyer wasn't having any better luck than I had.

Finally after weeks of back and forth communication, the State agreed to provide me with copies of my medical records. Upon hearing the news from Alan, I grew uneasy. What would I read about myself in those records? What awful things would they say about me? Would they confirm that I was the monster that I had believed myself to be?

I always knew that I had been in a seclusion room on a locked back ward when I was eighteen years old. I knew that I had been in leather wristlets. I knew that I had been kept in a straightjacket. I just never knew or even thought about how long I was kept in those conditions. No subsequent caregiver, even Kathy, had ever asked me directly about my time in a straightjacket. I have no way of knowing if I would have remembered anything about it even if someone had asked me. To this day, I only have fragmented memories of that time. I also knew that I had been violent toward myself and toward the VSH staff in 1970-1971. I wondered how Kathy would feel about me after she read the record and even more troubling for me, was the question of how I would feel about myself.

When Kathy learned that I had retained a lawyer she was understandably concerned. It hadn't been a year since I underwent the integration process and I was still fragile. She had suggested that I get my records and believed that the information would help in my therapy. Kathy was as surprised by the unwillingness of the State to provide me with my records as was everyone else. The last thing she wanted for me was to become involved in a battle with the State of Vermont.

Alan called me when the records arrived at his office. He remarked that he didn't see anything out of the ordinary in the records. Another lawyer working with Alan, Kim Hayden, dropped the records off at my apartment. I was trembling as I began to read.

The records were not in chronological order and were difficult to follow. I spread them out on the living room floor, stacking doctor's orders, nurse's notes, drug charts and other sections in the proper places. As I began to locate the 1970-1971 seclusion room charts, my heart began to pound

The charts were dated, daily logs of my time in seclusion. At the top of every page was printed, "Seclusion, wristlets and full straightjacket." I stared at the pile of seclusion charts stacked on my carpet. The seclusion began in October, 1970, and went on almost without interruption until June 21, 1971. I couldn't believe what I was looking at. How could I not have known this? How could I have been kept like this for almost nine months and not have remembered? I was horrified at both the conditions I was kept in and by the realization that I could not remember a substantial portion of my own life.

I stared at drug charts that showed I was given massive amounts of multiple drugs, sometime seven or eight drugs at a time. I was frequently given placebos. There were electric shock treatment charts. I was administered vaginal suppositories for months while tied to a bed in seclusion. There was no indication in the records as to the reason why the suppositories were ordered. Despite warnings printed at the top of each page of the drug charts indicating that I was allergic to phenothiazine drugs, I was given the drugs anyway.

I stared at letters to and from the VSH Superintendent, George Brooks. There were letters to and from the Mental Health Commissioner, Jonathan Leopold. There were letters from the Rutland court where I had been involuntarily committed in 1965 and in 1970. I read letters my mother wrote to George Brooks and to Leopold where she pleaded with them not to treat me harshly. She tried to schedule a meeting with VSH doctors and she bitterly complained about Dr. Otto Havas. I was overwhelmed by what I was reading. What did it all mean?

I shared my alarm with Kathy, who was understandably shocked by the things I told her were in my records. The next day I met with Alan and Kim. They had more closely read the records and quickly determined that not only had my civil and Constitutional rights been violated, but that I had been experimented on. There was going to be a lawsuit. Alan needed an expert medical witness and I suggested a former psychiatrist I had successfully worked with, Dr. Thomas Fox. Tom had recently become Commissioner of Mental Health in New Hampshire after leaving his position as Director of Psychiatry at the Rutland Regional Medical Center.

I spoke with Tom on the phone and Alan sent him a copy of my medical records. It didn't take long before Tom agreed to be an expert witness. Kathy had known Tom for a long time and my opinion of him couldn't have been better. Tom had been one of the very few psychiatrists I had ever had who actually helped me. I trusted him.

The 1965 and 1971 Medical Center Hospital records contained disturbing and confusing information as well. In 1965, despite being warned by doctors called in to consult on my condition to immediately stop the phenothiazine drugs, the Fletcher psychiatrists not only continued to give me the drugs I was allergic to, they increased the dose. There were records showing I was given frequent massive doses of Sodium Amytal, a drug commonly used in the 1960's as a "truth drug."

I was transferred from almost seven months in seclusion in VSH to the neurology unit of the Degoesbriand Hospital, a part of the Medical Center. There were numerous EEG's conducted and one in particular stood out. During the EEG, conducted only days after I was admitted, I was given

1800 mg of a drug called Metrazol. It was obvious in reading the chart notes that the drug caused me to hallucinate and experience substantial physical and psychological pain. At one point during the administration of Metrazol, I accused the doctors of causing my distress and I accurately blamed the drug for the hallucinations. It would take me months to learn what Metrazol was used for and who routinely used it. It was apparent that the Burlington hospitals had also engaged in experiments without my knowledge or consent. I was simply stunned.

In my 1970 VSH records was a letter to my mother from Mental Health Commissioner Leopold. In it he named several psychiatrists who were involved in my treatment: Dr. George Brooks, Dr. H. P. LaQueur, Dr. Otto Havas, Dr. Karl Trieal and Dr. Robert W. Hyde. I didn't recognize LaQueur or Hyde's names. After discovering that I had been used in experiments, I decided to learn all that I could about the VSH and about the doctors who worked there. I was able to obtain two books written about VSH. I also obtained information about the Human Radiation Experiments, a program conducted during the time when I was in VSH. Not only was Robert Hyde's name in the list of participants, but so was the University of Vermont College of Medicine.

Kathy helped me to try to identify Hyde and LaQueur and it didn't take long before we both realized that the same Robert W. Hyde who was Director of Research at VSH was the very same Robert W. Hyde who worked for the Central Intelligence Agency and conducted extensive drug and mind control experiments. The revelation was beyond shocking for me, for Kathy and for my lawyers.

Dr. Robert W. Hyde was born in Vermont and graduated from the University of Vermont College of Medicine. He was an only child. He and his wife Elizabeth had no children. He worked at the Marine Hospital in Louisiana and when WWII broke out he became an officer with the rank of Lt. Colonel. Hyde became Assistant Superintendent at Boston Psychopathic Hospital and went on to become Superintendent at Butler Hospital in Rhode Island. By 1964, Hyde was Assistant Commissioner of Mental Health in Vermont and became Director of Research at VSH. Hyde was on site at VSH the entire time I was a patient, 1965-1972. Hyde died in 1976, one year after the Rockefeller hearings about CIA mind control experiments and one year before the Senate Select Committee hearings in 1977. Newspaper articles written during the 1977 hearings make only brief references to Hyde. In an article published on August 4, 1977 Hyde is described as being, "Vermont born...and having died in 1976."

Hyde began working for CIA in 1952. He tested LSD while at Boston and acted in the capacity of consultant to CIA covert mind control programs. According to John Marks in his book, *The Search For the Manchurian Candidate*, Hyde was one of the CIA's primary consultants. Hyde is connected to the major figures and the primary research sites during MKULTRA. I realized that I was looking at a major player in the secret CIA experiments.

It seemed curious to me that such a major figure in the CIA experiments would have remained relatively overlooked by journalists. As I began to search for information about Hyde, I would slowly begin to suspect that he wasn't overlooked, but that he had been carefully protected.

I have no memory of ever seeing or meeting Hyde. This would have been highly unlikely considering the amount of time I spent in VSH and because after I returned to VSH from four months in the Burlington psych unit, Baird 6, I spent over another year at the state hospital. Hyde would have been onsite. He ran a regional ward and would have walked the grounds and wards of the hospital just like all of the other VSH staff doctors. My records state that he was active in my treatment and fully informed about my case. My search for Robert Hyde would span the next fifteen years and would lead me to shocking evidence of the covert CIA research conducted in Vermont.

It's difficult to explain the emotions that I had after learning that I had been experimented on by the CIA. After the initial shock came deep-seated feelings of fear, anger and an almost indescribable feeling of having had the CIA traipse through my mind, doing God only knows what and leaving their footprints all over my unconscious. It was akin to a psychological rape as far as I was concerned. It took me some time to adjust to the new reality in my life and over the next few months the fear changed into anger and then changed into a fierce determination that I would find definitive proof that the CIA had conducted MKULTRA in Vermont. CIA entered my life as a thirteen-year old child and their tactics shattered my life for decades after. I made a very conscious decision that I would never again be afraid of the CIA.

One of the positive emotional effects that came with learning that I had been used in CIA experiments was that, for the first time since I was thirteen years old, I realized that it wasn't because of something terrible about me. It was because of the terrible things that were done to me. It was a life altering realization.

I located Dr. Colin Ross, internationally respected specialist in multiple personality disorder and recognized expert on the CIA drug and mind control programs. We spoke on the phone a couple of times and Alan sent him a copy of my medical records. They never arrived. Alan resent the records and they were received. Dr. Ross agreed that I had been an unwitting subject of drug and other experiments. He agreed to act as an expert witness in the lawsuit.

As much as I wanted to name the CIA as a defendant in the suit, I agreed with Alan when he said that to do so would tie me up in the courts for possibly decades. This had been the pattern of CIA when they faced lawsuits. I would also have had to be interviewed by a CIA psychiatrist. There was still uncertainty as to exactly what CIA had done to me and this would have potentially placed me in danger. The lawsuit would bring out the experiments but we left CIA out as a defendant.

I began to gather everything I could find on the CIA experiments. The 1961 book, *The Vermont Story: Schizophrenic Rehabilitation* written by VSH doctors was particularly helpful to me. The very first time I read it, I knew that the story being told in this book was a lie. Despite the fact that I couldn't remember most of what happened to me in VSH, I did remember the months and years I was there both before and after the 1970-1971 experiments. The kind, caring treatment described in this book was something I never saw and I was pretty sure no one else who had been a patient there had ever seen either.

The book's bibliography was filled with the names of other researchers who were cited as having participated in VSH research or had an influence on VSH research. I set about to identify these researchers. A second book written about VSH history, *Empty Beds*, was extremely valuable and not only identified Hyde as Director of Research, but it gave me many more names to search for. There were also research grants identified and the book contained information about VSH research and personnel exchange sites. One in particular stood out: Boston Psychopathic Hospital.

Boston Psychopathic was a primary CIA site where LSD and other experimental drugs were tested under MKULTRA. VSH had a long-term research and personnel exchange relationship with the Boston hospital. I doubted that this was a coincidence. I went on to learn that the University of Vermont College of Medicine conducted behavioral research under the Department of Energy Human Radiation experiments. A list of participants includes the UVM College of Medicine, the White River Junction, Vermont Veteran's Hospital and the Agricultural College in Burlington, Vermont. UVM doctors staffed the Burlington hospitals and their resident doctors rotated to VSH. I also learned that McGill University, the infamous site of Dr. Ewen Cameron's experiments, was a research and personnel partner of VSH, UVM and the Burlington hospitals. McGill doctors were onsite in the

Vermont hospitals during the MKULTRA years.

The declassified CIA documents I obtained from the National Security Archives included Hyde's MKULTRA subprojects 8, 10, 10a, 63 and 66. A key document related to Boston Psychopathic hospital identified researchers who belonged to CIA cover groups. Not only did some of these names match the VSH book bibliography, but VSH Assistant Superintendent Dr. H. P. LaQueur was identified as a member of the Society for Biological Psychiatry and the Manfred Sakel Foundation. LaQueur worked for the Office of Strategic Services (OSS) during WWII. OSS became CIA in 1947.

A few months after Alan became my lawyer, his partnership with the law firm broke up and he joined another law firm. The new firm was headed by a former Vermont Governor. I continued to search for information about the CIA. I understood that because the very first thing taken from me when I was a patient in VSH was my credibility, I would need to be able to prove through documents that CIA experiments were conducted in Vermont. Despite the fact the CIA wasn't named in the lawsuit, I was determined to find out the extent of their activities in Vermont and, hopefully, learn all of what they did to me and why.

My VSH records were clearly incomplete and no matter how Alan tried to get the rest of the records, the State denied that they existed. As I continued to gather information about the CIA, my lawyers began to scrutinize my VSH medical records. The information in them raised many questions and only months after obtaining the records unusual things began to happen.

I was committed to VSH in October 1965 at the age of thirteen and again in October 1970 at the age of eighteen. I was served commitment papers in October, 1970 and the record shows that I asked to be present at my court hearing. Dr. George Brooks, Superintendent of VSH, notified the Rutland court that I would be transported by VSH to the hearing.

One hour before I was scheduled to be transported to the Rutland court, records show that I was taken to a seclusion room. There is nothing in the records to explain why I was taken there. VSH and Brooks notified the court that I would not be able to attend the hearing and Brooks suggested that Judge Howard Douglas conduct the hearing without me. VSH staff psychiatrist Dr. Otto Havas sent a letter to the court describing my condition as "severely psychotic." There is nothing in my records to support the diagnosis made by Havas.

Two Vermont legal aid lawyers, Charles Currington and J. Frederick Strong, were appointed to represent me during the hearing but never contacted me. They never spoke with me and they never offered any evidence on my behalf. They never raised objections to the fact that although I had requested to be present at the hearing, I was not allowed to attend. The judge held the hearing without me.

Alan said that the hearing should have been rescheduled so that I could attend and it was clear to him that not only had my civil and Constitutional rights been violated but that I had been illegally committed. There was a discussion between my lawyers as to whether or not one of the counts in the lawsuit should include kidnapping. It was decided not to use the word kidnapping but the illegal commitment was part of the lawsuit.

It's apparent to me after reading the VSH records that VSH locked me in a seclusion room to prevent the judge from seeing or speaking with me. If the judge had spoken with me he would have quickly determined that I was not psychotic and very likely would not have committed me to VSH.

Given the extremes VSH went to insure that I would be involuntarily committed, it's clear that the CIA research was far more important to them than the law or my civil rights were. I asked Alan to find the legal aid lawyers who were appointed to protect my rights but he did not attempt to locate them.

Declassified CIA documents note that during MKULTRA, CIA

enlisted the help of judges, police, family doctors and others in positions of power in order to obtain subjects for their experiments. I will very likely never know how much if at all this played into what happened during the involuntary court commitment. The 1970 court hearing would not be the only time I experienced questionable behavior by the court.

Before Alan joined the new law firm, Kim began contacting McGill University in Montreal, Canada about the CIA research. McGill and the Allen Memorial Institute admitted their role in the CIA experiments during the 1977 Senate hearings. Kim was in the process of developing at least the beginning of a communication process with McGill when Alan called a halt to the telephone calls to McGill.

Kim was noticeably frustrated by Alan's decision. Despite not naming CIA as a defendant, any information that McGill could have provided would have been very helpful. I began to notice that after Alan changed law firms, he gave subtle and not so subtle hints in his actions or lack of actions, of a change in attitude about the lawsuit. It wasn't that his expectations about the suit had changed, but I became uneasy watching him walk away from evidence that might have helped us. Over the months and years to come, I grew frustrated and angry and I remained completely in the dark about why Alan did some of things he did. I told myself that having no experience with how lawyers operated, maybe I was interpreting things the wrong way when it came to questioning Alan's handling of the lawsuit.

Alan and Kim had voiced their shock and disgust with the way I had been treated in the Vermont hospitals. Alan and I had several conversations about his confidence that I would prevail in the lawsuit. I liked Alan and in 1997 there was no reason not to trust the things he told me.

My lawyers requested copies of my Social Security medical records in an effort to find the information missing from the copies sent to us by the State of Vermont. I went on Social Security disability in the mid 1970's. Weeks went by without a response from Social Security and Kim finally contacted them by phone

The woman from Social Security explained to my lawyers that, "Everyone's records are kept in the salt mines in Baltimore, Maryland."

The problem was that my records hadn't been found there. The search continued until we were informed that my Social Security records were located in St. Louis, Missouri.

Kim attempted to speak with Social Security in Wilkes Barre, Pennsylvania. I was with her that day when during her phone conversation I heard her say, "Are you telling me that the Social Security Administration does not have a phone number that I can call and speak with someone who might be able to answer my questions?"

When Kim hung up the phone she expressed shock at the conversation. She told me she had never heard of such a thing and she was unable to explain what had just transpired on the phone. When Alan came into the office Kim told him about the phone call. Alan listened and then without answering Kim, he turned and walked into his office, leaving Kim and I standing in the hallway.

My Social Security records finally arrived and I sat in the hallway of the law firm to read them. I was immediately perplexed by the content of the records. Although I had been granted disability because of my time in VSH, there was little reference to VSH. I read brief summaries about my 1978 Johns Hopkins hospitalization and other brief summaries of my condition. There were only a couple of pages total and the information was nothing that helped me.

A couple of years after my 1972 release from VSH, I applied for Social Security disability after being urged to do so by personnel in the Morrisville welfare office. I had been receiving $20.00 a week for room and board and $8.00 a week for personal use. Up until this time I had no idea that I would be eligible for disability benefits.

I was initially reluctant to open all of my medical records to Social

Security and I withheld permission for them to obtain the VSH records. I carried a deep-seated fear that somehow the records would prove that I was the monster that I believed myself to have been in VSH. A friend finally convinced me to open all of my medical records to Social Security.

A few months later I opened my door to find a man who introduced himself as a representative of Social Security. He told me that he worked out of the Morrisville office and that he had never made a home visit like this before. He appeared to be visibly shaken.

The man told me that he had just come from VSH where he had gone unannounced to read my medical records. I never forgot what he said next.

"I want to extend an apology to you from the entire state of Vermont and I promise you that no one will ever bother you again. You will receive disability benefits."

I remember feeling confused by his remarks. I didn't ask him any questions, maybe because I was stunned by what he said. In the 1970's I had no idea what he might have seen or even what he was referring to. I remember feeling relieved that I would receive benefits. I never forgot his remarks to me that day.

It is at least possible that what the man from Social Security read in my VSH records involved the CIA experiments. His visit to me was prior to the 1977 Senate hearings and the resulting public knowledge of the CIA programs. Whatever he saw in my VSH records was enough for him to make a personal visit to me and to extend an apology to me. I will very likely never know if he did in fact see evidence of the CIA research.

After the 1977 hearings, CIA enlisted Social Security in identifying and locating possible unwitting subjects of the CIA experiments. In my opinion it is highly unlikely that CIA revealed Vermont hospital's participation in the experiments to Social Security. The Vermont CIA research has been too well covered up for too long. I consider the Social Security Administration to have been lied to by CIA, just like CIA has lied to the rest of the country. Despite my requests to Alan to try to locate the man who visited me that day, Alan chose not to.

In the mid 1980's when I was living with my parents in Brandon, two men who claimed to be representatives from the Social Security Administration paid me a visit. I remember them getting out of their car and following me into my parent's house. My mother went into the living room to give us privacy to talk in the kitchen. I recall sitting down with the men at the kitchen table. My memory ends there.

I have no memory of anything that was said by me or by the two men. I have no memory of them leaving. It would be decades before I would realize that Social Security doesn't make home visits to people receiving benefits. Kathy and I have discussed this incident many times since I learned about the Vermont CIA experiments. My mother and I have also talked about this. We all agree that the likelihood was that these men misrepresented themselves and that the distinct possibility exists that they were in some way checking on me. Was it a check on my memory? Was it to insure that my memory loss remained? These would be only two of the many questions that I would have about the actions and behavior of the CIA.

In 2008, I phoned Social Security in St. Louis to try to obtain my own copy of my medical records. I learned that there were duplicate sets of my records and for reasons the woman at Social Security couldn't explain to me, the duplicate sets had been destroyed on June 30, 2004. She didn't know who authorized the destruction of the records and she didn't know why there were two sets of records.

The woman tried to be helpful but she did not know the answers to my questions. I asked if there was someone else I might speak with but she said she had no idea who to refer me to. I hung up the phone with more questions than I'd had before I called.

If I've learned anything over the fifteen years I've investigated the CIA in Vermont, I've learned that CIA has the power to keep certain information covered up. Social Security was likely a victim of the cover up. I learned an interesting piece of information a few years ago about how CIA insures that certain activities remain secret. The scenario goes something like this:

CIA briefs Governors, Congressman and Senators on classified programs, insuring that the official can never speak publicly about the information. The penalty for doing so is treason. I suspect that this method goes a long way in keeping certain CIA activities quiet. I'm sure there are situations when this is vital to national security, but using these methods to keep Americans from knowing about CIA illegal activities conducted on American soil is a whole other ballgame.

The day I sat in the law firm reading my Social Security records I noticed a man walking down the hall toward me. I recognized him as the senior law partner, F. Ray Keyser, a former Vermont Governor. Keyser was Governor from 1961-1963. The expression on his face confused me. He looked afraid.

I continued to watch him walking toward me and I tried to understand what I was seeing. Why would this man look afraid? It made absolutely no sense to me and I strained to see if maybe I was misinterpreting his facial expression. I wasn't.

I told Kathy about the incident and I brought it up many times over the next few years. It would take almost 15 years before I would be able to even speculate about why the former Governor might be affected by me or by the content of what I had learned in the lawsuit being handled by his law firm

Another former Vermont Governor and former U.S. Senator, Robert Stafford had an office in the law firm. Stafford, a highly respected official was a member of the 1977 Kennedy hearings on CIA MKULTRA and was

Vermont's Governor from 1959 -1961. It's highly improbable that during behind closed-door meetings, Vermont's role in the drug and mind control programs wasn't discussed. Was Stafford held to secrecy? I don't know. I tried to have Alan arrange for me to meet with Stafford but the meeting was never set up.

During the preparation for the lawsuit, we tried to obtain the Church Committee report on CIA MKULTRA. We weren't having any luck getting a copy. Alan was a long time friend of U.S. Congressman James Jeffords of Vermont. Alan and Jeffords played golf together and during one of their golf games, Alan tried to talk with Jeffords about the CIA MKULTRA experiments. He told Jeffords that he had a client who wanted a copy of the Church report. Apparently every time Alan tried to speak with Jeffords about the CIA, Jeffords walked away from him. We never obtained a copy of the Church Committee report.

By 2008, I had enough original source documents to prove that CIA experiments were conducted in Vermont and that they were covered up by state and federal officials. I began to scrutinize my contacts with government officials and agencies. I also began to take a closer look at Vermont state officials.

It seemed improbable that CIA could have conducted a 20-year long research program in Vermont hospitals and in the University of Vermont without someone in Vermont state government knowing about it and allowing it. During the lawsuit I didn't have the documentation that I would obtain in the years after the lawsuit ended. What I didn't know in 1998 was that I was looking at a massive, coordinated state and federal cover up.

Alan tried to locate the defendant doctors named in the suit. Several who were named had died and Alan was almost totally unsuccessful in locating the others. Ironically, in the years after the lawsuit ended I was able to locate several of the defendants with relative ease. Alan did locate Dr.

Robert Hugel, the psychiatrist who treated me in Mary Fletcher in 1965. A sheriff armed with papers to serve on Hugel waited unsuccessfully at the foot of Hugel's driveway to serve him.

Dr. George Brooks, VSH Superintendent during the 1970-1973 hospitalization was in a nursing home and Alan was asked by Brook's attorney to demonstrate sympathy and drop Brooks from the lawsuit. Alan suggested to me that it would be better to drop Brooks from the suit. I found that I had no sympathy available for George Brooks and I refused.

One VSH doctor I had always remembered for removing me from terrible conditions in a seclusion room in 1970 was Dr. Frederick Curlin, who was Assistant Superintendent in 1970-1971. My VSH records show that upon my admission to the Medical ward in October, 1970, Curlin and Brooks were my doctors of record while I was on the Medical ward. I have no memory of seeing either during that time. I cannot stress enough how unusual it would have been to have the Superintendent and the Assistant Superintendent actively directing a patient's care on the Medical ward.

The scattered memories I have of Curlin include him coming to the locked ward, 1A where I was being kept naked, with my arms secured behind my back in leather wristlets in a seclusion room. There was no bed and no mattress on the floor. I recall nurses' aides opening the door as Curlin ordered them to remove the restraints, remove me from the seclusion room and dress me.

Curlin led me toward the exit and the nurses shouted at him that he could not take me off the ward.

"The hell I can't!" Curlin yelled back. My memory ends at the door exiting 1A.

My medical records match my next memory of standing next to Curlin on Weeks 3 where he told me that Dr. O`Shea would take care of me. I have no additional memories of this episode.

The other memory I have of Curlin involves him bringing a red chestnut horse behind the locked ward for me to see. The horse was held by a boy I knew, Vern, who wore a bright blue shirt. I never learned how Curlin knew I loved horses or why he brought the horse for me to see. It seems unlikely that I would have brought the subject up the day he removed me from seclusion.

I recounted the fragmented memories to Kathy over the years before the lawsuit. I believed that Curlin had been a good guy who had rescued me. In 1998, I began searching for Curlin. I was certain that he had information that would help the lawsuit and help me understand what had happened to me. My mother, who had also believed that Curlin was a good guy, had several phone conversations with him in 1970 and he told her that he was originally from New York state. I located a Curlin listed in New York and called the number.

The woman who answered the phone was hostile. I could barely get a word in as she barked at me, demanding to know who I was and what I wanted. I told her my name and that Dr. Curlin had been my doctor in VSH in 1970. Her attitude immediately changed upon hearing my name. I found this curious.

I left my phone number with her after confirming that she knew how to reach Dr. Curlin. The next day, Dr. Curlin phoned me, and much to my surprise and confusion, I couldn't contain my emotions upon hearing his voice. The pain that surfaced from deep inside of me when I heard him speak frightened me. I couldn't seem to stop crying and the emotion was coming from an unfamiliar place inside of me. I told myself that my reaction must be because he removed me from the terrible conditions in that seclusion room.

When I was finally able to speak I told him about the lawsuit and about the abuse I had discovered in my VSH records. I asked him simple, direct questions and his responses immediately disturbed me.

"How did you know I was in that seclusion room?"

"Being Assistant Superintendent has its advantages."

"Did someone tell you that I was there?"

"Brooks and Havas were out of town."

"But how did you know I was there?"

"Being Assistant Superintendent has its advantages."

"Did you know Robert Hyde?"

"Yes. He was always cleaning horse's stalls and always wore jodhpurs."

"Was that horse you brought for me to see, yours? What was its name?"

"Yes. Her name was Beauty. You need to sit across from me and look into my eyes. Let me buy you a plane ticket to California."

"I don't like to fly."

"Let me buy you a bus ticket."

"Dr. Curlin, I'm not going to leave Vermont. Why did you leave VSH? When I returned from Baird 6, you were gone."

"I was only there for a year. You don't remember the Kennedy Assassination do you?"

"Yes, I remember the assassination."

"You don't remember the Kennedy Assassination, do you?"

"Yes, I told you that I do."

"You don't remember the Kennedy Assassination, do you?"

"Dr. Curlin, yes I do remember it. I was eleven years old. Did you know that VSH was conducting CIA experiments?"

"Call me Doc. I love you Karen,"

"Are you CIA, Dr. Curlin?"

"Not every good Indian is a dead Indian. I do love you."

I took notes during my conversation with Curlin. His responses were strange and made me feel very uncomfortable. I tried to persuade him to come to Vermont and meet with my lawyer. He flatly refused, saying that he didn't have good memories about Vermont. He tried to portray himself as having been misused in some unexplained fashion while he was in Vermont.

I spoke with Curlin again and I tried to stress to him that he needed to answer my questions. He refused. I was suspicious of his involvement in the experiments I was subjected to and when the phone call ended I had decided to name him as a defendant.

Kathy and her husband Jimmy traveled to California to visit friends and Kathy set up a meeting with Curlin. Kathy testified at a deposition about the meeting at a restaurant. She said he and a woman he identified as his wife entered the restaurant after Kathy and Jimmy had taken a table in the center of the nearly empty restaurant. Curlin immediately had them move to a table directly in front of a large window overlooking the street.

Curlin evaded Kathy's questions about what happened in VSH. Several times he expressed his love for me, which made both Kathy and Jimmy uncomfortable. In a story Curlin told to Kathy and Jimmy about an Irish couple who had angered the wrong people, Curlin described how the couple was killed when a bomb planted in their car exploded. Kathy testified that she had previously told Curlin that she and Jimmy were Irish and that she felt Curlin's story was meant as a threat.

When Curlin was served with the lawsuit papers, he phoned Kathy. He was angry. Kathy explained that he was given every chance to tell what he knew but that he chose not to. Curlin was clearly upset when the call ended.

It would be ten years after this before I would learn very disturbing information about Curlin and about our interaction in VSH. It would also take another ten years before I would learn that information about Curlin's conduct with me in VSH was apparently kept from me and hidden in the closing of the lawsuit. The information would shock me.

In the years preceding the lawsuit, I had weeks and weeks of repetitive dreams. The dreams were filled with images including a piece of land my parents bought for me to safely ride my horse. Graphic images of guns and sexual symbolism also filled the dreams. Both Kathy and I initially thought the images were entirely symbolic, until I was able to learn from relatives and other people from my early childhood that the images were from real events.

Kathy and I spoke frequently about the memories on the phone. It was during this time that I began to receive 3 A.M. phone calls. When I answered the phone, whoever was calling always hung up. This continued for weeks and became an every night occurrence. I finally notified the phone company.

A trap was set up on my phone and immediately the 3 A.M. calls stopped. Within literally a few hours after the trap was removed from my phone, the calls began again. The trap was reinstalled and the calls once again stopped. When the second trap was removed, the calls began again.

I spoke with a representative of the phone company who told me that the phone company believed that my phone was tapped. I was shocked. Why would anyone want to tap my phone? The phone company failed to find a physical tap on my line and they were able to rule out the source of the tap as anyone in my neighborhood. Over the next several years, telephone technicians frequently reiterated that my phone was tapped. I remained mystified as to why anyone would bother to wiretap my phone.

On one memorable occasion, phone techs stood in my kitchen and said that the problem was the same problem that caused me to have the trap placed on the phone.

"The trap was put on the phone because of the 3 A.M. phone calls. This is different. Now there are strange noises and clicks and people's voices," I said to the techs.

"You have the same problem you first had," they replied.

As of the writing of this book, my phone remains tapped. This has been verified numerous times over the years by the phone company. I learned that after September 11th and the Patriot Act, the small room inside the phone company where wiretapped phones were visible to phone techs by the red lines, was off limits and locked. The security manager at my current phone company has informed me that regardless of whether or not I change my phone number, which I have several times, or I move, the people tapping my phone have the ability to continue the wiretap. He even suggested that satellites are responsible for the tap. This appears to be very sophisticated. I've asked myself many times, why after all of these years would CIA remain interested in my activities. I have no satisfactory answer.

I've become accustomed to the fact that nothing I say on the phone is private and that someone is listening, but the situation makes me extremely angry. In the 1990's I had no idea who might have wiretapped my phone or why. I now understand why my repetitive dreams, which were filled with actual memories, would be of interest to CIA, given the fact that CIA's top goal in the experiments was to create permanent amnesia. I may not have known who was tapping my phone in the 1990's but I have no doubt now that it is CIA and directly related to the experiments conducted on me in VSH.

Shortly after the lawsuit was filed in 1998, I began to notice strangers who appeared to be following me. At first I thought it must have been my imagination, but as the months passed I realized that I really was being followed. I complained frequently to Kathy and then I decided to keep a record of the car license plates, a description of the vehicles and a description of the men in those cars.

It didn't take long before I saw that the same cars were always behind me and always parked near me. The men in these cars seemed to go out of their way to insure that I saw them. This made no sense to me.

On several occasions I was approached on the street by men I did not know who tried to engage me in conversation. I was not receptive, in fact, I reacted angrily. They always hurried away when they found that I would make a scene.

One man in particular followed me everywhere. On one day in particular, he followed me around the grocery store. I found it strange that when I went from aisle to aisle, there he was, just standing there with nothing in his hands and no shopping cart. He followed me into the check out line and never made eye contact with me. I remember thinking to myself that I could follow someone better than he could.

After seeing this man for months, I turned on the television one evening and saw his photograph on the local news. I couldn't believe what I was seeing. The man was wanted and apparently had a criminal background. I phoned Kathy and told her that I was certain this was the same man who had been following me.

Months after this incident I was able to learn that this man was not a criminal but that he was an undercover federal agent. I even learned his name. My head spun. What was going on? Why would a federal agent follow me? I subsequently learned that more than one of the car license plate numbers I recorded was traced back to federal agents. Someone was very clearly worried about the information I was uncovering.

It took me years to realize that very likely the federal agent who followed me around grocery stores and stayed so close by me might have been protecting me. I never looked for anyone else who might have been out of place or paying close attention to what I was doing, but apparently he was either aware of someone or watching for someone. I asked Dr. Colin Ross for his opinion and he speculated that I might have created a division within the intelligence community. I had my protectors and my non-protectors.

By 2009, I was still being followed. I'd almost grown accustomed to seeing the strangers, yet at the same time their presence made me very angry. I made Senator Bernie Sander's office aware of my situation back in 2000 and Sanders was the only elected official to ever try to help me. In 2009, the actions of one of the men following me began to disturb me.

I noticed him parked in his car next to mine when I exited a local pharmacy one Sunday morning. There was no one else inside the store, so I realized that he wasn't waiting for someone to come out. He stared at me. The expression on his face was hostile. I noted that he was blondish, wore wire rim glasses and I had the eerie feeling that I had met him before. I drove away that day hoping that I wouldn't encounter him again.

Weeks later I stood in the check out line of a store, and I realized the man standing behind me was standing too close to me and I moved away from him. He moved closer. I stepped forward again, this time making sure that my back wasn't to him. Again, he moved closer. I turned around and looked at him and I recognized him as the blond man with wire rim glasses. He never made eye contact. I exited the store and as I got into my car, I realized that he was parked directly in front of me. I watched him get into his vehicle. I didn't drive away. I wanted him to leave first and after what seemed like a long time, he drove away. There was something I couldn't put my finger on about this guy and the more I thought about it, the angrier I became.

The next day, I phoned Senator Sander's office and reported the activities of this man. By 2011, Sander's office was fully informed about the CIA in my life and I was told that the office would send a Congressional Liaison officer to complain to CIA about what Sander's staff termed "stalking."

In 2009, I also filed a FOIA request with the FBI in an attempt to learn if FBI was following me. I doubted that they were but I wanted to make sure. I had never found FBI participation in MKULTRA.

The FOIA came back no documents located. After the incidents with the blond man, and my growing anger at the behavior of CIA, who I was certain was behind the harassment, I phoned the FBI office in Albany, New York and explained the situation I had been involved in with CIA. I recall telling the FBI that I realized it all sounded crazy and that the behavior of the CIA was indeed crazy, but that what I was reporting to FBI was accurate.

I told the woman on the phone about being followed for months by a man I was able to identify as an undercover federal agent and I gave her his name. I asked the FBI to help me stop the harassment I was being subjected to by CIA and asked them to check with Senator Sander's office if they still didn't believe me.

I never saw the blond man again and as the weeks went by, I noticed I wasn't being followed. My new lawyer thought it was unusual for the FBI not to open a case file on a complaint, but I never heard from FBI. By May 2011, I had only one encounter with a stranger in a parking lot. It was similar to the other encounters, without the hostility demonstrated by the blond man.

The harassment stopped in late 2010, except my phone remains tapped. I stopped seeing strangers following me, and my mail stopped being stolen. I did however note that by 2010 I stopped sending FOIA requests and no longer requested the help of elected officials. I suspect the reason the harassment stopped was because of the complaints I made to Sanders and the FBI. I don't doubt that CIA was responsible. Who else would have the sophistication to pull off the types of surveillance that I was subjected to for years after I filed the lawsuit and discovered the Vermont CIA experiments?

The lawsuit was extremely stressful for me and during the first court hearing, I witnessed something that troubled me. I sat beside my lawyer, listening in disbelief as the judge spoke in glowing terms about one of the defendant doctors. The judge talked about his experiences with the doctor who acted as an expert witness in previous legal cases. The judge couldn't say enough good things about the doctor and as I looked over at my lawyer, he remained silent. I had never been involved in a court hearing before but the lavish praise coming from the judge didn't seem appropriate to me.

Shortly after this incident the lawyers for the doctor and the Burlington hospital petitioned Alan to request that we drop his clients from the suit. In the letter he wrote to Alan, the attorney included a cryptic line: "No good deed goes unpunished."

Over my strong objections, Alan dropped the doctor and the hospital from the suit after laying out all of his reasons to me. In the years after the suit ended I would obtain damning information about the hospital and about the University of Vermont College of Medicine.

Alan believed that the medical records made the case and although he understood that the CIA experiments were the reason I had been treated the way I had, he wanted to stay clear of talking about CIA during the trial. He doubted the jury would believe CIA was behind the research. I remained incredibly frustrated by the things Alan did and didn't do; all the while trying to tell myself that he was looking out for my interests.

During Kathy's deposition, the lawyers for the State brought boxes marked MSIS. I knew that a few of my medical records in 1970-1971 were marked MSIS and I asked Alan to request copies of the records the State obviously had. The lawyers frequently referred to information during Kathy's deposition that we didn't have. Alan never obtained the information

Alan was provided with a list of potential witnesses who were on staff when I was in VSH. These people could have provided valuable information about what happened to me. None of these people were deposed, not even Dr. Curlin. I was almost constantly in an emotional uproar over how the suit was being handled and about the information I continued to obtain about MKULTRA.

By the spring of 1999, I didn't feel well. I assumed it was due to the stress I was under. I had been diagnosed with macular degeneration, a disorder that could potentially cost me my eyesight. Tom believed that high doses of the drug Mellaril given to me in VSH when I was 13 years old were responsible. I had a difficult time with the diagnosis. The State of Vermont notified Alan that VSH had located more medical records and asked us to come to VSH to read the material. I never knew why the documents couldn't have been mailed, but Alan, Kathy and I drove to VSH to read the new material.

I felt sick inside at the thought of returning to that Hell-hole and when we entered the hospital I remember a terrible feeling of dread enveloping me. The documents located by the State were not informative at all. I felt relief when we drove away from VSH but I continued to not feel well.

On the morning of June 14, 1999, I felt a single, brief, searing pain in my chest. Over the next several hours my left arm began to throb until by 6 P.M., I could no longer stand the pain in my arm. I went to the emergency room.

I don't remember much of what happened in the emergency room. I knew the doctors suspected I was having a heart attack. Kathy was called and after what I later learned was several hours spent stabilizing me, I was taken to intensive care. During the middle of the night I had chest pains again. I saw a doctor standing outside of my hospital room and for the first time I wondered if I would die.

I spent five days in intensive care. Tests revealed that I had suffered a heart attack and that there was also evidence of damage from a previous heart attack. The doctors said they weren't sure if the heart attack was due to a sudden spasm, but that I did not have coronary artery disease. I went to cardiac rehab and during my recovery the lawsuit was put on hold.

When I was strong enough to continue the suit, I gave a deposition. Kim had left the Keyser law firm and I missed having her participation. The State's lead lawyer pretended to sleep through the deposition. I found his behavior both disgusting and revealing and I told myself that the State was more worried about my lawsuit than they would like me to know.

When the lead lawyer for the State finally questioned me, he was insulting every chance he got. He tried to learn how much I actually knew about the CIA and Hyde. He tried to find out if I could in fact remember what had happened to me and although I told him that I could remember some things, he chose to not ask me what those things were. I was exhausted by the end of the deposition. Although I wasn't aware of it at the time, Kathy and Tom realized that I was dissociating again.

Dr. Tom Fox gave three depositions in all. He stated that in his opinion I had been experimented on and that he had never seen such brutal treatment before. I had the chance to talk with Tom in the months before his depositions and he told me how important it would have been for him to have known what happened to me in VSH. He remarked that he, the Rutland hospital staff and Kathy had all been working in the dark with me.

"If only we had known how you had been treated. We could have helped you so much more and so much sooner," Tom told me.

In 2001, Tom was diagnosed with pancreatic cancer. He somehow managed to give the third deposition and appear at a court hearing, but by the summer of 2002, Dr. Tom Fox lost his battle with cancer. Everyone who knew him was devastated. I know that I was.

The suit dragged on. We no longer had an expert medical witness and I suggested that Alan contact Colin Ross, who had agreed to testify on my behalf. I couldn't understand Alan's reluctance to involve Dr. Ross, especially given the fact that he was one of the top specialists in the country on MPD and an expert on the MKULTRA program.

The State wanted me to be interviewed by their psychiatrist, which greatly disturbed me. Alan tried to fight the order from the court but I ended up having to meet with the psychiatrist. I guarded myself against the doctor but I remained pleasant. I wasn't about to give the State a window into my mind. As far as I was concerned, the State of Vermont had already taken more than enough from me.

Several months after the heart attack, my rheumatologist diagnosed me with a third autoimmune disease, antiphospholipid antibody disorder. He determined that the disease had been the cause of the heart attack when it thickened my blood, causing a blood clot. He prescribed a blood thinner

By the early spring of 2002, I was deposed again. The lead lawyer for the State was insulting and ridiculed me at every turn. I knew he was trying to elicit a dramatic response from me. I remained calm and quietly answered his questions, but on the inside I was fuming. I'd been interrogated before and the tactics of the lawyer felt familiar.

The lawsuit was sent into mediation and we met with the judge assigned to run the mediation. After he talked with the State lawyers, the judge told us the State offered a settlement. The sum was so small that it was obvious it was meant to be insulting. I told Alan that I was leaving and Alan too, walked out of the mediation.

My health began to rapidly decline and after blood tests revealed that the antiphospholipid disease was active, and producing cells that could kill me, my doctor told me that if I continued the lawsuit, I could die. He prescribed a powerful drug to attack the dangerous cells developing in my bloodstream. My anti-DNA was escalating rapidly.

I couldn't believe what was happening. I struggled with the diagnosis and what it might mean and I was facing the end of my battle to hold the State accountable for its actions. It was days before I finally decided that I had to drop the lawsuit. It was a painful decision, but I knew how sick I really was.

Alan was shocked when I told him that I had to drop the lawsuit and why. Alan believed that we had a good case and would have won the lawsuit. He agreed to notify the State. I remember thinking to myself that I couldn't believe that I had come this far only to have to stop before I learned what had really happened to me. I was determined to get well, and to once again continue to obtain the information that would prove the Vermont CIA experiments. I never could have foreseen how long it would take me to unravel the CIA experiments and the information sitting in my medical records.

Alan phoned me several weeks after the suit was dropped to tell me that the State offered a settlement. I was surprised. I was the one who dropped the lawsuit. The State wasn't obligated to pay me a cent. Even more surprising to me was that the amount being offered was over three times the amount that was offered in the mediation.

I questioned Alan about the amount. Why was the State even offering me money? Alan suggested that I take the offer. Again I asked him why were they settling when I ended the suit? He told me to take the money. I agreed to settle at the amount offered but the whole thing gnawed at me. It didn't make any sense.

I was pretty sure that Alan hadn't really believed that the CIA was responsible for my treatment in the Vermont hospitals. He knew that Hyde was CIA and he knew about a few other doctors' connections to CIA, but he had a hard time wrapping his head around the idea. He wasn't alone in that. I was still struggling with the revelation. I would remain on the powerful drug Imuran for a couple of years and the drug would eventually produce a remission in the antiphospholipid disease. I launched what would be an additional ten-year search to identify the connections of the Vermont hospitals to the CIA.

The lawsuit was over in the spring of 2002 but information that I was unaware of in 2002 would surface again years later and that information would be shocking.

2
MARY FLETCHER HOSPITAL – VERMONT STATE HOSPITAL, 1965-1969

I grew up in Brandon, a small, rural town in Southern Vermont. I was a friendly, curious and sensitive child who loved horses, idolized my older brother and adored my Grandfather. I was close to my parents and spent countless hours playing with my cousins and my friends. My family lived on Maple Street and there were acres of pastureland we played in. We swam in the summer, played baseball and hide and seek. We walked back and forth to school everyday and we counted the days until summer vacation. As far as anyone, including me knew, there was nothing unusual about my life.

My father worked in a lumber mill, and my mother stayed home to raise my brother and me. My parents married young; my father was twenty-two and my mother was sixteen. They lived a quiet, simple life in the small rural town of Brandon. I was born ten years after my brother and I idolized him.

When my brother enlisted in the Air Force in 1960, I fell into a deep depression. I missed him terribly and to make matters worse, my mother suffered a near emotional breakdown over Kip's enlistment. Even a television commercial for the Air Force sent her rushing out of the room sobbing. I began to feel very alone. It was because of my reaction to Kip being gone that my parents bought me a horse in March of 1960.

I had wanted a horse for as long as I could remember. The horse was pastured in a neighbor's field next door. Both Kip and I had grown up close to the neighbors and we spent many hours at their house. My cousin got her own horse a year later and our families spent their free time watching us ride and helping us learn how to take care of the horses. My

Grandfather prided himself on his knowledge of horses and we grew even closer during this time.

In 1963, my parents bought a piece of land across the river that ran behind our house from the next-door neighbors who had allowed us to pasture the horse in their field. It was after I began riding my horse on this piece of land that I began to be preoccupied with suicidal thoughts. At the time, no one including me had any reason to factor the land into my emotional condition. It would be another 30 years before I would know about the violent trauma I had suffered on that land.

The suicidal thoughts and feelings grew. My behavior at home and in school dramatically changed and I made several minor attempts to kill myself. I managed to hide this from my parents. My friends knew that I was suicidal, but in an effort to protect me, they kept the knowledge to themselves. I stood on the streets of Brandon and timed the cars and trucks as they passed. I decided to step out in front of an oncoming vehicle, but couldn't make myself take that final step into traffic.

I knew that there was something wrong with me and I was frightened. I became withdrawn and obsessed with the dark thoughts I was having. I felt completely isolated from family and friends. I shut myself away in my room and stopped doing all of the things I had always done before.

My parents, especially my mother, attributed the changes in my behavior to adolescence and I found it impossible to tell them that I was consumed with the idea of killing myself. In 1963, while Kip was home on leave, President Kennedy was assassinated and I had an unusually intense reaction to the tragedy. I became even more withdrawn and secretive at home.

In the fall of 1964, I attended seventh grade at the union high school and the adjustment was very difficult for me. When I was in the first grade, the elementary school burned to the ground during Christmas vacation and all of my subsequent elementary school years were spent in church basements and office space substitutions for a school. There was a building for first and second grade, another for third and fourth and one for fifth and sixth grades. It was difficult to make the adjustment to the new school with all of the many students there.

Within weeks of starting classes at the new high school, I suffered an outburst at school and I was required to see a psychiatrist in Burlington. I remember very little about the session with Dr. Cohen except that I didn't like him and I wasn't open to talking with him. He set up a consultation at the Degoesbriand hospital outpatient clinic where I met German psychiatrist, Dr. Robert Hugel for the first time.

I immediately disliked Hugel. His approach was aggressive and I withdrew even deeper into myself over the next few months. The more he pushed me, the deeper I drew back into myself. When he said to me that there was nothing wrong with me, I agreed with him. I simply wanted to be left alone. The intense preoccupation with suicide became worse. I began to load and unload my father's 30-30 rifle and tried to fight off thoughts of shooting my mother or myself. The thoughts and feelings I was having were frightening, but the worst part for me was that it was becoming more difficult for me to hide the fact that there really was something serious going on.

My mother and I clashed frequently. The more distant I became, the harder she pushed to get closer to me and the angrier I became. When my relatives tried to tell her that I was sick and needed help, she resisted the idea, attributing my behavior to my age.

As more people noticed that something was very wrong with me, my mother became more convinced that my acting out was simply to defy her. She couldn't allow herself to believe that there could be anything emotionally wrong with me. I never doubted that my parents loved me, and that knowledge made the thoughts and feelings I was having even harder for me to contend with.

I had another meltdown at school. This time I was found wandering around the hallway confused and disoriented. I made a suicidal gesture, slashing my wrist. When my family doctor arrived at the school, I told him that if he sent me home I would either kill my mother or kill myself.

When my father and brother came to take me to the Mary Fletcher hospital I reassured myself that I would be able to escape by leaping from the car as it traveled along the highway. I was seated between my father and brother, which prevented me from jumping out of the moving car. Although I don't have any memory of the ride to the hospital or of my admission to the psychiatric unit, I do know that in September, 1965 my life would be changed forever by the events that would unfold.

The 1965 Mary Fletcher medical records show that I was immediately prescribed the phenothiazine drugs, Thorazine and Stelazine. Over the next thirty days I was also given frequent large does of Sodium Amytal. It's interesting to note that Sodium Amytal was used in MKULTRA as a way to allow the researchers to map the subject's unconscious mind so that the subject could be successfully exploited later. It's also noteworthy that the dangers of combining large doses of phenothiazine drugs and Sodium Amytal were well known by the medical establishment in 1965, yet this is exactly what was done in my case.

I don't have much memory of my 1965 hospitalization, but I do recall hiding under the bed sheets. I was frightened. This was the first time I had ever been in a hospital and the first time I had ever been away from home. The record notes that I was severely depressed and suicidal and that within days of starting the Thorazine, I had symptoms of an allergic reaction.

The records note that I had a rash, a fever, a sore throat and muscle spasms. Dr. Hugel and Dr. W. Stewart Agras continued the drug. Only days after my admission, I woke up to see a glass urine specimen bottle sitting on the table beside my bed. I got out of bed, grabbed the bottle and went into the bathroom. I broke the bottle and slashed my wrist. I felt nothing until

I saw the blood gush from my wrist with the force of a fire hose. I didn't know that blood could come out of a body like that and I was frightened. I began screaming and running wildly around the room.

The record shows that pressure was applied to the 2 inch across and 7/8 of an inch deep wound. The severed tendon, noted to have been the palmaris longus tendon was operated on for hours and my wrist was placed in a cast. Hugel and Agras visited me the next morning and threatened me with transfer to the Vermont State Hospital. Hugel remarked that the only reason they weren't sending me directly to VSH was that no one had told me beforehand that suicide attempts were not tolerated.

During a psychological test days later, I complained to the psychologist that I did not feel well. He berated me and accused me of only pretending to feel sick to avoid taking the test. I couldn't understand what it was about me that made the doctors treat me so badly. The records show that I was never given any psychological counseling and I don't recall any of the doctors ever talking with me except to berate and threaten me.

My answer to one of the questions in the psychological test would bring about a dramatic reaction from the doctors and their reactions to my answer would alarm me.

"What does two heads are better than one mean?"

"If you are crazy in one head, you still have one more head to save," was my response.

The doctors stood in my hospital room and demanded to know why I gave that answer to the question. They demanded to know if I lied. Over and over they shouted at me until I finally told them yes, I lied. Their reactions to my answer frightened me and made me realize that whatever it was about me, I had better keep the truth, whatever it was, hidden.

During the 30 days I was in Mary Fletcher, I never showered or washed my hair. I was afraid to take my clothes off and enter the shower. No one seemed to notice or tried to help me. In retrospect I find this suspect.

I was a thirteen-year old child who was clearly emotionally ill and in need of help, yet I was left in conditions that few others would have been left in.

Kip was scheduled to be married that October and the timing of my breakdown cast a pall over the ceremony. I liked Sue, my future sister-in-law but it wouldn't be until after my integration in 1996 that I could finally explain to her that her marriage to my brother was not the cause of my hospitalization.

The records note that I continued to have allergic reactions to the drugs I was given. I began to have dystonic reactions, which were very frightening. My muscles went into severe spasms, twisting the muscles in my face and extremities. After each allergic reaction, the doctors gave me medication to counter the reaction and then continued to give me drugs they knew I was allergic to.

By October 21, 1965, the adverse drug reactions had become so serious that Dr. Agras asked for a medical consult. The consulting doctor's notes include: pulse: 120, temperature: 38.4, blood pressure: 110/60, white blood cell count: 22, 700, mild ache in throat, tonsil pain, cough, nodes in neck, tenderness in right lower stomach, covered with a rash, weak and unable to eat.

The consult diagnosed me with a severe allergic reaction to phenothiazine drugs and advised that the drugs be immediately stopped. Agras wrote in the records that he would not stop the drugs. He continued to give me the drugs I was allergic to and my condition rapidly deteriorated.

I began to lose control. For reasons unknown to me at the time, I began screaming uncontrollably. Agras, Hugel and two female psychiatrists, Dr. Elizabeth Forsberg and Dr. Rosemary Brewster stood in my hospital room and demanded that I stop screaming or they would send me to VSH. No matter how I tried, I couldn't stop screaming and I was terrified.

It's noteworthy that during my month-long stay at the Mary Fletcher psychiatric unit, none of the psychiatrists attempted to learn the reasons for the breakdown that led to my admission. After the serious suicide attempt in the hospital, no doctor tried to learn why I attempted suicide. Not once during my stay did any psychiatrist counsel or engage me in psychotherapy of any type. Instead they used Sodium Amytal and powerful tranquilizing drugs that they knew I was allergic to. Forty years later, I would find documents about the research being conducted in the Vermont hospitals where I was a patient that would raise questions about the use of LSD and whether or not my transfer to VSH had been the plan all along.

On October 24, 1965 I was transferred via ambulance to VSH. The admission record notes that I was covered with "a rash all over face, arms, legs and body, had bruises on arms and legs, had attempted suicide severing the palmaris longus tendon in left wrist and allergic to Thorazine."

The records show that I was placed in a straightjacket and given injections of Trilafon and Compazine, both phenothiazine drugs.

The record notes that, "Patient remained awake much of the night in a very disturbed state. This noon she was given 10 mg. of Trilafon and toward the end of the afternoon she was given 10 mg. of Compazine... following these injections she had a reaction which was felt to be a dystonic reaction. She has spasms in the corner of her mouth and the side of her face. She has spasms in her extremities and apparently in her diaphragm causing a loud moan. The patient was very frightened by this."

Dr. Covey administered an injection of a side effect drug. The injection helped and he repeated the injection. The symptoms gradually subsided. I stopped screaming. VSH nurses aides removed me from the straightjacket and from seclusion. I could barely walk.

In 1965, VSH and the University Of Vermont College Of Medicine had been conducting research using unwitting subjects for over a decade. Experimental drugs obtained from two CIA-contracted pharmaceutical companies were being given to VSH patients. VSH staff psychiatrists participated in experiments at verified CIA test sites and CIA researchers participated in experiments conducted at VSH. In 1963, VSH-UVM began sending the test results of child patients directly to CIA Chief Psychologist John Gittinger at CIA headquarters in Washington, DC.

In 1965, Dr. Robert W. Hyde, longtime CIA researcher and CIA Technical Services Division employee was officially Director of Research at VSH. He would remain in that position throughout the years I was a VSH patient. In 1965, my family and I didn't know about the CIA research in Vermont hospitals. In 1965, I was thirteen years old and involuntarily committed to the Vermont mental institution. In 1965, the experiment had begun.

The locked adult women's ward, Weeks 3, held patients with all types of mental illness and as I looked around the ward, none of the women appeared to pose any threat to me. The nurses' aides didn't seem to be terrible people, but I wasn't about to make the same mistake I'd made in Mary Fletcher and trust any of them.

The doctor who gave me the shot that stopped the drug reaction, Dr. Covey, was a resident doctor from UVM. He was kind to me. My medical records note that he asked me if I heard voices and that I told him, yes. When he asked if the voices were coming from inside of my head or from outside, I answered that they were inside of my head. Over the next few days he asked me again and again about the voices, signaling to me that I had made a mistake answering truthfully. My stay in Mary Fletcher taught me that whenever the doctors reacted to something I said, trouble would follow unless I told them that I made up the whole thing. I told him that I made it up and it wasn't true. It worked. He backed off.

The record also notes that I described an incident in Mary Fletcher when black figures surrounded my bed and urged me to cut my wrist. I said that I didn't want to hurt myself but that these black figures frightened me and I couldn't resist obeying them. I have no memory of these black figures.

In the record, the notes quote me and then contain the written remarks of the nurses; "At the Mary Fletcher Hospital they used to say, get your wrist." She states that she did not want to lay her wrist open but that she was afraid of them. "I felt I should do what they said. It was like they were controlling my life. I didn't know who they were. They were like shadows."

"The figures were described as black all over and had no particular shape or form but she felt that they were men. She states that she was afraid of them. Patient states that she has not seen the black figures at the Vermont State Hospital, only at the Mary Fletcher Hospital. Patient also states that she has a weakness for broken glass."

In CIA mind control experiments conducted by Dr. Harris Isbell, he notes that a few of the experimental subjects he dosed with LSD reported that they, "...felt their experiences were caused by the experimenters controlling their minds."

A December, 1965 meeting of VSH doctors regarding my case notes that Dr. George Brooks stated that I was, "not the garden variety type and that it is thought that hysteria at this age becomes schizophrenia."

Dr. Rupert Chittuck, VSH Superintendent stated that I should remain in the hospital for "a considerable amount of time." It was decided that I not be allowed to attend school and that they would keep me on an adult ward, despite the fact that VSH had a children's ward. Many of the Weeks 3 nurses aides objected to having a thirteen-year old child on a locked adult women's ward.

In this meeting my diagnosis was stated to be "a differential diagnosis between schizophrenic reaction of the acute undifferentiated type and a severe anxiety reaction, with depressive, dissociative and hysterical symptoms...the latter diagnosis is favored."

On December 21-22, 1965, I was given a psychological test by Dr. Donald Eldred. The three-page summary of that test would show that the test was a PAS or a Psychological Assessment System. PAS was a specific psychological test created by CIA Chief Psychologist, John Gittinger. The PAS was routinely used by CIA to learn how to compromise and exploit a person's weaknesses. It was used to "get at" people. I wouldn't identify the VSH PAS until after the lawsuit ended, and I would not know until the mid-2000's that VSH sent the test results directly to Gittinger at CIA headquarters in Washington, DC.

On several occasions, Dr. Chittuck came onto Weeks 3 accompanied by several doctors who I didn't recognize. Chittuck called me over to introduce me to the men. I recall standing surrounded by the men and hearing Chittuck say, "This is Karen."

I have no memory of what they said to me or what I said to them. I did notice that Chittuck never introduced any of the other patients to the groups of men who came onto the ward. In 1965, the identities of these men wouldn't have meant much to me, but decades later when I identified CIA personnel on site at VSH, my suspicions about who those men might have been were answered in the documents I obtained. I would also learn that the reason VSH doctors were so interested in me was because of the disorder that they knew I had; the disorder that the CIA was very interested in for its MKULTRA experiments.

VSH doctors prescribed up to 1800 mg a day of a phenothiazine drug called Mellaril despite the fact that I was allergic to phenothiazine drugs. A side effect drug was also ordered. The doctor in charge of my case, Dr. Caron, had little to say to me and rarely asked me questions. He frequently turned his back to me when we were in a room together. A patient told me one day what a great doctor he was and how much he was helping her. I wondered why he never tried to help me.

My parents provided VSH doctors with information they believed would help the doctors help me. My mother told them about my love for horses, my close relationship with my grandfather and about my unusually intense reaction to the Kennedy Assassination. She also told them that I ran away when I was only five years old and that when I was two, my brother was shot in the back in a deer hunting accident. She said I watched when the dressing on his wound was changed after he hemorrhaged.

There are no nurse's notes in the VSH records or in the 1965 Mary Fletcher records. This is also true for the 1970-71 VSH hospitalization and for the return to Weeks 3, VSH from the Burlington Baird 6 stay in 1971. Records are also entirely missing for the 1970-71 stay on 10B, where Dr. Otto Havas was the doctor. There is a single doctor's note by Havas for the 10B stay.

Despite the fact that I was not schizophrenic and the records note that the doctors were well aware of this in 1965, they labeled me as schizophrenic. The diagnosis would change to dissociative and the word dissociative appears in the 1965 PAS and in later records. VSH would mislead subsequent caregivers for years with a diagnosis they knew to be false. I learned decades later that the term "schizophrenic rehabilitation" was a cover for the true nature of VSH-UVM research. Countless VSH patients during the 1950's, 1960's and 1970's were labeled with an illness they didn't have.

My parents visited when they could and there were times when I wouldn't see them. I couldn't explain why I had the feelings I did about my mother and every time I refused to see them, I felt torn apart. I wanted to run to my mother and go home with her. I wanted things to be the way they had been before all the craziness had taken over my life. There was something causing my conflicted feelings toward my mother but I wouldn't know the cause of the terrible feelings for three decades.

Weeks 3 was chaotic and unpredictable. The women patients, who only moments before seemed fine to me, would suddenly erupt in screams or violence. There were times when I behaved the same way and I had no idea why. The night that one patient was dragged away to the dreaded 1A ward I had heard so many awful things about, was a frightening experience. She screamed and begged the aides not to send her to 1A. I told myself that it must have been a very bad place to be.

After I visited home a few times, I was discharged on a six-month visit in March 1966. I was taking 1800 mg of Mellarill and I knew that I had been changed by my experiences in the hospitals. I realized that the ways in which I had always believed the world to be were wrong. Doctors, nurses and hospitals were supposed to be good and safe but I knew this wasn't true. I had no more idea what had caused me to be hospitalized than I had before the breakdown. Now I was the crazy girl. I was the one who had been in the state mental hospital. I didn't share my feelings with anyone.

My friends went to school without me. I remained on the outside watching as their lives went on. I was overwhelmed with feelings of shame and I spent almost all of my time alone. There aren't many memories for me of the year or so after I was released from VSH but by the time I was fifteen, one event stands out above everything else - meeting Phil Cram.

Phil moved onto Maple Street with his parents and two brothers in 1967, and I was immediately interested in getting to know him. I returned to VSH in early 1967 but it was a short, uneventful stay, not quite six weeks. Phil was attracted to me too, especially when he learned that like him, I played the guitar. Phil was tall, slender and had an open, engaging personality. He had a beautiful singing voice, one so strong and clear that most people were surprised at just how talented he really was. We began spending much of our time together.

Phil's parents accepted me into their lives as my parents welcomed him into theirs. I stopped taking the Mellarill and I felt better. I wasn't isolated and lonely anymore and as I expanded my world I began to spend more time with other kids. We rode our bicycles together, played baseball and sat for hours on the railroad bridge on Pearl Street talking. When Phil and I played guitars and sang together, his younger brother Bernie practiced playing drums on any solid object he could find. Even my mother, who also played the guitar and sang, sometimes joined in. It was a good time.

There were times when Phil and I argued. I'd cry and he'd cry and then we'd make up. After one argument, he came to make up and gave me a single rose. Phil and I discovered that we were both better together than apart and we began to spend even more time with each other. He had a strength that I drew from and whenever I had problems, he seemed to be able to reassure me that everything would be okay.

I spent time at his house and he spent even more time at my house. By the summer of 1969, Phil and I were talking about getting married and both of our families were concerned that we were too young. Phil repeatedly said that when he turned eighteen, he would do what he wanted and that what he wanted was for us to be married. I agreed. All I wanted was to be with Phil forever.

In July, 1969 my parents stayed with Phil, Bernie and I at my uncle's lakeside camp. We swam and canoed. We fished and took long slow boat rides at sunset. Those two weeks were the happiest time in my life. I belonged in the world again, I loved Phil and he loved me.

On Sunday, August 3, 1969, I went to work with Phil at a local hamburger drive-in, despite being sick with a hard cold. I tried to stay at work but as the day progressed, I became too sick to work. Phil drove me home and I went to bed.

I had a very disturbing dream and when I woke up I told my parents about it. In the dream, Phil and I were sitting in the back seat of a car. I couldn't see who was driving. I looked out the car window to see the body of a large black dog dead in the road. When I turned back to tell Phil, he was gone.

The dream upset me but my parents reassured me that being sick had probably produced the nightmare. That evening Phil and I talked about getting married and we planned to go to Rutland the next day to shop for furniture. He told me that he would pick me up in the morning.

Phil and I lingered at the door that night, kissing and holding each other. I never loved anyone before and Phil had changed my life forever. Even now, forty-three years later, I can still see his face and feel the very powerful emotions I felt that night.

Monday, August 4, 1969 was a gloomy, rainy summer day. I waited for Phil to pick me up so that we could shop for furniture in Rutland, but as the hours passed and he was nowhere in sight, I became worried. I phoned his house and his sister-in-law said she didn't know where he was. Only minutes later, Bernie came to wait with me.

By noon, I knew something was very wrong and I called his house again. His sister-in-law told me that Phil had been in a car accident and he was in the hospital. I couldn't believe it and as I waited to hear any news, I prayed that Phil would be okay.

It was hours later when the news finally came. I watched as my father whispered something to my mother at the door and when I saw the expressions on their faces, I knew. Phil was dead.

Phil was killed in a head on car crash as he drove on Route 7 from Rutland to Brandon. Halfway home he pulled out to pass the car in front of him when another car pulled onto the highway. Phil couldn't stop.

I sobbed in agony. My parents sobbed. I couldn't believe that he was gone. Not Phil, not my Phil, it simply couldn't be happening. Losing Phil was and remains the worst thing to have ever happened in my life and to this day, I have never really gotten over it. I'm convinced that if he had lived, my life would never have been what it was and that very likely I would never have returned to VSH.

The weeks and months after Phil died remain a blur to me. Unknown to me at the time, a diamond engagement ring was found in the dash of Phil's car. No one told me about the ring until forty years later. I never got the ring.

The morning of his death, Phil and his mother Helen had a terrible argument about us getting married. Phil swore at her and left the house angry. Apparently he decided to go to Rutland alone, buy the engagement ring and surprise me with it. Helen spent the rest of her life blaming herself for Phil's accident. Shortly before Helen died, she and I had a chance to talk. Although Helen refused to acknowledge that she kept the ring, she shared several memories she had of Phil and I together. I didn't remember the things she told me, but I was grateful to her for sharing them with me. I hope that Helen found peace when she died. Phil would have wanted it that way.

I managed to hang on for one more year without Phil. A very dark cloud had enveloped me. I attended an outpatient mental health clinic-sponsored group a few times but nothing seemed to help. It was during the visits to this clinic that I first met Kathy Judge, who would play an integral role in my life twenty years later. In September 1970, I had to put down my horse. I became very physically ill a short time later and it was determined that I had hepatitis. Several people in town were diagnosed with the illness. After Phil died, I began taking Mellarill again at the urging of my parents, who didn't want to see me return to VSH again.

I developed severe vomiting and a strange black fur appeared on my tongue. I would learn decades later that I didn't have hepatitis, but that I had a toxic reaction to Mellarill. I was admitted to the Rutland hospital under the care of psychiatrist, Dr. James Todd.

I don't remember anything about Dr. Todd and there are no memories of the short hospitalization in Rutland. The records show that my diagnosis was "anxiety, hysteria, hysterical personality." Todd ordered drugs including Paraldehyde. It's noted that I had panic attacks and that I was screaming uncontrollably. Todd didn't hesitate to send me back to VSH, despite what I learned later were the strong protests by the nursing staff.

Rosemary Johnson and I first met when she worked for Rutland

Mental Health and was on staff at the outpatient clinic where I went after Phil died. I spoke with Rosemary when I was investigating VSH and she told me that the Rutland nurses were in an uproar over my transfer to VSH. She said it was clear to the nurses that my reactions were fearful and not in any way dangerous. Todd refused to be swayed and sent me to VSH. My parents also tried to stop my return to VSH but their efforts were in vain.

No one, including me could have imagined the horrors I would be subjected to for the next three years. No one could have imagined that the CIA had already singled me out for experiments and no one, especially me, could have imagined that it would be over 30 years before I would learn the truth about the CIA experiments I was swept into.

3
THE EXPERIMENT, 1970-1973

"By 1962 and 1963 the general idea we were able to come up with is that brainwashing was largely a process of isolating a human being, keeping him out of contact, putting him out of control, putting him under long stress in relationship to interviewing and interrogation and that they could produce any change that way without having to resort to any kind of esoteric means."

John Gittinger, testimony, Senate Select Committee on Intelligence Hearings on CIA Drug and Mind Control Programs, MKULTRA

The VSH records show that upon admission on October 12, 1970, I was covered with a rash, unconscious, suffering from hepatitis and "uncontrollable." The records also note that, "within five minutes the rash disappeared." I was admitted to the medical ward, MS3, where my doctors were George Brooks and Frederick Curlin. The record shows that I was placed in restraints on my arms and legs and that I had severe vomiting.

I now know that I did not have hepatitis but that I had a toxic reaction to Mellarill. Blood tests taken during this time make no mention of hepatitis. My blood was sent to Biochemical Procedures, a Mead Johnson laboratory in California. It would take me until early 2012 to be suspicious of Mead Johnson's involvement with the CIA. I searched for Biochemical Procedures and found several connections to CIA back in 1971, but as of yet I cannot absolutely determine that Mead Johnson was a CIA lab. CIBA and Smith, Kline and French pharmaceutical companies also contracted with VSH-UVM research and all three were identified in declassified CIA documents as CIA contract labs.

The records show that I became violent on MS3, stating that I threw chairs at women patients. Although I have no memory of this incident, I doubt its accuracy. If I did indeed throw chairs, I'm sure I threw them at the VSH nurses, not at the patients. I do remember my transfer from MS3 to the infamous locked ward, 1A.

On October 19, 1970 the record shows that the doctor who signed the seclusion order was Dr. Elizabeth Forsberg - the same German psychiatrist who was part of my care in Mary Fletcher in 1965. She called my mother that night in 1965 to tell her that I was being sent to VSH. Despite the pleas of my mother not to send me to VSH, Forsberg refused.

I was placed in a wooden wheelchair with my hands and legs secured to the chair by strips of cloth. A cloth tie was wrapped around my neck and secured to the back of the chair. They wheeled me into the underground tunnel that ran beneath the entire hospital.

The nurses screamed at me, and one of them pulled my head back by pulling my hair. I have no memory of why they behaved so violently, given the fact of the way I was tied down, I posed no threat to them. I don't remember actually arriving at 1A but I do remember waking up in the seclusion room.

I heard terrible stories about 1A when I was thirteen. It was the most dreaded ward in the hospital and it was considered the end of the line. There was no worse place they could send a patient.

I woke up on the floor, naked, with my arms secured behind my back in leather wristlets. The gnawing, searing pain in my arms, neck and shoulders was impossible to relieve. It didn't matter how I held my body or the position I was in, it was impossible to escape the constant pain the wristlets produced. I heard frightening screams and strange shrieks coming from outside the seclusion room. The record shows I was held in these conditions until October 23, 1970.

Many of the women patients on 1A had been there for years and they were considered to be hopeless. There were old women who shuffled when they walked and middle-aged women who sat on wooden benches all day. There were young women with severe autism and there were severely retarded women who spent their days propped up against the hallway walls. A few of the women howled and screamed almost constantly and others could carry on a conversation. At least a few of the women were only on the ward temporarily, having been sent there in response to behavior that was unacceptable on open wards.

When I obtained the research project documents from VSH-UVM experiments, I realized that these women had been the target VSH population for the use of experimental drugs. In retrospect, I realize that many of the women's conditions were very likely created, if not exacerbated by the unethical experiments conducted by VSH-UVM.

Included in my medical records is a letter written by my mother to Commissioner of Mental Health, Jonathan Leopold after this incident, in which she complains about my treatment and begs him to stop treating me so harshly.

Leopold's letter of response wasn't written until months later and in it he adamantly denied that I had been kept in these conditions. The VSH records contradict Leopold. Apparently the reason I was removed from these conditions was because Dr. Frederick Curlin personally removed me from seclusion and took me off the ward with him.

The record shows that before Curlin took me to Weeks 3, I had already met Dr. Otto Havas, on October 21, 1970. Havas ran the Rutland County ward 10B. I don't remember the first time I met Havas, but I do know I did not like the man.

Havas was Hungarian and both his accent, which was similar to the German accent of Dr. Robert Hugel, from Mary Fletcher, and his uncanny resemblance to Hugel, immediately affected me. Havas had a cruel streak and over the next almost three years, I would learn just how cruel he could be.

By 1970, VSH had implemented regionalization, or the lodging of patients on wards designated by the country they were from; 10B was the Rutland county ward. Weeks 3 held Chittenden county patients and after Curlin brought me to Weeks 3, Havas met with me again.

I have no idea what Havas might have said to me or what he had said during our initial meeting, but I do know, from memory and from the record, what happened when Havas told me that I would be transferred to his 10B ward.

I ran wildly down the hall of Weeks 3 and smashed my head through the pane glass window of the door to the porch. I remember staggering and falling to the floor. There was blood gushing from my face, near my eyes. As I lay on the floor, several male aides ran toward me and I responded by fighting them. While I was pinned to the floor, face first, one male aide kneeled on the back of my thighs and repeatedly smashed my forehead on the floor. This aide would later say that I had kicked him in the groin.

I was again placed in a seclusion room on 1A, with my arms secured in wristlets. I spent three days on 1A before being transferred to 10B. I lasted eight days on Havas's ward before returning to 1A, where I again spent time in seclusion and wristlets.

Because there are no records for the 10B ward except for scattered notations by Havas later in the record, I have only a few scattered memories of being on 10B. One includes a strange incident between Havas and me.

After a morning meeting on the ward, Havas walked up to me and whispered something that I do not recall into my ear. Whatever he said upset me enough that I ran from him and off the ward. Havas chased after me. This would have been highly unusual. Doctors didn't chase patients through the hallways. Aides did that. When I reached the area in front of the dining hall, I inexplicably ran straight into a chalkboard that was propped up in the hall. I could have continued running, but for some reason I crashed head first into the chalkboard.

Havas threw himself on top of me and held me down until the aides came and took me to 1A. It would be a very long time before I unraveled this scenario.

On November 12, 1970, the day of my scheduled Rutland court hearing, which I had requested to be present at, I was taken to 1A at noon and locked in a seclusion room. There is nothing in the record to explain the circumstances that led to this incident.

I went back and forth from 1A to 10B until late December, 1970, when I was secluded and in restraints. Beginning on December 30, I was kept in wristlets and seclusion for up to ten straight days at a time without relief. The records show that on three separate occasions I was kept in wristlets and in seclusion for up to fourteen days at a time. Each time the wristlets were removed, I was placed in a straightjacket.

When in seclusion, I was often kept naked. My arms were secured behind my back day and night. There was no bed. There was no mattress on the floor. There were no blankets. There was no access to a toilet. I remember relieving myself on the floor like an animal and then being forced to remain in the small room with my own excrement. It was a degrading experience and the searing pain caused by the wristlets was constant and maddening.

While in seclusion and wristlets, I began smashing my own head into the door and against the walls. I learned during my investigation that self-injury of this type is common among people who are kept in extended periods of isolation.

The records show that on several occasions, I was left for two and three days at a time with no food or water. From December 30, 1970 until June 21, 1971, I was kept in seclusion and in wristlets and beginning on January 31, 1971, I was placed in a straightjacket. My arms and feet were tied to the bed. I remained this way until June 21st.

December 30, 1970 is a key date. The records show that it was the day I was transferred to 1A where I would remain until the following June.

A doctor's note written by Havas states that, "10B is not chemotherapeutically equipped to handle this patient."

Essentially this means that whatever experimental drugs VSH was preparing to give me would cause me to be unable to be on an open ward.

A computer-generated form dated December 30, 1970 includes biographical and clinical information about me. The information was transmitted via computer to an unknown computer terminal. Over the next several months, additional computer-generated information about me was transmitted via the computer data base system. During my investigation I learned that the computer- generated information was a component of the Rockland Project.

In the 2000's, I would learn that the Rockland Project, a $6.1 million dollar sophisticated computer network that connected to sites in several states, including Washington DC, was a project no one in the state or federal government wanted to talk about.

VSH continued to transmit clinical updates via the computer system throughout my time on the locked ward 1A and again in 1972 after I returned to VSH from four months in Fletcher's Baird 6. The transmissions suddenly end in 1972.

At CIA headquarters located at 1834 Connecticut Avenue, NW, Washington, DC, the site of John Gittinger's Psychological Assessment Associates, a CIA front, Gittinger kept the tests scores of each subject's PAS, or Personality Assessment System on a computer data base system. Test subjects' biographical information and clinical patient updates were kept with the PAS results. CIA spent "a small fortune" computerizing the PAS data bank. The CIA computer system was a multi-million dollar project, handled by CIA Project OFTEN and installed by the Office of Research and

Development in 1968.

Vermont installed a $6.1 million dollar computer data base system in 1968, which became operational late the following year, and which is described in original source documents as "the most sophisticated computer system in the country." VSH had the primary computer terminal on site. Every one of the other states listed as sites for the computer data base system and connected into Vermont's data base were CIA research sites during MKULTRA.

Beginning with a 1959 research project, VSH sent the results of PAS's conducted on child patients directly to John Gittinger at Psychological Assessment Associates, 1834 Connecticut Avenue, NW, Washington, DC, according to original source documents.

John Gittinger created the PAS for CIA, who relied heavily on these tests, describing them in CIA documents as "the key to the entire clandestine business." PAS is described as being used "to compromise people," "to look for soft spots" and "to get at people." The PAS is described by CIA as "planned destructiveness."

CIA described the primary motive in using the PAS in a 1963 CIA Inspector General Technical Services Division assessment: "PAS objectives are to control, exploit or neutralize. These objectives are innately anti-ethical rather than therapeutic in their intent."

The test was given to VSH child patients and the results were sent directly to Gittinger at CIA headquarters in Washington, according to UVM-VSH documents. Hyde routinely used Gittinger's PAS during his LSD experiments under the covert CIA funding source, Human Ecology. According to author John Marks, "Hundreds of thousands of dollars in Human Ecology grants and even more in Psychological Assessment contracts - all CIA funds - flowed out to verify and expand the PAS."

A bibliography of references on the use of Gittinger's PAS, compiled by Richard York and Barbara Allen, contains three citations for

UVM-VSH research projects in 1959, 1965 and 1966. VSH doctors Rupert Chittuck, Superintendent at VSH until 1968, George Brooks, who became Superintendent in 1968, and Donald Eldred, are cited in the bibliography. York notes that the criteria for inclusion on the list required, "explicit and specific mention of the PAS in a paper, article or book."

Richard York is identified in declassified CIA documents and he was an employee of Gittinger's Psychological Assessment Associates. York frequently conducted CIA-funded research with Hyde and UVM-VSH documents identify York as a "Consultant" who visited VSH during the experiments.

The sophisticated computer system was abruptly cancelled in 1973 when CIA Director Richard Helms ordered a halt to all MKULTRA projects and the destruction of all MKULTRA documents. In 1973, after MKULTRA became public, VSH never again conducted active patient research. The federal funding agencies that poured money into VSH research during the MKULTRA years admitted their witting participation in MKULTRA. VSH obtained all of its research monies through these federal agencies.

During my investigation, I filed FOIA's with the National Institute of Mental Health and the United States Public Health Service, both of which funded the Rockland Project. No documents were located. I contacted Rockland State Hospital in Orangeburg, New York for Rockland Project documents. The main processing terminal was located at Rockland State Hospital. No documents were located. I contacted Vermont Department of Health, seeking this information. No one in Vermont government knew anything about the Rockland Project and they were not able to locate documents. Yet I obtained a Vermont Biennial Report that provided details about the Rockland Project.

I contacted former Vermont Governor, Phil Hoff, by phone. Hoff was noted in the documents I had about the Rockland Project as a part of the process that brought the computer data system into VSH. My initial conversation with Hoff was pleasant, but he denied knowing about the Rockland Project and also claimed not to know Robert Hyde or anything about the CIA research in VSH-UVM. The phone conversation ended on a positive note and I thanked him for his time.

Much to my surprise, Hoff phoned me back three separate times. It was clear to me by the third time he called me back, that he was either unwilling or unable to answer my questions about the Rockland Project. Governor Hoff then made a curious statement.

"It's just as if it never existed," Hoff told me.

"But Governor, it did exist. I have the documents that prove it existed," I replied.

"Karen, it's just as if it never existed."

I understood the meaning behind the Governor's cryptic remark. The Rockland Project was a component of the CIA covert research. Almost all documents were destroyed in 1973 when MKULTRA was going to be made public. I am convinced that Vermont officials, past and present, have knowledge of the CIA covert research, allowed it to take place and continue to cover it up.

During the lawsuit, my lawyer Kim Hayden contacted the Vermont State Archivist in an attempt to locate certain documents thought to be in the possession of former Vermont Governors.

Gregory Sanford wrote in his letter to Kim: "We do not have the bulk of the Governor Philip Hoff records; as I noted, he is the only 20th century governor to largely ignore the requirements of 3 V.S.A. 4 and, instead placed his records with Special Collections in the Bailey/Howe Library at the University of Vermont."

The VSH medical record notes that I was seen once a week for several weeks, in my seclusion room, by Patrick Sullivan, from UVM Department of Psychology. There are no notes by Sullivan in the records and I have only one brief memory of seeing him.

Sullivan introduced himself when he entered the seclusion room. He wore a green suit coat and a vest. He had thick brown hair and wore black rim glasses.

He said to me, "You can't be hypnotized."

My memory ends there.

Experts have told me that the quickest and surest way to disarm someone when planning to conduct hypnosis is to tell that person that they cannot be hypnotized. The tactic was apparently successful.

On December 12, 1970, Dr. Otto Havas began writing orders for vaginal suppositories. There is no medical reason noted anywhere in the records for the use of these vaginal suppositories. They would be administered twelve times while I was tied to a bed in a straightjacket. Havas wrote the order to be used at the discretion of the doctor. During these months in seclusion and restraint I was prescribed placebos, along with up to eight different types of drugs at a time. I was subjected to two complete drug washouts.

Dr. Tom Fox explained to me that drug washouts are typical in experiments and a hallmark of experimentation. All drugs would be completely stopped and a period of time would elapse so that the chemicals would leave my system. Then new drugs would be started. I was also administered regular enemas. I have no memory of the administration of the vaginal suppositories or the enemas.

A November, 1970 doctor's orders chart from my VSH medical records lists the following drugs administered to me: Haldol, 2 mg three times a day; Artane, 2 mg three times a day; Reserpine, 2 mg IM, twice a day, PRN; Chloralhydrate, 500 mg, HS; Darvon 60 mg PRN; and Sodium Amytal, 250 mg IM, PRN.

A doctor's orders chart from April-May, 1971 contains the following drugs administered to me: Lithium, 300 mg three times a day; Dilantin, 100 mg three times a day; Elavil, 50 mg twice a day; Sodium Phenobarbital, ½

AMP, IM; Sodium Amytal 250 mg PRN; and Kemadrin, 5 mg twice a day.

In my investigation into the CIA drug and mind control programs at VSH-UVM, I obtained 1957 research project documents using FOIA. These documents showed that VSH-UVM disguised active experimental drugs by using placebos. This insured that no staff or patients would suspect that the placebo contained an active chemical substance. I believe that there was an active experimental chemical in the placebos I was given.

After prolonged periods in wristlets, I was, on several occasions, allowed out of seclusion. I began attacking the aides and I tried to plunge my head through windows on the ward. I was selective in which aides I targeted for violence. Only the aides who had abused me were attacked.

The night nurse on 1A, Alice Laplant, was a tough old Vermonter. She brought me water by the pitcher and allowed me to drink until I was satisfied. Alice removed me from seclusion one night and brought me into the nurse's station where she gave me a cigarette. The nursing supervisor came through the ward and reacted angrily when she saw me sitting with Alice. I remember the conversation between them

"What is she doing here? She is dangerous!"

Alice took a long, slow drag off from her cigarette and replied, "I know I don't have any reason to worry about Karen. Can you say the same?"

The supervisor left the ward. I believe Alice knew that I targeted only the abusive aides and she was right. She never had anything to fear from me. I entered Mary Fletcher very depressed, withdrawn and suicidal and left totally out of control, driven to the extreme by repeated doses of drugs I had severe reactions to. I entered VSH a thirteen-year old kid who was in obvious need of psychiatric help only to be repeatedly subjected to drugs that were known to cause allergic reactions. At eighteen I was no closer to knowing why I had the 1965 breakdown or why I had been sent to VSH in the terrible condition that I arrived there in. In October, 1971 my world had just begun to disintegrate.

I sat on the floor of the seclusion room with my arms bound behind my back in wristlets. I don't know how long I had been there. I cried to God, asking Him what I had done to deserve this. I agonized over the fact that no one in my family had come to take me out of the horror I was trapped in. I wondered how they could leave me like this. I was helpless and sinking deeper into hopelessness.

My mother was frantically trying to see me on 1A, but she was repeatedly told that I refused to see her. The North office supervisor, Ruth Phillips told my mother that the best thing she could do was to go back home and forget about me. My mother was shocked and angry. She had no intention of going away and leaving me, but her attempts to visit me were routinely blocked by VSH staff.

I recall being in seclusion and seeing Ruth Phillips at the door. She told me that no one in my family was coming to take me home and that I would die in VSH. My parents and I were being played by the VSH personnel. VSH couldn't allow anyone to see the conditions I was being kept in and I learned that several people tried to see me, but were turned away.

By April, 1971, rumors about what was happening to me reached Rutland County Mental Health staff members Rosemary Johnson and Judy West. They traveled to VSH as part of their job representing Rutland county patients in VSH. While at VSH they reviewed the medical records of Rutland county patients and visited each patient - except for me.

Rosemary told me in the mid 2000's that she and Judy were not allowed to view my VSH records and that they were prevented from seeing me on 1A. They strongly complained but it got them nowhere. They left VSH unable to see me.

In April, 1971, Judge Henry Black signed the visitor log in VSH North office and tried to see me. VSH refused to allow him to see me.

My mother also unsuccessfully tried to see me that day and Judge Black stopped her in the hall and introduced himself. He was visibly angry. Judge Black, who was accompanied by a female attorney, left VSH without either seeing me or apparently following up.

Judge Henry Black was described in an August 4, 1977 front page *Rutland Herald* article about his death as, “one of Vermont’s most influential lawyers.” Black was a member of the American Bar Association House of Delegates. He was president of the Vermont Bar in 1957.

How one of Vermont’s most influential Judges learned about me is a question I cannot answer. I don’t know why he allowed VSH to turn him away or why he didn’t follow up. I do know that there was no way that VSH would have allowed him to see me locked in seclusion and bound to a bed in a straightjacket. I remained in those conditions for almost two more months.

In an ironic twist, the obituary of Judge Black on the front page of the August 4, 1977 *Rutland Herald*, is next to an article entitled, “CIA Experiments Confirmed; Turner Says None Going Now.”

During the brief time I wasn’t on 1A in the first couple of months I was in VSH in 1970, I met Goddard College students who worked at VSH as part of their studies. One student, Phil Fass and I immediately clicked, although the first time he said his name was Phil, I turned and walked away. Phil was sensitive and intelligent and we enjoyed each other’s company, however brief the times we spent together were. When I was placed in seclusion in December, Phil was worried. The longer I remained in seclusion, the more concerned he became.

Over the next several months, Phil contacted Vermont Governor Deane Davis and explained my situation. Davis initially assured Phil that he would attend to the situation and Phil would be able to see me. A follow up contact with the Governor became a dead end. Phil contacted the ACLU and met with lawyers. He stressed that he simply wanted to see me and make sure I was okay. The ACLU told him that if he could find information for them about conditions inside VSH, they would make sure he was able to see me.

A second meeting was scheduled between Phil and the lawyers from ACLU. They met at a local diner. The lawyers told Phil that they had no idea what he was talking about after he asked if he could see me. The two men told him that if he didn't shut up and leave the situation alone, that they would make sure that Phil was locked up in VSH. Phil was stunned.

Phil wrote several letters to the Editor of the *Barre Times Argus* and the responses, many by personnel at VSH, were harsh and negative toward Phil. They wanted him to shut up and go away. Phil would remain in my life for the next few years, but in 1971, all that he could do was wait.

In April, 1971, I received electric shock treatments or ECT. The ECT chart shows that I had eight treatments and that each treatment involved the use of 30-35 shocks. The standard number of shocks given by medical professionals was one shock maintained for a fraction of a second. The records show the shocks were sustained over a 40-second period of time. On two separate occasions, the ECT failed to produce a seizure and the entire process was repeated.

CIA employed a type of ECT known as Paige-Russell. These ECT's used 35-40 shocks in each session, sustained over a prolonged amount of time. These ECT's produced a regressive state of confusion, disorientation and amnesia. Dr. Ewen Cameron, CIA researcher employed by McGill University and Director of the Allan Memorial Institute in Montreal, Canada, used Paige-Russell ECT in his MKULTRA Subproject 68 "depatterning" experiments. CIA and VSH-UVM were longtime research and personnel exchange partners with McGill, and personnel from McGill populated VSH and the Burlington psychiatric units, both before and during the times I was a patient in the hospitals.

I spoke with former Goddard student, Jane Youngbaer in 2009.

Jane was a friend of both Phil and I in 1970-1971. Jane described seeing me brought back to 1A after an ECT. She said I did not recognize her and that I was very different after the treatment. Jane was very disturbed by my condition.

On June 8, 1971, Havas made arrangements with neurologist, Dr. Hebert Martin at the Degoesbriand hospital in Burlington, a part of the Mary Fletcher hospital, known in 1971 as the Medical Center Hospital of Vermont, for me to be transferred to the neurology unit on June 21, 1971. Havas notes that I would be sent to the unit for "necessary brain studies and special treatment."

Havas writes that I was given eight ECT treatments in April and that there was no improvement. He also writes that ECT was given in an "effort to tame her."

In the book, *Acid Dreams*, by Martin Lee and Bruce Shlain, the use of LSD by CIA researchers is described: "LSD would be employed to provoke a reality shift, to break someone down and tame him, to find a locus of anonymity and leave a mark there forever."

The VSH medical referral form signed by Havas on June 18, 1971, lists my diagnosis as Neurosis, Hysterical, Dissociative Type and Personality Disorder, Schizoid. Drug sensitivities are listed as Penicillin, Darvon, Thorazine, Compazine, Tofranil and Mellarill. Noted as drugs currently prescribed are Mysoline and Thorazine.

Despite the pleas by my mother to Havas and other VSH doctors for information on my condition and for access to me, VSH did not inform my parents about my transfer to the Burlington hospital until June 21.

On June 18, 1971 the record shows that Havas conducted four ECT's. The record appears to have been written over showing 4 treatments. The number 6 is visible under the number 4. That night the doctor on call, Dr. Fontaine, treated eye and facial injuries I suffered. Dr. Fontaine was from McGill and her name appears again in the Baird 6 records in July of

1971.

ECT is known to cause amnesia and I believe that Havas conducted the treatments not only as part of the experiment, but also to insure that my memories of 1A were gone. For the most part, he was successful.

I woke up lying on a mattress in a seclusion room. I wasn't wearing wristlets. I tried to get up, but I couldn't. Nurses' aides brought me out of the seclusion room where Dr. Clare O`Shea conducted a neurological exam. O'Shea was the doctor Curlin brought me to on Weeks 3 after he removed me from seclusion in October, 1970

I was showered, dressed and placed in wristlets, with my arms in front of my body. 1A head nurse, Peggy Raymond and three other VSH aides accompanied me to a state-owned vehicle. Peggy gave me a cigarette. The car exited the grounds of VSH and pulled onto Interstate 89. It was June 21, 1971.

I remember looking out of the window of the car as it headed toward Burlington. The sky was a crystal clear blue, the sun was out and the pastureland and fields were a deep, rich green. I began to cry. I was overwhelmed by the knowledge that I had made it out of that terrible place alive. I stared out of the car window, smoked my cigarette and thanked God.

The next memory I have is of walking into the admission office at the Degoesbriand hospital. My arms were secured in leather wristlets, and I was accompanied by two VSH male aides and two VSH female aides. The woman conducting the admission suddenly left her chair and returned with a man who ordered the VSH aides to remove the wristlets and leave the premises. People sitting in the admission area seemed to react negatively to the event. I wondered what I had done to upset people.

I have few memories of the almost three weeks on the neurology unit. The records show that I was in a regressed child-like state and that I referred to myself, not as Karen, but as Skippy. The nurses began calling me Skippy. I would later say that Karen had died in VSH. I was prescribed Thorazine and Stelazine, despite a long-noted history of being allergic to the drugs.

CIA documents may help explain why, despite my repeated, well-documented allergic reactions to Thorazine and other phenothiazine drugs, VSH, Degoesbriand and Baird 6 doctors prescribed the drugs throughout the years I was a patient in the hospitals.

In the book, *The C.I.A. Doctors: Human Rights Violations by American Psychiatrists*, Dr. Colin Ross refers to CIA ARTICHOKE documents. ARTICHOKE was a CIA research program, the forerunner of MKULTRA. One of those documents reads:

"Still problematic is the use of drugs for deconditioning. Chlorapromazine (Thorazine) ought theoretically to have some value...It may be that this is exactly what we are looking for; perhaps it could decondition an enemy agent out of his simulated personality and back to his real one."

I was given a psychological test in which I was apparently not very cooperative. The record shows that I refused to use both hands during portions of the tests because I was holding a stuffed animal. The psychologist conducting the test was clearly checking my memory. It's noted that although I complained about my treatment in VSH, when pressed for details, I couldn't provide any.

Several EEG's were conducted. During one, I was placed in a strange room with walls on all four sides that looked like plastic. Suddenly as I lay hooked up to EEG leads, a man rushed into the room and broke a glass bottle on the floor. I reacted by crying.

The record states that, "The patient was purposefully upset by the breaking of the bottle."

On June 28, the records show that Dr. Charles Poser ordered an

EEG with Metrazol activation. Prior to the EEG I was given phenobarbital. The record shows that I was given 1800 mg of Metrazol. I had hallucinations. I complained that I was in severe physical pain. Apparently I recognized that I was, in fact, hallucinating and I accused the doctors of giving me drugs that caused me to hallucinate. The doctor refused to give me more than 1800 mg of Metrazol, noting that I had an unusual tolerance to the drug. No seizure was produced.

Metrazol is described in declassified CIA documents as being used on POW's in Soviet gulags.

It causes excruciating physical and psychological pain, so severe that a POW is said to, "Say or do anything to avoid another dose of the drug."

CIA documents describe the effects of Metrazol and the CIA reason for using it. In his book, *The C.I.A. Doctors*, Dr. Colin Ross refers to CIA documents that read:

"Metrazol, which has been very useful in shock therapy, is no longer popular because, for one thing it produces feelings of overwhelming terror and doom prior to the convulsion. But terror, anxiety, worry would be valuable for many purposes from our point of view."

Metrazol was used in MKULTRA to produce amnesia and as a way to negate the effects of LSD. A pre-treatment of phenobarbital was routine. The use of Metrazol was stopped throughout most of the world in the 1950's because of the excruciating effects it produced. Yet, in 1971, in the Degoesbriand hospital, in Burlington, Vermont, a nineteen-year old patient who had just been removed from almost seven months in seclusion and restraint was administered 1800 mg of Metrazol. I have no memory of the Metrazol activation and learned of it only when I obtained my medical records in 1997.

The record shows that the hallucinations continued after I returned to my room. I complained to the nurses that I heard "men in my head."

The record shows a notation that I was suffering from "hallucinatory effects of Metrazol."

That night I went into the bathroom and tried to set myself on fire.

A psychiatric consultation was ordered and Dr. Charles Ravaris from Baird 6, the Fletcher hospital inpatient psychiatric unit visited me. It was decided that I would be moved to Baird 6 and on July 2, 1971, I was taken to the psychiatric unit.

I can only imagine that when I was transferred from the brutal conditions in VSH to the Burlington hospitals, that I must have believed that I was finally safe. I suspect that after the administration of the Metrazol, I understood that I was not safe in the new hospital. During my investigation I obtained documents that show that I was very definitely not safe.

Documents obtained from the Department of Energy include its list of participants in the Human Radiation Experiments; they show that, in 1955, the University of Vermont College of Medicine entered into a contract with the Air Force School of Aviation Medicine, in Texas. UVM Department of Pharmacology handled the research. The Human Radiation Experiments were the forerunner of the CIA MKULTRA experiments. The Department of Energy list of participants includes a designation for UVM for conducting behavioral experiments. Robert Hyde is named as a participant by DOE.

In 1955, the Chief Scientist at the School of Aviation Medicine was Hubertus Strughold, former Chief Scientist for Research at the Dachau concentration camp in Nazi Germany. Strughold's Dachau experiments were unspeakably horrific and caused the agonizing deaths of thousands of concentration camp victims.

Strughold conducted experiments using drugs and mind control in Dachau and is widely regarded as having been the first to do so. Strughold was brought into the United States after WWII through the Paperclip

Project, which allowed certain Nazi war criminals to work for the American government.

The SAM-UVM contract grant, AF 18 (604)1093 was funded in part by the DOE, yet in the 2000's, DOE claimed to have no documents. UVM's Department of Pharmacology and VSH went on to conduct experiments using VSH patients. VSH secured a contract for the drugs, Thorazine and Reserpine, as well as other experimental drugs used in their research from Smith, Kline and French pharmaceutical company. Another contract was secured with CIBA and later a third contract was obtained with Mead Johnson.

In 1955, the CIA MKULTRA program was well underway at Boston Psychopathic Hospital where Robert Hyde conducted LSD and mind control experiments. VSH's research and exchange program with Boston Psychopathic was also well underway. UVM-VSH launched "schizophrenic rehabilitation" in 1955.

In 1961, UVM's first Chairman of the newly created Department of Psychiatry was Dr. Thomas Boag. Boag came to the UVM position from his position as Assistant Director to Dr. Ewen Cameron at McGill and the Allan Memorial Institute in Montreal, Canada. Boag's appointment to the position at UVM was reported in a 1961 American Psychiatric Association bulletin. Cameron was actively conducting CIA drug and mind control experiments at both Canadian institutions beginning in the 1950's. In 1959, when VSH-UVM administered experimental drugs to unwitting VSH patients as a part of the schizophrenic rehabilitation project, Dr. George Brooks traveled to the Allan Memorial Institute to present his paper on VSH experiences with schizophrenics.

In a search of Boag's research, I found that Boag had conducted numerous experiments using LSD with Dr. Paul Maclean. Maclean was a Boston neurophysiologist. Boag's position as UVM Chairman of the Department of Psychiatry, and UVM's use of Special Interrogations, LSD, mescaline and other experimental methods and agents, certainly helped facilitate the covert research conducted at UVM, VSH and the Burlington hospitals during the 1960's and early 1970's.

A 1963-1966 VSH-UVM research project, "Programmed Instruction with Disturbed Students," lists Boag, from UVM's College Of Medicine and George Brooks from VSH as the primary researchers. This project used the PAS and sent the results of the tests on child patients directly to John Gittinger at CIA headquarters in Washington, DC. The December, 1965 PAS conducted on me in VSH would have been sent to Gittinger.

In 1965, I have a faint memory of doing testing, some of which involved manual dexterity tests. I remember having my photograph taken. I also recall asking why the other patients didn't have their photographs taken and I was told that the other patients had already been photographed. No photo was included in my medical records. It's not a stretch for me to believe that my photograph landed on Gittinger's desk with my PAS.

Boag wasn't the only Ewen Cameron associate involved in UVM-VSH research. Dr. Heinz Lehmann, who would become Chairman of the Department of Psychology at McGill in 1971, is cited in UVM-VSH research documents. Two other Cameron Associates, Dr. Robert Malmo and Dr. Charles Shagrass are also cited in UVM-VSH research project documents.

In 1956, Brooks received the first fellowship from Smith, Kline and French and was sponsored by the drug company to spend six months on site at Boston Psychopathic Hospital. He was there for "special drug studies."

It's interesting to note that CIA academic funding came through and was paid through the use of "special study contracts" awarded through the use of CIA-connected foundations and groups. Smith, Kline and French Pharmaceuticals is identified in declassified CIA documents as providing drugs to CIA.

At the Burlington hospitals, where UVM doctors and medical students rotated to the units as well as to VSH, doctors from McGill populated all three hospitals. I spoke with several former staff members of Baird 6, who described McGill psychiatrists as routinely participating in the care of patients. One former staff member said that the McGill psychiatrists were simply part of the medical staff.

In 1955, Eric Wittkower, from McGill, created a CIA front group known as Transcultural Psychiatry. Wittkower's research is cited by VSH-UVM in the 1961 book, *The Vermont Story,* written about the VSH-UVM schizophrenic rehabilitation project.

A citation in the 1961 book, *The Vermont Story* was under the name of Eric Wittkower. The citation was for a conference held in Zurich, Switzerland on September 7, 1957. A Symposium on the Chemical Concepts of Psychosis was held in Zurich, Switzerland, September 1-7, 1957. A corresponding article was included in a 1958 book edited by Max Rinkel and Herman Denber - both CIA-LSD researchers. Rinkel is cited in UVM-VSH documents and Denber published with and conducted research with George Brooks.

Participants in the Symposium included CIA and LSD researchers, Paul Hoch, Hudson Hoagland, Abram Hoffer, Amedeo Marrazzi and Humphrey Osmond. These men were part of the CIA network that conducted LSD, brain implant and other mind control research, according to Dr. Colin Ross.

Hoch edited and published UVM-VSH research papers. Rinkel is cited in UVM-VSH documents and conducted extensive LSD research with Hyde. Hoagland conducted CIA-LSD research with Hyde at Worcester. Marrazzi worked out of Rockland State Hospital in New York, another UVM-VSH affiliate, under an Army contract.

During the summer of 1971, when I was a patient on Baird 6, a member of Transcultural Psychiatry, Dr. Thomas Chiu, was onsite. Chiu worked out of UVM's Department of Psychology. I have no memory of Chiu and learned of him through a former Baird 6 staff member. It's interesting to me that I have no memory of Chiu, who was on site at Baird 6 during the full four months that I was there. I can recall most of the doctors and the nurses on the unit.

For years in therapy with Kathy Judge, I told her numerous times before I obtained my medical records, that I had unexplained negative feelings about Chinese people. To my knowledge, I had never met a Chinese person and I had no reason to feel anything negative toward the Chinese.

After my investigation into CIA experiments in Vermont, Kathy and I spoke about the fact that Chiu was on site at Baird 6 and that he appears to be someone I cannot recall. Chiu, as a member of a CIA front group, has made me suspicious that I very well may have had contact with him and that it is no coincidence that I can't remember him.

Chiu worked out of UVM's Department of Psychology and he had been previously advised by Dr. Henry Murray, a well-known Harvard CIA researcher According to author Alston Chase in his book, *A Mind For Murder*, written about Unabomber Ted Kaczynski, Murray obtained LSD from Robert Hyde and conducted drug and mind control experiments on Kaczynski.

Author H.P. Albarelli, Jr. wrote in his book, *A Terrible Mistake*, that during the 1960's and early 1970's, UVM conducted drug and mind control research. CIA Director of Research and Robert Hyde's CIA boss, Sidney Gottlieb, stated in an interview that UVM "conducted Special Interrogations." Gottlieb also said that the CIA cover front groups, Human Ecology and Josiah P. Macy, Jr. Foundation "may have funded" UVM's research.

Special interrogations involved the use of electric shock treatments, chemical shock treatments including Metrazol, sensory deprivation, drugs such as LSD and mescaline, hypnosis and the creation of amnesia. In the

2000's, UVM denied a FOIA request I made about the SAM, LSD and mind control experiments. UVM claimed to have no documents or knowledge of CIA drug and mind control research and denied ever using unwitting subjects in their research. Documents I obtained contradict UVM's claims.

According to H.P. Albarelli Jr.:

"CIA's BLUEBIRD project focused almost exclusively on situations deemed "special interrogations" - or SI - in which the quick and complete inducing of full disclosure was paramount. Documents from the project's earliest meetings reveal a laundry list of methods including: heroin, morphine, polygraph, and electric shock, the use of "mechanical aids," lobotomies, hypnotism, fatigue, isolation, sensory deprivation and torture."

"BLUEBIRD laid the foundation for all of the CIA psychological manipulation and mind control programs to come."

BLUEBIRD was renamed ARTICHOKE in 1951. ARTICHOKE and MKULTRA ran alongside each other. In Montreal, in 1957, Ewen Cameron began conducting CIA funded brainwashing experiments known as depatterning.

According to John Marks, the President of Human Ecology, Dr. Harold Wolff, was "offered CIA access to everything in its files on threats, coercion, imprisonment, isolation, deprivation, humiliation, torture, brainwashing, black psychiatry, hypnosis and a combination of these with or without chemical agents."

"People with specific skills for special ARTICHOKE projects had been recruited from the U.S. Department of Agriculture, FDA, HEW and NIH...ARTICHOKE officials attempted to forge collaborative lines with Army, Navy and Air Force."

UVM secured a research contract with the Air Force School of Aviation Medicine in 1955. The contract was issued to UVM Department of

Pharmacology.

The book, *A Father, A Son and the CIA*, by Harvey Weinstein, notes that:

"The Air Force was interested in sensory deprivation with space flights in mind. They sponsored numerous research projects through Human Ecology...Gittinger helped connect Cameron and McGill to the Air Force interest in brainwashing, sensory deprivation and isolation research."

In 1971, Baird 6 was a newly built psychiatric unit and I walked onto the unit to find the nursing staff dressed in regular street clothing. One of the nurses told me that my doctor was the "best looking doctor in the hospital." Dr. Richard Ellison was indeed a handsome man and as I would learn over the time that he was my doctor, he was also a very kind, caring psychiatrist. Ellison was still a medical resident physician. His superiors were co-Chairmen of the Baird 6 unit, Dr. Richard Lippincott and Dr. Charles Ravaris. Baird 6 head nurse, Karen Esty would become a person I would not only fondly remember, but who went out of her way to try to help me.

My first few weeks on Baird 6 are pretty much a blur. I was manic after only a day on the new unit and unable to settle down long enough to sleep. I could eat when I was hungry and I could drink soda and coffee. I could smoke cigarettes, sit in comfortable chairs, watch television and actually talk to other people. I could walk the hallway without being bound in wristlets or secluded in a locked room. I could sleep in a bed with sheets and blankets and not on the bare floor of a seclusion room. I'm sure it must have been like heaven for me.

Former staff at Baird 6 told me during my investigation that they, as nurses were not told that I had been kept in the conditions I was kept in VSH. Baird 6 nurses did not know that I had spent almost seven months in a straightjacket. They also said that this information was kept out of my patient chart. My medical records support their assertions and contain no mention of the long seclusion and restraint in VSH.

Also withheld from the Baird 6 nurses, was the fact that at the age of thirteen, I had been a patient in the Mary Fletcher psychiatric unit. The former Baird 6 staff told me that the information kept from them would have been vital patient information and information normally provided to the nursing staff. They expressed their shock and were very disturbed to learn that the information had been kept from them. I also learned that, in 1965, McGill psychiatrists were also on site at the Burlington hospital.

My diagnosis when I became a patient on Baird 6 was once again shifted upon admission to the unit, back to schizophrenic, despite the previously noted diagnosis of hysteria, dissociative and schizoid. The former Baird 6 staff members described for me the frequent staff conversations in 1971 about my diagnosis. The staff recognized that I was dissociative and were split as to whether or not I was a multiple personality.

When I was able to speak with one of the Baird 6 staff in the 2000's, her response to learning that I was diagnosed as a multiple personality, was, "I'm not surprised at all. Most of us thought so in 1971."

On each page of my Baird 6 medical records my name is noted as "Skippy." The staff called me by this name, as did the doctors. Beginning with my admission to the neurology unit on June 21, 1971 and throughout the four months I spent on Baird 6, it appears that I was no longer Karen.

After learning that I had been an unwitting CIA experimental subject and learning the details of the research I was subjected to, valid questions surfaced. Did the researchers create a new personality in VSH? Did they create more than one personality? I entered VSH locked ward 1A as Karen and walked out of the locked ward eight months later referring to myself by another name. This name was accepted without question by the Burlington doctors and used in my medical records. I learned later that in the CIA's BLUEBIRD and ARTICHOKE mind control programs, new personalities and amnesia were created in subjects known to be dissociative. In the summer of 1971, the experiment continued.

The Baird 6 records show that over the course of the four months I was a patient, painkillers were prescribed. There are nurses' notes describing my complaints about pain in my head, jaws and face. The pain was apparently severe. No cause for the pain is noted. The VSH drug charts also show that during my time in seclusion, painkillers were given on a regular basis.

During the 1997 lawsuit years, a small scar was discovered behind my right ear. A plastic surgeon described the scar as "surgical." Other doctors I consulted agreed that the scar was surgical. There is nothing in my medical records that shows any surgical procedure or notes any reason for a surgical procedure to have been done.

In 2009, while brushing my teeth, I spit into the sink what I initially thought was a tooth filling. When I examined it, I quickly realized that the object was not a filling. My doctor examined the object and examined the inside of my mouth. On the inside right cheek was a small slit. My doctors referred me to an Ear, Nose and Throat specialist who also saw the small slit in my cheek. The specialist jokingly asked me if I had been kidnapped by aliens. I answered that it wasn't aliens.

The small slit inside the cheek of my mouth turned into what looked like an injection site and eventually disappeared. Another doctor told me that the object could not have been part of a dental procedure. If it had been, the object would have emerged from my gums, not from my cheek. He agreed that a surgical procedure had likely been conducted.

In 2009, I gave the object to Dr. Colin Ross, who examined it under a powerful microscope. He concluded that the object appeared to be rock, not metal and contained no electronic or computerized components. How the object got onto my mouth and why I had a surgical slit inside of my mouth, and behind my ear, remains unknown. The scar behind my ear remains clearly visible upon inspection.

The Baird 6 records show that I was child-like at times and then at other times openly defiant and angry. I frequently stormed around bitterly complaining about VSH. The nurses wrote in the records that there was a coordinated plan to discourage me from talking about VSH and it's clear from the records that they did so. They also asked me during these times to be specific about my complaints about VSH. I couldn't be specific. It's very clear that I could not remember.

I also had unexplained episodes where I ran head first into walls, doors or people. These episodes appear to be similar to the VSH 10B episode when I ran head first into the chalkboard trying to get away from Havas. Several EEG's were done as well as skull x-rays. The record also shows that Dr. Fontaine, the McGill psychiatrist who treated my eye and facial injuries in VSH, saw me on Baird 6 at least two times. It looks like she was the doctor on call. The records also show that I attempted suicide on several occasions, usually cutting my wrist. It's also clear from the records that there was a concerted effort by the psychiatrists to have me accept the fact that I was "schizophrenic." I fought the diagnosis.

One EEG stands out. The records show that I was taken across the campus grounds with a medical student I was fond of. We stopped and had ice cream and then he took me for the EEG. He wrote that I immediately changed. My mood went from happy and enjoying myself to angry, unresponsive to him and finally totally mute.

When reading the reference to the EEG, I wondered why it was necessary to exit the Fletcher hospital and cross the "campus" to have the EEG. Was this EEG done in the lab of UVM College of Medicine? The Fletcher hospital had its EEG lab on site inside of the hospital. There was no reason to leave the hospital grounds.

I now know that I would have had reasons to be very frightened to have an EEG after the terrible effects of the Metrazol activation done in

Degoesbriand. There would be another similar reaction to an EEG later in my life as well.

The Baird 6 nurse's notes contain descriptions of my condition and quotes from me on July 15, 1971. The record notes that I said I felt like, "clawing my eyes out." The record notes that I reported hearing a "whisper telling me to do things" and that I was unable to remember what these things were.

On August 28, 1971, the record shows that I complained of "sensations of something crawling all over her...that her arms and shoulders weren't hers...that she didn't feel like herself and that the cigarette in her fingers felt as thin as a piece of paper."

On August 29, 1971 the record shows that I was, "hyperventilating, frightened...apparently in great distress and tearful."

The record goes on to describe that I had, " feelings of depersonalization...detached from self, hands look funny, not herself... visual hallucinations, tactile hallucinations, things crawling up legs, visual distortions, hallucinations, things look bigger and smaller, rain falling from under the table...most preoccupied with going completely crazy...appears very frightened and out of control."

The record notes that I felt like I was losing control and that I was afraid I would remain this way forever.

Many of the symptoms described in the Baird 6 chart match symptoms reported by people who have been given LSD. In the book by CIA researcher, Harold Abramson, *The Use of LSD in Psychotherapy*, symptoms reported after taking LSD include quotes by patients:

"One half of my body feels different from the other half;" "It's as if half of my body is split off and independent of the rest;" "Parts of my body don't seem to belong to me;" "My hands and feet feel peculiar;" "Objects seem superimposed...in a strange fluid fashion." "My body seems to be doing strange things all on its own; changing size, growing younger and older;" "I have a fear that I might become permanently insane;" and "I have to struggle to keep things in control."

Phil Fass learned I was on Baird 6 and visited frequently. I liked Phil. He was an excellent friend to me and as we spent more time together, I began to fear that closeness. Phil wanted our relationship to grow and I realized that he felt more for me than I did for him. I might have been able to love him if things had been different, if I hadn't lost my Phil Cram and if all the terrible things that had happened to me hadn't happened. Phil and I remained in contact for a while longer.

I grew particularly close to head nurse Karen Esty. She tried hard to help me, as did most of the Baird 6 nurses. I was trying as hard as I knew how to be well, but my problems were overwhelming. Karen hung in with me.

It's notable that the Baird 6 records show no plan to help me transition out of the unit. There are no plans for my discharge or for where I would go when I left the Baird 6 unit.

In August, I was given ECT treatments. The chart shows that in one ECT I had a "prolonged recovery of respiration." In another ECT I stopped breathing for five minutes and had to be medically supported to breathe. The records show I expressed a significant amount of fear at having the ECT treatments, saying that they had made me worse before.

In October of 1971, a female patient confined to a wheelchair became the focus of most of the patients including me. She was a sweet person who was conflicted about going home on a weekend pass. She was suicidal and we were all worried about her. A few years before, she jumped from a sixth floor window of the Mary Fletcher hospital and ended up in a wheelchair. I vividly recall her promise to us that she would not do anything to harm herself.

It was Sunday morning and it was unusual for the doctors and the staff to call a meeting. We all gathered in the day room and were told that the woman we had all worried would harm herself, had committed suicide. The news hit everyone hard.

For reasons I cannot explain, the next day I went to the stairwell, opened a window and was preparing to jump when Dr. Ellison entered the stairwell and grabbed me. The incident was witnessed by a nurse from another floor.

I recall Dr. Ellison telling me, "You could have done anything else except this."

The hospital couldn't keep me on Baird 6 after this incident and when I was told that I would have to go back to VSH, whatever hope I had managed to find for myself, slipped away. My records note that I said numerous times over the four months I was on Baird 6 that I would rather be dead than ever go back to VSH.

I expected to be immediately transferred to VSH and as one day passed, then two days and then three days, I asked what the hold up was. I figured it would be easier to just get it over with. I never got an answer about the reason for the delay.

Karen Esty told me that I was going to be placed on Weeks 3 in VSH and that in January, Dr. Ellison would be the doctor on Weeks 3. She asked me to hold on until he came. I was familiar with Weeks 3. It was nothing like 10B and certainly nothing like 1A. I told her I would hang on until Dr. Ellison came. Karen and several of the nurses promised that they would visit me and the record shows that they kept their promises.

During my investigation, I learned from a former psychiatrist on Baird 6 the details of a behind-the-scenes arrangement that took place regarding my transfer back to VSH. The administrator of the Burlington hospital was in poor health and in his absence, Dr. Hans Huessy took over the position.

Huessy made arrangements with VSH and Superintendent George Brooks that I would be placed on the Chittenden county ward Weeks 3, which was overseen by UVM and the Burlington hospital. The arrangement included a provision that I would not be placed back on Havas' ward and that Havas would have no contact with me while I was a patient in VSH. Brooks and VSH agreed to the arrangement. It was a very unusual set of circumstances and it would take me years after I began my investigation to fully understand what it all really meant.

During my investigation of CIA MKULTRA, I was able to cultivate reliable sources of information from people who were on site at the three Vermont hospitals and from others who had valuable information that I never would have been able to find in documents.

I learned disturbing information about Dr. Curlin and I followed up on this information by filing a Vermont Records Act request in 2008. I requested documents regarding his dismissal as Assistant Superintendent from VSH. In August 1971, my source told me that Curlin was told by Superintendent George Brooks to leave VSH so as not to cause "a mess." Brooks had been informed that Curlin had sexual contact with female patients.

My Vermont Records request asked for documents held by the State in regards to the incident with Curlin. I spoke with an Assistant Attorney General about the matter and I learned, much to my shock, that it was assumed by the Attorney General's Office that I knew that Curlin had admitted "sexual misconduct" with me in VSH. I learned that Curlin's personnel records were made available to my former lawyer Alan George during the lawsuit and that in the closing of the lawsuit was an admission by Curlin about "sexual misconduct."

I told the Assistant Attorney General that I was never told about this and that I would speak with my former lawyer. Alan denied that he was provided Curlin's personnel records and that Curlin's admission was in the closing. I phoned the Attorney General's office again and told him what my former lawyer said.

"Your lawyer is a liar!" the Assistant Attorney General told me.

I initially defended Alan. I couldn't believe that he would have kept such important information from me. The Assistant Attorney General told me during our first conversation that he spoke with the lawyer who defended Curlin during the lawsuit and he stated that Curlin's admission was in the closing of the lawsuit.

The Assistant Attorney General denied saying these things to me during our second phone call, but he did tell me that he had read the closing and Curlin's admission of "sexual misconduct" was in the documents.

I decided not to challenge the State of Vermont and I withdrew my appeal on the records request. I stated that there was a "mutual misunderstanding" between the Assistant Attorney General and myself. The last thing I wanted was to get tangled up in any type of struggle with the State of Vermont again.

I went to the Rutland court and spoke with the court clerk who told me that when there is a settlement between the sides in a lawsuit, the details of the closing remain between the lawyers and are not part of the official court documents.

Suddenly things made sense to me. When the State offered me three times the amount they initially offered to settle after I ended the lawsuit, I repeatedly asked Alan why they would even pay me a single cent. They didn't have to because I ended the suit. His answer was only to take the money.

I was absolutely shocked that my lawyer would have kept the information about Curlin from me. It made no sense to me and it made no sense to Kathy. What did make sense to me was that Curlin insured that I would never come back on him in another lawsuit by paying me money. He knew that eventually I would find out about his "sexual misconduct." I was left to surmise that this was why the State paid me the amount they finally did.

Alan denied knowing about Curlin's admission. I asked him if he had ever been threatened during my lawsuit and he denied that he had. When I asked him to send the lawsuit documents to my current lawyer, a great deal of the documents had been " lost."

During the lawsuit one lawyer made a startling claim. He stated that, "People have been murdered over this before!"

I thought about his revelation and things really began to make sense to me, despite the steadfast denials by my former lawyer.

I will never know for sure what was actually in the closing of the lawsuit. I was never provided a copy of the closing. The information I have been able to obtain from several reliable sources tells what I need to know.

Curlin and Havas were friends, I learned from sources who knew them both. Even Curlin told me on the phone during the lawsuit that he and Havas were friends. Havas is the doctor who wrote the orders for vaginal suppositories when I was on 1A and his behavior with me in VSH is suspect at best. The behind-the-scenes arrangements between the Fletcher hospital and VSH to keep Havas away from me in 1971 also raise disturbing questions.

VSH Superintendent George Brooks very clearly knew that Curlin was involved in sexual misconduct, apparently with me. Brooks did not want a "mess" for VSH or for the covert CIA experiments being conducted at VSH-UVM. Any investigation into VSH would have put the CIA project in jeopardy. The last thing VSH wanted was a nasty sex scandal. If the information I received from multiple sources is true, Brooks covered up a crime.

It appears as if the Fletcher hospital was also privy to information about Havas. Whatever they knew caused them to make special arrangements with VSH to insure that Havas had no contact with me in VSH.

The behavior of Havas during the 1970-1971 months he was my doctor raise disturbing questions as to his involvement in sexual misconduct as well. If the Fletcher hospital did in fact know anything about sexual misconduct by VSH doctors, they too committed a crime by covering it up. Havas wrote the orders for vaginal suppositories and they were used twelve times between December, 1970 and May, 1971. Did Havas write the orders for Curlin or was Havas also involved in "sexual misconduct?" It appears as though I will never know for sure. But my medical records and the valuable information provided to me by sources in positions to know the truth, tell a story.

I realized, in 2008, that someone working at VSH had to have told Brooks about Curlin and me. It's obvious that Curlin didn't bring the information to Brooks, so someone out there saw something and knows even more. It's also clear to me that Curlin knew I could not remember, when no allegations of sexual misconduct were included in the lawsuit I filed.

It's difficult to realize that if the information about Curlin is true, personnel in two Vermont hospitals kept it covered up. The Vermont Attorney General's office apparently knew about Curlin, if the information I obtained is accurate, and they too kept it covered up. In 1971, all that mattered to VSH, UVM and the participating Burlington hospitals and personnel, was the experiment. In October, 1971, I returned to VSH where the medical records and my memory show that the experiment continued.

I was admitted to Weeks 3 on October 29, 1971 where charge nurse, Viola Littlejohn got me settled in. I'd known Littlejohn since I was thirteen. She was the nurse on duty the first night I was in VSH in 1965. Littlejohn was someone I trusted and thought highly of. She was a tough, no nonsense woman with a heart of gold. She liked me and I always got along well with her. I always knew where I stood with Littlejohn. I liked the fact that she had no hidden agenda. If she had something to say, she said it. She was one of the very few VSH staff I had positive feelings about.

Being back in VSH hit me hard. I was very depressed and overwhelmed by feelings of despair. It seemed that I would never leave the hospital. Somehow, I kept going. I waited for Dr. Ellison to come in January and when he finally arrived, I hoped that maybe he and I could work toward getting me out of the hospital. Several Baird 6 nurses, including Karen Esty visited me on Weeks 3 to provide support. I appreciated their visits.

Dr. Ellison encouraged me to study for my GED and he started helping me study. I was enrolled in the VSH school working toward my high school diploma. In addition, Phil Fass kept in touch, sometimes in person and other times by phone. Phil wanted me to move to New Jersey where he lived. I was hesitant, but we remained in contact for several months until for reasons I cannot recall, Phil stopped contacting me. It's possible I asked him to stop, but I don't know for sure.

While I was in Baird 6, I began to escape the hospital and the first time I did, raises questions. I was in a room directly across from the nurses' station under close observation. During the middle of the night, dressed in nightclothes, I managed to somehow leave the observation room, take an elevator down to the main floor and leave the hospital grounds, all the while unnoticed by anyone. I was found by a police officer downtown in Burlington. He returned me to Baird 6.

I began to escape from VSH in the fall of 1971 and each time I escaped I was successful. Waterbury, where VSH was located, is a small town. Many VSH staff reside on the same streets I took to make my way to the Interstate. There were even several instances when I escaped that I encountered the Waterbury Chief of Police on my way to the Interstate. He used to wave and say hello. He called me by name.

I stuck out my thumb and got a ride quickly. I was headed toward Waitsfield on Route 100. I noticed that the back seat of the car was filled with camera equipment of all kinds. I asked the man driving the car about it. He said he was a photographer. I told him where I was from and we talked for miles. When we got to the junction of the road I told him that I wanted to get out.

"I'm going out of the country on a job. Do you want to come with me?" he asked.

I was surprised by his offer, but I declined, saying I'd go back to VSH.

The man said he would turn his car around and drive me all the way back to VSH and when we arrived in the VSH parking lot, he extended his offer again.

"Are you sure you don't want to come with me?"

Again I declined his offer and as I watched him drive away, I thought that the entire incident was a little strange. I told no one in VSH about it.

I left VSH one night and hitchhiked on Route 100. I was picked up quickly by a priest who drove me as far as Waitsfield, where I asked him to let me out of the car. It was very rural and there were no streetlights. I couldn't see my hand in front of my face as I tried to walk. I finally went to a house where I told the people inside where I was from. They called VSH and I was returned to the hospital.

The next day, the same priest came up to me on Weeks 3. I asked him what he was doing there and he told me that he was the priest at VSH. I knew this was not true because I knew the priest at VSH. The man who claimed to be a priest left the ward and I never saw him again. Whoever he was, he wasn't a priest.

I escaped again. I would have been very aware of the fact that escaping VSH brought consequences, yet I escaped time after time for reasons I cannot explain. The records note the escapes but show nothing that might explain the reasons why I might have run.

I easily slipped out of the hospital, made my way through the streets of Waterbury and stood again on the Interstate. I looked closely at the young man who stopped to give me a ride. He was blond, with a short, military-styled haircut. I noticed he wore a pale yellow, button-down collar, short sleeve shirt. I decided that he looked safe and I got into the car.

He drove on Interstate 89 as far as the exit to Richmond and when he took the exit off the Interstate and began driving on the secondary road, I asked him why. He didn't answer me. He pulled his car off from Route 2 and when he began driving on a dirt road, I became very uneasy. Several miles up the dirt road he pulled down into a logging road and I knew I was in danger. He clearly knew where he was going.

He stopped the car at the bottom of a very steep hill, at the end of a logging road and turned off the engine. The area he parked in was remote and secluded.

He never looked at me and then said, "Get out of the car."

I knew he was going to hurt me and as I exited the car I decided that I was going to do as much damage to him, including kill him if I had to. I looked around the ground for a rock and when I found a suitable rock I picked it up and waited for him to come near me.

He opened the driver's side door and stood beside his car, resting his right arm on the roof of the car.

"Get out of here!" he announced.

I couldn't believe what I was hearing and I didn't move, expecting that he would come after me any minute.

He shouted to me again, "I said get out of here!"

Stunned, I began to walk away, carefully watching him to make sure he wasn't going to suddenly run up behind me. I walked up the logging road hill, still clutching the rock in my hand. I refused to run.

I reached the dirt road, still expecting him to change his mind and come after me. I walked along the dirt road picking out spots along the way I could jump into to hide myself if he came for me. Suddenly I heard a car coming. I didn't wave the driver down. I didn't step onto the road or let him know that I was in danger. To this day I don't know why I didn't signal for help.

The vehicle coming down the road was an old pickup truck and the old man driving it drove on by me and disappeared from sight. I kept walking and waiting for the blond man to come after me. I realized that the pickup truck had turned around and was coming back. The driver turned his truck around again and stopped next to me.

"I have a Granddaughter your age and I wouldn't want her out here alone so I came back. Get in," the old man said to me.

I got in.

I began telling the old man what had happened with the blond man and as I talked, I nervously looked back expecting the blond man to come racing up behind us. The old man pulled onto the Interstate and drove fast. When we neared the Waterbury exit, the blond man raced his car up behind us. He pulled his car up close to the rear of the truck and pulled back several times as if to try to intimidate the old man. He pulled alongside the truck and glared at us.

"That's him!" I shouted to the old man.

"Don't be afraid. He isn't going to hurt you," the old man replied.

The blond man slowed his car and eventually backed off and we lost sight of him when we exited into the town of Waterbury. I asked the old man to take me to the police, but he said that he would take me back to VSH and he would go to the police for me. The old man returned me to the VSH parking lot and drove away. I waited for the police to contact me but they never did.

Only after I learned that I had been experimented on was I able to understand this incident and the conclusion I reached is disturbing. As I would find in other situations related to the experiment in VSH, certain pieces of information that were contained in my medical records, particularly information given to VSH by my mother when I was thirteen, were apparently used in the experiments. Whether it was my love of horses, used by Curlin in

1971, or my intense reaction to the Kennedy Assassination, key information was pulled directly from my medical records.

"You can't remember the Kennedy Assassination, can you?" I was asked by one of the psychiatrists.

My close relationship with my Grandfather, noted in my 1965 records, was also used. They used information from my mother about my running away when I was five years old and the history I had with guns, including my brother being shot and my preoccupation with them. I am convinced they learned about my early childhood traumas in 1965 using Sodium Amytal. They used the information, like Gittinger said in reference to the PAS, to exploit, get at and compromise people.

It is not difficult for me to believe that the blond man was part of the experiment. Once he saw me pick up the rock, he knew that I would fight for my life. Those conducting the experiment already knew that when pushed I would react violently. They witnessed that behavior on 1A. The old man said something key when he told me that he had a granddaughter my age.

I also realized years later that the two men were clearly working together. All the time I was in the truck I looked back, fearful that the blond man would come after me. The truck went miles before the blond man actually pulled up behind us. How did he know what vehicle I got into? When I got into the truck on the dirt road, the blond man was still at the bottom of the logging road. It would have been physically impossible for him to have seen the truck or seen me get into it.

Even more disturbing for me is the young blond man, whose face I could never fully recall. He is the first person I thought of in the 2000's when the blond man with the wire rim glasses began to harass me. Something about the blond man with wire rim glasses was familiar. I felt that I had met him before and he was the only one of the many who tried to harass me in the years after I filed the lawsuit, that I felt threatened by. The threat I felt and told Kathy about many times was that I knew this man from my past. I will never know if the blond man in 1972 and the blond man in the 2000's is the same man.

The admission form in the October, 1971 records includes a physical done upon admission. One area stands out. Under the section where my face, neck and ears are examined, it is noted that I have an "old fibrosis" on the right TM joint. The admission physical in October, 1970 contains no such fibrosis.

The Baird 6 record shows that in July of 1971 the nurses noted my complaints about severe pain behind my right ear. They noted a large "sac" and inflammation present behind my right ear. No examination by a doctor is noted to have taken place and there are no further notes in the Baird 6 records that would indicate I was seen by a doctor or treated for any medical condition related to this problem. The 1972 VSH record also notes complaints by me about pain behind my right ear. A nurse's note describes a "bunch" behind my right ear. There was, according to the records, no further follow-up.

The surgical scar behind my right ear that was discovered during the lawsuit, combined with the large amounts of painkillers I was given on Baird 6 for facial, jaw and head pain and the extensive use of painkillers in VSH when I was in seclusion and restraint, lead me to the disturbing possibility that I was surgically implanted as part of the experiment. I may have been implanted while on 1A and the implant may have been removed when I was transferred to Burlington. It is also possible, based on information about the MKULTRA experiments, that I was triggered to escape by preprogrammed hypnotic suggestions. CIA used this method during Special Interrogations research. My VSH escapes suggest that one or both of these methods may have been used. The people who appeared in the escapes also strongly suggest that not only was I being closely monitored when I escaped, but that the people monitoring and following me had no intention of allowing anything to happen to me. It was during my final escape from VSH that I saw this play out.

Dr. Ellison began escalating his plan for me to leave VSH. He was due to leave his 6-month position in June, 1972 and he wanted me out of the hospital before he left. I obtained my GED in May and arrangements were made for my discharge on June 19, 1972.

On June 19, 1972 CIA Director Richard Helms ordered the destruction of all MKULTRA files, saying the files were "dynamite and could damage CIA operations." The files were actually destroyed on June 30, 1972. In June of 1971, Attorney General John Mitchell viewed secret files and was reportedly sickened for days by what he read.

I find it to be an extraordinary coincidence that I was discharged from VSH, an active CIA experiment site at the same time when CIA ceased MKULTRA operations, destroyed the files and faced public exposure for its covert experiments.

I went back to my parents' house and tried to begin a normal life. I got a job and tried as hard as I could, but it was no use. I left my parents' house and hitchhiked back to VSH. I walked onto the grounds in the middle of the night and was readmitted to Weeks 3. In retrospect, I can only assume that by this time I was institutionalized. I must have believed that I could not make it outside of the hospital. It's difficult for me to imagine that I voluntarily returned to VSH, but I did.

I don't remember what happened, if anything, to cause me to escape again only days later. I have no explanation for why I ran and the records provide me with no information as to the cause of my escape.

I easily escaped the grounds of VSH and quickly got a ride on the Interstate. The heavy-set man behind the wheel asked me if I would like to stop at McDonald's on the Barre-Montpelier road and I said, yes. He bought me a meal and we were on the Interstate again. I had no idea where I was going and as the miles passed, the man began to talk in a way that made me nervous.

He patted the seat of the car and asked me to slide over closer to him. I reacted immediately by sliding nearer to him and placing a knife to his throat. He had no way of knowing that the knife was a blunt-ended butter knife I took from the Weeks 3 ward, and I wanted to keep it that way. His arms were bigger around than my thighs and I knew if he realized that the knife wouldn't cut him, I was in deep trouble.

I saw a place up ahead on the highway and told him to pull over and stop. I immediately got out of the car, ran down into the wooded area and disappeared from his view. I came out of the woods to find a farmhouse, which I entered. No one seemed to be in the house. I have no idea why I entered the house or what I planned to do.

A man came in the door and was understandably startled to find me there. I told him I did not want to hurt him or hurt anyone and that I was from VSH. I told him that VSH had done terrible things to me. I noticed a rifle hanging on a rack over a door and told him I needed it.

He said, "You don't want this old BB gun."

I looked at the rifle and decided that I didn't need it. I left the man's house and ran into a large field. I found a hunting camp and since it was starting to get dark, I decided to enter the camp and stay the night. I curled up on the bed and tried to figure out what to do.

I heard voices outside and saw the light from a flashlight. It was the Vermont State Police. They came into the camp and brought me back to VSH. During my escapes from VSH, I had repeated contact with the Vermont State Police. Every time I was picked up by the troopers, they treated me with kindness and respect. They bought me cigarettes and sodas and listened to my hatred of VSH. Apparently, I was unable to provide specifics about the treatment I received in VSH.

The Vermont State Police were practically the only people during those years that consistently treated me like a human being. I will always have the utmost respect and regard for the Vermont State Police. Thanks guys.

I was initially returned to Weeks 3 but it was soon apparent that I was to be transferred to the locked ward, now called 2A. Weeks 3 aide, Edie walked me to the locked ward and I can only imagine the despair I must have been feeling as I approached the ward.

Edie and I were met at the door by seven or eight aides. They were clearly prepared to do battle with me. Edie spoke up and stressed that I had walked peacefully with her. The aides led me into the ward, down the hall and into a seclusion room. As I undressed, I noticed that of one of the aides, who I had known before and had no problems with, was trembling.

"Don't worry, Sherry, I'm not going to give you any trouble," I said.

Sherry looked surprised and responded, "I hope not, Karen."

I was Karen again. I had been Skippy from the moment I had left 1A over a year earlier. All throughout my time on Baird 6 and during the nine months on Weeks 3, I was called Skippy by staff and patients. But when I walked into the locked ward in July, 1972, I was once again Karen.

I wasn't forced to sleep on a bare floor and I wasn't restrained in wristlets. I slept in a bed and in the morning, I was allowed out of the locked room for a shower and to get dressed. I recognized many of the aides and patients from my time on 1A, but I also noticed new faces.

Dr. Karl Trieal, the Russian doctor who ran the 1A ward when I was there before, tried to talk with me, but I refused to speak with him. The records show that during the brutal months in seclusion on 1A, Trieal may have been the doctor of record, but that Havas was clearly in charge of my treatment. I had nothing but contempt for Trieal and he knew it.

One of the new faces on 2A was an aide named Debby. She approached me the first day and tried to engage me in conversation, but I wasn't interested in talking to anyone.

Debby later described the expression in my eyes as, "Like mirrored sunglasses. You can look out but nobody can see in."

Over the next several weeks, Debby continued to try to make friends with me.

I caused no problems on the ward and it was apparent, even to these aides who had participated in the brutal seclusion room months, that my time in Baird 6 had helped me. I was allowed to have ground privileges as long as an aide was with me. On August 8, 1972, there is nothing in my records to show what if anything had happened to cause me to run.

An aide named Sherry took me and another patient named Jane out of the ward and onto the hospital grounds. The record notes that we were on our way to the hospital canteen. I knew when I exited 2A that I was going to run and I lagged behind Sherry and told Jane to catch up to Sherry because I was running. Jane asked me if she could come with me and I told her it was up to her what she did. I had always made my escapes alone and I wasn't comfortable with someone else coming along, but I agreed. Sherry, a young, new aide was walking quite a distance in front of us, and not paying close attention to what we were doing and when I saw the opportunity, I took it.

Jane and I ran across the grounds and headed for the street. Initially Sherry thought Jane and I were playing a joke on her but she quickly realized that we were not. Jane and I reached the railroad tracks, climbed up the hill and made our way easily to the Interstate. Within moments, we got a ride and were gone.

An elderly couple gave us a ride into Montpelier, where they stopped at a store. Jane went into the store and bought two sodas and a pack of cigarettes. I remained in the car. We were soon on the Interstate again when Jane and I asked the couple to let us out of the car. I'm not sure how many miles away from VSH we were by the time we left the first vehicle. We stood hitchhiking for only moments before a young man in a fast car stopped to give us a ride.

It didn't take long before I realized that Jane and the young man knew each other. I sat in the back seat and she slid very close to the young man in the front seat as we sped along the Interstate. I became increasingly uneasy and finally I asked them to stop and let me out of the car. The young man pulled to the side of the road and I got out of the car. As I watched the car disappear up the Interstate, I suddenly felt overwhelmed by despair. I stood by the side of the Interstate for several minutes staring as the car sped down the Interstate. I was still carrying the glass soda bottle in my hand, and I stepped over the guardrail and made my way down the steep embankment. At the bottom of the embankment I found a small cluster of cedar tress where I laid down. I cut my wrist, closed my eyes and waited to die.

When I first heard the men's voices I thought I was dreaming or hallucinating. I have no idea how much time had passed.

"She's over here!"

I opened my eyes to see three men standing over me. They reassured me that they would not hurt me and said that everything would be okay. Two of the men picked me up, carried me up the steep embankment and placed me in the backseat of their car. One man stayed in the back with me while one drove the car and the third man looked back at me from the front passenger seat. The men repeatedly told me not to be afraid. I've always remembered what they said but I have never been able to recall their faces.

The record shows that I was brought to the New London, New Hampshire hospital by, "A man who refused to give his name and refused to give any other information except that he found her near the Exit 13 on the Interstate."

The record goes on to say that the man left the hospital and that New Hampshire State Police were notified and went to Exit 13 to check to see if I might have been in a car accident. I don't remember being brought into the hospital by the man. My memory begins again when I was in surgery.

At first I felt confused and then wary of the doctors. I refused to answer their questions until I was taken to a hospital room where I told them my name and where I had escaped from. The record shows that Dr. Karl Trieal informed the New Hampshire hospital that I was a "paranoid schizophrenic." Nothing in any of my medical records supports Trieal's diagnosis.

I have no doubt that Trieal told the New Hampshire hospital that I was a paranoid schizophrenic for a reason. The last thing VSH or Trieal wanted was for anyone, especially an out of state hospital staff and the State police, to believe me if I told them about VSH conditions. The diagnosis of paranoid schizophrenia would have insured that nothing I said would be given any merit,

I was taken to the Vermont state line by two New Hampshire State Troopers, who treated me very well. Two Vermont State troopers transported me back to VSH where I was taken back to 2A. I was not placed in seclusion.

A few days later, I asked an aide where Jane was and she said that, "Jane was probably back in Massachusetts."

This statement meant little to me in 1972 but in the 2000's it meant a great deal, given the fact that VSH-UVM conducted research with Boston Psychopathic Hospital and placed staff at VSH.

When I was first placed back on the locked ward 2A, I asked an aide where another patient I had known before was. Her name was Janie. She was about my age, blond and in horrible condition. Her coordination was severely impaired and she could barely walk. She had terrible seizures.

I was told that, "Janie died. She is a good example of what happens when you take too much LSD."

When I discovered the evidence of experimental LSD use at VSH and UVM, I wondered if Janie had been a victim of the experiments. I would later find shocking evidence that Janie may not have been the only death at VSH caused by the covert experiments.

After learning about the CIA experiments, I took a close look at this escape, the circumstances of which had always bothered me. Kathy and I talked about it many times over the years before I obtained my records. I always insisted that there was simply no way that the three men could have seen me at the bottom of the steep embankment. I knew they couldn't have seen me from the Interstate. How did they know I was there?

During the lawsuit, I went with Alan to New Hampshire to see Dr. Tom Fox and we drove past Exit 13. It was clear that it would have been impossible for those three men to see me at the bottom of the embankment. Alan agreed that it would have been impossible.

I thought about Jane going into the store while I remained in the elderly couple's car. Did she phone the young man she so clearly knew who picked us up? This was the only time I ever escaped with someone else. I always escaped alone. I realized that the three men had to have been following me. They knew I went down the embankment because they had been watching me during the escape. The man's refusal to give his name at the New Hampshire hospital is also key. There were three men in the car that day, yet only one went into the hospital.

I concluded that the three men were part of the continuing experiment as was Jane. Although I will never be completely certain, I learned about an interesting tactic used by CIA in their LSD experiments known as the "stable mate project."

CIA placed a non-mentally ill employee on a hospital ward to befriend a specific research subject. The employee was from outside the hospital and the same age as the intended subject.

The stablemate or the "running mate" is based on the concept of two horses from the same stable entered in a race.

According to the book, *The Use of LSD in Psychotherapy*,

by Harold Abramson, a well known CIA researcher and research partner of Robert Hyde, "The horse, by having in the race a familiar partner to whom he is conditioned, is motivated to overcome the stresses of the strange competition because of adaption to a familiar and safe object."

Abramson goes on to say, "Earlier experiences led us to hope that under the action of LSD this process of identification with a stablemate might be potentiated."

My suspicions about having been given LSD in VSH while on 1A and in the 1965 Mary Fletcher hospitalization were supported by Dr. Tom Fox and by Kathy. Both believed that I had been given the hallucinogen, based on their experiences with others who had taken the drug. I would also have an experience in 1987 that would suggest that the chances of prior LSD use were high. I never willingly or wittingly took any drugs except those prescribed by a doctor.

I believe that my escapes were not only part of the experiment but that they involved the use of a triggered response mechanism set up in me by hypnosis and implants. CIA declassified documents show that CIA was very invested in controlling a subject's behavior. Numerous books on the CIA research and declassified CIA documents detail the use of hypnosis to achieve this control. The subject would not know or have any awareness that his or her actions were triggered by pre-programmed commands. I may never know for sure that these tactics were used on me, but my records and the memories I have of the escapes suggests that they were.

The new VSH aide, Debby, called the ward one day in August, 1972 and had an aide ask me if I wanted to go out on a pass with her and go swimming. I was surprised but very happy to go. Debby came to VSH and took me with her back to Moscow, Vermont, a small town near Stowe.

I remember walking along the quiet road with Debby on that summer afternoon. Debby bought us sodas in the small store in Moscow and she took me to a pond behind a house in the town. I felt free for the first time in almost three years. I almost felt normal. Debby was fun to be with and we laughed and swam in the pond.

Debby brought me to meet the people she lived with, Henry and Joyce. They welcomed me into their home and invited me to have dinner with them. I hadn't had a home cooked meal in a long time and Joyce was an excellent cook. I ate heartily.

We sat in the living room after dinner, talking and watching television. I remember sitting on the floor, resting my back on the chair Debby sat in. I hadn't spent time in a home in three years and I savored the experience. That evening, Henry drove me back to VSH and told me that I was welcome to visit anytime. It was the best day I had in a long time. Over the next few weeks, Debby took me back to Henry and Joyce's house many times and I enjoyed every minute of my time with them. I began to hope again.

4
RELEASED, NOT FREE, 1972-1981

When a person is involuntarily committed to a state mental institution, the Board of Mental Health is required to meet every six months and decide if the person can be released on conditions or continue to be confined. My records show that from October, 1970 until August, 1972, the Board met once, without my being present. Records show that in August, 1972 the Board finally allowed me to be present at the meeting.

If I was told ahead of time that I was going to meet with the Board and possibly be released, I have no memory of it. I was taken from 2A by an aide and led into a room where several doctors, including George Brooks sat at a table.

I had nothing but contempt for the doctors sitting in front of me asking me questions and it took me a few minutes to actually realize that this meeting might free me from VSH. I don't recall the questions I was asked or the answers I gave but I vividly remember watching George Brooks' reactions to my answers.

Brooks frequently glanced at the other men in the room and smiled, as if satisfied by my responses. I quickly figured out that Brooks had some type of investment in my success at this meeting. Two years of fighting these people had profoundly affected me. I hated everything they stood for. I began to give inappropriate answers to their questions.

I watched Brooks closely. He was visibly upset by my responses. At one point he physically almost flinched and lowered his head as if in disgust and disappointment. I couldn't understand why Brooks cared whether I stayed in VSH or not. I wondered why he would be so invested in my leaving. I failed the Board of Mental Health meeting.

It would take me thirty years to understand why George Brooks was so intent on my leaving VSH in 1972. Dr. Karl Trieal, who was the doctor for the locked women's ward 2A, where I was being kept, was preparing to retire. Dr. Otto Havas was going to take over the ward. Because of the arrangement made by Dr. Hans Heussy, VSH and Brooks could not allow me to be on the same ward as Havas.

Additionally, by the summer of 1972, the CIA drug and mind control programs had been canceled. It wouldn't be long before the first Senate investigation would begin and within a few years, every national news agency would report the CIA MKULTRA programs to the American public. Brooks and VSH, including Dr. Robert Hyde had a lot to concern themselves with in 1972.

I obtained documents and reliable information about several VSH staff psychiatrists, including former VSH Assistant Superintendent, H. Peter LaQueur, who held this position until Curlin replaced him in 1970. LaQueur had been an agent with the Office of Strategic Services during WWII. OSS became CIA in 1947. LaQueur was found in CIA declassified MKULTRA documents as a member of two CIA front groups. His name is listed as a member in a 1962 Society For Biological Psychiatry document and he is also listed as a member of another CIA front group called the Manfred Sakel Foundation.

John Bockoven was a former VSH staff psychiatrist and was a frequent research partner of Hyde and of CIA researcher Richard York. Bockoven was onsite at Boston Psychopathic Hospital during the MKULTRA LSD testing and is noted in VSH-UVM research project documents as having been onsite at VSH in the role of consultant to VSH-UVM research.

I filed a Vermont Records Act request with the Vermont Department of Personnel for verification of John Bockoven's employment by VSH. The request was granted and the one-page document on Bockoven was completely redacted.

I filed similar requests with the Vermont Department of Personnel seeking verification of employment of Dr. Otto Havas. No documents were found. Havas is noted in several VSH publications as an on-staff VSH psychiatrist, yet he was not found to be employed by VSH or by the State of Vermont. The Hungarian psychiatrist's employer has not been identified.

Dr. Karl Trieal, the Russian psychiatrist, began working at VSH as a staff psychiatrist in 1952, using the name Karl Trieal-Kink. He was on staff at the hospital until his retirement in 1972. No documents were located on Trieal. He was not employed by VSH or by the State of Vermont. The identity of his employer is not known.

VSH-UVM research project documents list the names of numerous, verified CIA researchers who acted in the capacity of consultants to VSH-UVM research programs. Dr. Milton Greenblatt, former Director of Research at Boston Psychopathic Hospital and a well-documented MKULTRA researcher is noted in VSH-UVM research documents as acting is the capacity of consultant to the Vermont experiments.

Dr. Richard York worked at Boston Psychopathic Hospital during the MKULTRA years and conducted CIA research. York was a frequent research partner of Hyde's and was on staff at Butler Hospital when Hyde was Superintendent at the Rhode Island hospital conducting LSD research for CIA. York worked for John Gittinger's Psychological Assessment Associates in Washington, DC from 1962-1966 and is noted in VSH-UVM project documents as having consulted on Vermont research and as visiting the VSH site.

In addition, almost a dozen more verified CIA-employed researchers and several known CIA research sites are named in VSH-UVM documents as participants in the Vermont hospital's experiments. These researchers and sites will be more fully detailed in later chapters.

I continued to go to Henry and Joyce's home with Debby and in September after driving me back to VSH, Henry and Debby asked me if I would like to live with them. I couldn't believe what I was hearing. I was excited and happy.

The next day I found my way through the VSH administration building and walked into George Brooks' office. Brooks was standing behind his desk when I went in and he looked both surprised to see me and uneasy that I was standing only feet from him. I was confused by the fact that Brooks was afraid of me. I had no memory of ever interacting with him.

I told him about Henry and Joyce and about Debby. I pointed out that Debby worked at VSH. I said I had a chance to leave VSH and live with them. I asked Brooks to let me go.

Much to my surprise, Brooks answered, "If you don't do anything for one week, I will let you go."

I assured him that nothing would happen and as I thanked him, I couldn't help but notice that he was still standing behind his desk as I left his office. Less than two weeks after I failed a Board of Mental Health discharge meeting, George Brooks kept his word and I walked out of VSH, never to return again.

Henry and Joyce welcomed me into their home. Joyce was severely crippled by arthritis and needed help around the house. I helped her with household chores and Debby and I helped her grocery shop. Joyce required the use of a wheelchair when going out of the house and Debby pushed the wheelchair, while I pushed the grocery cart. There were trips made to McDonald's and other outings that Joyce clearly enjoyed. Over the years to come I would learn much from Joyce about cooking and baking. I valued her as a friend for years.

Henry was Road Commissioner in Stowe and I also grew close to him. He and I rode dirt bikes together, rode snowmobiles and hiked on snowshoes through the woods. Henry put his motorboat into the Waterbury Dam on many occasions, giving Joyce, Debby and I an enjoyable summer. In the summer I helped Henry tend to his vegetable garden and Joyce and I froze many bags of those vegetables.

Henry and Joyce's home had a fully finished basement where Debby and I had rooms. I had frequent nightmares for the first few weeks I was out of VSH and after a particularly bad nightmare in which I woke up screaming, Debby brought me into her bed to sleep the rest of the night. Over the next weeks, the situation became sexual.

I wasn't gay and Debby knew this. After she insisted that we make out in the woods after we had ridden the dirt bikes deep into the woods, I was overwhelmed with shame and guilt. I jumped onto the dirt bike and intentionally crashed it. I was taken to the emergency room with a mild concussion and various bumps and bruises. The side of the motorcycle helmet I was wearing had two places where the helmet had cracked when I crashed.

My relationship with Debby became disturbing for me and she became frustrated by my lack of sexual interest in her. She often remarked that I was asexual because I never initiated contact with her or actively participated in contact. I tried to push the sexual aspect of our relationship out of my mind. Life was so much better for me living with Debby at Henry and Joyce's home. I told myself that my freedom was worth putting up with Debby's sexual advances. Most of the time I enjoyed being with her.

I left VSH with no money and only the clothes on my back. Debby used her own money to buy me clothes, winter boots and a warm jacket. She brought me to the Morrisville welfare office where I got twenty dollars a week for room and board and eight dollars a week for personal use. I grew more dependent on Debby.

It's hard to describe the effect being locked in VSH had on me. I hadn't been able to remain in my parents' home and every time I tried, I ended up back in VSH. I began to credit Debby for freeing me from VSH and the longer I remained free, the more I credited being with Debby as the reason. I carried a deep, pervasive fear of returning to VSH and that fear dictated my life for decades.

In the spring of 1973, Debby and I moved out of Henry and Joyce's home and we rented an apartment in Stowe. Debby continued to work at VSH and I tried to work at several places in Stowe as a dishwasher and chambermaid. The one job I had that I kept was at a Stowe motel where I did chambermaid work and I would have remained there except that the owner went out of business.

I had no friends, knew few people and pretty much lived in my own small world. I drove Debby's car, took care of our apartment, spent time with Henry and Joyce and considered myself fortunate to be free. VSH required that I be seen by the Lamoille County Mental Health clinic and I reluctantly complied. It was better than having to be seen by VSH doctors.

I have few memories of seeing counselors at Lamoille County Mental Health, but I did begin to regularly see a woman counselor. I was guarded, wary and unable to gain much insight into my problems. I doubt I was at all receptive to any attempts to analyze me.

Debby bought a house in Waterbury Center in 1976 and it was exciting to move into the brand new home. I took care of the household duties, played my guitar and tried to live my life. Debby, who was several inches taller than I was and outweighed me by over a hundred and fifty pounds, began to be physically abusive.

Debby threw me across the room and I crashed into the television. I have no memory of why she was so angry, but the physical abuse continued. She underwent a dramatic change in her personality. She was angry and sullen and we rarely spent time together without outbursts from her about how stupid and worthless I was. She seemed to take pleasure in ridiculing me. I began to try to distance myself from her.

I began to run cross-country in the fields near the house. One chilly fall day, after there was a small chimney fire in the house, I went out for a run. I reached the field several miles away from the house when I was suddenly bombarded by strange images that flashed in my mind. I saw railroad tracks, broken glass scattered on the ground, and images of my own bare feet. I felt frightened and confused. The images made no sense to me and I told no one about them. Years later, I realized that this was my first flashback related to my early childhood trauma.

In 1955, my father took me to a house fire in town. He held me in his arms as he stood near the railroad tracks. I had no shoes or socks on when he placed me in his car and drove to the fire. A crowd of people gathered as the house burned and when the people in the crowd were told that a woman was trapped in the burning house, the crowd reacted in panic. The woman died in the fire.

Several of my relatives provided the information about the fire to me during the 1990's when I was in therapy with Kathy. I learned that I struggled to escape my father's arms when the crowd panicked but because I had no shoes on, he didn't let me go. I was three years old and one year earlier, at another house fire, I became hysterical when the windows of the house exploded during the fire. My father finally had to leave the scene because of my hysterical reaction. I have no memory of the first fire and only bits and pieces of memories of the fatal fire.

While living with Debby, I began to lose weight and have fevers, and I developed a painful rash on my fingers. I was referred to a doctor in Burlington who suspected that I might have an autoimmune disorder. He wanted to hospitalize me for tests in the Mary Fletcher hospital, but I couldn't bear the thought of returning to that hospital again for any reason.

Debby was having financial problems. She told me that she quit her job at VSH because they wanted her to pass out medication and she refused. She held several jobs during this time but never seemed to be able to keep them. She decided to rent the house we lived in and move to Baltimore, Maryland with her parents. She suggested to me that I would find better health care at Johns Hopkins Hospital.

Baltimore was a whole new world for me. I grew up in rural Vermont and had never been in a big city before. Debby's parents allowed us to live with them but as time progressed, tensions grew. Debby's mother couldn't understand why Debby insisted that I go to Johns Hopkins when there was a very good hospital closer to where we were living. Debby insisted, and I was seen by doctors at the famous Baltimore hospital.

I was admitted for tests and during the admission I truthfully told the doctors about my medical history and that I had been in VSH. A social worker visited me and suggested that I be seen by a consultant from the Phipps Clinic, a noted psychiatric clinic at Hopkins.

Prior to the consult, it was found that I had a "connective tissue disorder." The doctor told me that she suspected that I had lupus and she felt that the "L cell" that would confirm her diagnosis, would eventually be detected.

I was seen by a psychiatrist from the Phipps Clinic and arrangements were made for me to go to the Clinic once I was discharged. The psychiatrist who conducted the consult interview while I was still an inpatient on the medical ward told me that there was a very long waiting list to get into the world-famous clinic, yet I was immediately accepted. I went into the Phipps Clinic several days later and filled out paperwork. A woman asked me to follow her and I was led into a room where, much to my surprise, a dozen or so men were seated in chairs.

The chairs formed a circle in the small room and I sat down in one of the chairs. I was uncomfortable at how close together the chairs were. I recall looking around the circle of men in suits and ties and my memory ends there. I have no memory of any question I was asked or my responses or how long I was in the room.

I learned during my investigation into CIA programs that Johns Hopkins was a primary CIA research site. Several of the psychiatrists at Hopkins were major figures in the covert research: MKULTRA Subproject 87 was conducted there. Johns Hopkins would have been aware of Robert

Hyde's CIA experiments and very likely would have been aware of the role that VSH-UVM played in MKULTRA. Who the dozen or so men really were in that room, I don't know, but because of Hopkins' role in MKULTRA, and my memory lapse during our meeting, I have reason to suspect they may have been CIA researchers.

I had another disturbing incident several weeks after I began to see an outpatient counselor at the Phipps Clinic. We met in her office for weeks until one day she said her office was unavailable. She showed me into another office and I immediately noticed something that bothered me.

There was a large glass window with curtains drawn across it. I became suspicious and refused to remain in the office. She asked me why and I said there were people sitting behind the window watching me. She engaged me in conversation for a few minutes and then offered to show me what was behind the window.

She opened a door into a room that looked like a movie theater. Several movie theater-like chairs, in two rows, faced the one-way mirror. There were trays next to each chair.

"See, no one is here, " she told me.

I took one more look around and agreed to talk with her, but I didn't forget for one moment that it was likely that people were watching and listening. Years later I wondered why I seemed to be immediately suspicious about the strange glass window.

My emotional condition was getting worse. I had traveled into downtown Baltimore on the city bus many times after moving to the city, but I began to have trouble making my bus connections. On one occasion I became lost in an unfamiliar section of the city. I tried to find my way back to a street I might recognize but I couldn't. Thanks to a middle-aged African American woman who helped me find my way back safely, I was able to board the right bus and make it home.

The drugs I was prescribed were causing problems both physically and emotionally. Lithium made me shake all over and Haldol caused a variety of dystonic reactions. The Haldol was finally discontinued. When I lived in the Waterbury Center house with Debby, I quit taking all the drugs I was prescribed and I did much better without them

I spent a month as an inpatient in the Phipps Clinic and I didn't receive any help at all. By the end of the month, I was eager to leave. I'd had enough of hospitals. But I continued to struggle. Tensions were high in Debby's parents' home. Debby and her mother didn't get along well and I didn't particularly like her mother.

I wanted to go back to Vermont. The outpatient counselor I was seeing suggested that I voluntarily spend some time in Spring Grove State Hospital. I cannot imagine myself agreeing to this, but apparently I did, and Debby drove me to the hospital one night in February.

I don't remember much of anything until I was on the ward. I immediately realized that I had made a mistake. The ward was coed and from what I saw, the patients were severely disturbed. I decided to let the staff think that I couldn't speak, calculating that it would give me more time to decide what to do. I palmed the drugs they gave me and flushed them down the toilet.

The next morning the patients were lined up and taken downstairs for breakfast. As we approached the dining hall I realized that there was an unlocked door. I saw a man come in the door and another leave through it. I began to hatch my escape plan.

A woman psychiatrist came onto the ward that morning and gathered everyone for what appeared to be a group meeting. It didn't take long for me to see that she was drunk. Thankfully, she demonstrated no interest in me and I continued to prepare myself to escape. I was very aware of the fact that if I tried and failed to escape I would likely be held involuntarily, but I was willing to take that risk.

When the aide called us to line up for lunch, I prepared myself.

I followed in a line of other patients to the downstairs floor and when I reached the area where the unlocked door to the outside was, I lingered back. The aide's attention was directed toward the front of the line and I watched him closely, waiting for my opportunity. Another patient began to talk to me and I angrily whispered to him to leave me alone and go on his way. He did and I took one more glance at the aide, who wasn't looking in my direction. I bolted toward the door. It flew open and I ran out onto unfamiliar hospital grounds. I chose a direction, not sure where it would lead and ran. I was only wearing a sweater and it was very cold outside but I ran as fast as I could.

I came to a tall wire fence and hesitated for a moment before I saw an opening in the fence. It appeared to be a well-worn path leading off the hospital grounds and I slipped through the opening. I ran a few yards to find myself on the street. I kept looking behind me, but no one was chasing me. I walked into a Dunkin Donuts shop and paced around trying to decide what to do next.

I had change in my pocket and using the pay phone I called Debby. I told her that if she didn't come and get me my next call would be to my family, who would make sure I left Baltimore. I told her not to notify the hospital and that if she didn't do as I asked, she'd never see me again.

Debby picked me up at the Dunkin Donuts shop and drove me back to her parents' house. She went back to Spring Grove to pick up my jacket after I refused to walk back into the hospital for any reason. I told her I wanted to go back to Vermont. It was only a few weeks later that we left Baltimore and headed back to Vermont.

During the CIA MKULTRA experiments, Spring Grove State Hospital was a primary research site, especially for LSD testing. According to H.P. Albarelli, Catonsville, Maryland, where Spring Grove State Hospital was located and which was only a few miles from where I had been living with Debby's parents for months, was a hotbed for CIA and intelligence personnel, even in the late 1970's. Spring Grove conducted mind control experiments for CIA that according to Albarelli included successfully using LSD "in surfacing repressed material in the minds of patients, permitting transference of vital information to psychiatrists." In retrospect, escaping Spring Grove State Hospital was very likely one of the best things I did during those years.

Debby and I stayed with my parents for a couple of months before we moved back to the Waterbury Center house. My mother didn't like Debby at all and found it difficult to tolerate her, but she tried to make the best of the situation for my sake. I still found it hard to be in my parents' house, but finally Debby and I went home.

It was a relief to be back in the house, but Debby grew even crueler toward me. She clearly resented the fact that I was not interested in her advances toward me. She tried to make me believe that there was something wrong with me because I rebuffed her. I became angrier and more depressed over the next few months, until finally I went back to Lamoille County Mental Health to see a counselor.

The counselor told me that there was a new woman psychiatrist at the clinic and suggested I talk with her. Despite my reservations about sitting in front of another psychiatrist, I agreed to talk with her.

Dr. Judy Nepvue came to Lamoille County Mental Health from her previous employment in California. She was originally from Morrisville and brought her ten children back to Vermont to live. Dr. Nepvue was soft spoken and could easily have been mistaken for any other Vermont housewife, but for me she was simply one more psychiatrist to guard myself against.

I returned to see Dr. Nepvue over the next few months and continued to see the counselor. Life in the Waterbury Center house was becoming harder for me to tolerate. Debby began spending more time away from the house and I began playing my guitar for hours at a time. I'd never given up playing the guitar and I'd actually gotten quite good. Playing seemed to take me away from the stress of my life and one day I opened the front door to find a teenage boy standing on the step.

Shawn heard me playing the guitar when he walked by the house and he mustered the nerve to ask me to teach him how to play. I agreed to help him and Shawn spent many weeks absorbing all the instruction I gave him. I enjoyed teaching him and I enjoyed having someone to talk with. Within months of beginning lessons, Shawn was able to form a teenage rock band in which he played lead guitar. I was proud of him.

I played my electric guitar on a Stowe nightclub stage one night and my performance went so well that two musicians asked me if I'd play with them in the next set. One guy played guitar and the other sang and when we took the stage together, we brought down the house playing a rocking blues number. It was a fantastic feeling.

Unknown to me at the time, a counselor from Lamoille County Mental Health was in the audience that night and reported back to Dr. Nepvue that he watched me perform. Dr. Nepvue later told me that she had already discarded the diagnosis I came to her with. She said she knew almost immediately that I was not a "deteriorating schizophrenic." Hearing about me on the Stowe stage only helped her make the diagnosis she had already decided was accurate. Dr. Nepvue worked with an expert in multiple personality when she was in California.

A new next-door neighbor moved in during the spring of 1981. The woman had a young daughter named Becky who liked to talk with me when she and her mother walked by the house. The woman, Sharon seemed pleasant and I enjoyed listening to the little girl talk about all the things little girls her age talk about. I hadn't been around any children in years and I had always loved kids. Phil Cram and I had talked many times before his death about having children.

I was in the kitchen doing dishes when Debby came up to me, spun me around and kissed me roughly. I reacted instantaneously by violently biting her lip. The expression of both shock and pain was evident on her face. She was bleeding and I just stood there, not speaking, and stared at her. I felt nothing. Crying, Debby left the kitchen to tend to her bleeding lip. This was the last time Debby tried to interest me in her. I recognized the look in her eye after I bit her. Debby was afraid of me.

My emotional condition worsened and I became suicidal. I had prolonged periods of almost hysterical sobbing, and even more disturbing for me was the fact that I couldn't understand where the tears, or the pain that produced the tears, was coming from. I called the counselor at the clinic and told him that things were getting out of hand. He told me to get to the emergency room.

I called Debby at work and told her what was happening. She didn't want to hear and refused to drive me to the hospital. I hung up the phone as the panic overwhelmed me even more. There was a knock at the door and I found my next-door neighbor, Sharon. She saw I was in bad shape and came into the living room, where I began to tell her that I didn't know what was wrong with me, but that whatever it was, it was getting worse.

Sharon told me that she would drive me to the hospital and I agreed to let her. On the way, Sharon revealed to me that she had been suspicious of Debby's behavior every since she moved next door. She told me that she was a Vermont State Police officer and that she had concerns that Debby was abusing me. I was surprised to learn that anyone had been paying attention to me or to Debby, but I was relieved to know that a Vermont State Trooper lived next door.

Dr. Nepvue admitted me to the general hospital. Copley Hospital was a small hospital and I would be among the general patient population. Dr. Nepvue walked onto ward with me and I was frightened to be admitted to yet another hospital. Dr. Nepvue assured me that everything would be okay and that I had nothing to fear in this hospital.

The first days in Copley are a blur. I seemed to be slipping in and out of some strange, unfamiliar world where at times I couldn't speak or even move. Other times I tried to fight off the barrage of voices screaming in my head, telling me not to eat and not to sleep. I thought I was going crazy.

One of the nurses introduced herself to me as Cheryl and asked me if I remembered her. I didn't. Cheryl told me that she and I had been friends when we were both eighteen years old. She had worked as a nurses' aide at VSH on Weeks 3. As hard as I tried, I never recovered memories of Cheryl.

Cheryl spoke to Dr. Nepvue and told her that she had heard that really bad things had happened to me in VSH. This led Dr. Nepvue to ask me to sign a release so that she could obtain copies of my medical records. I refused, telling her that I was sure that if she read about me in the VSH records, she would find out that I was a monster and she wouldn't want anything to do with me. She tried to tell me that would not be the case, but I wouldn't allow her to obtain the VSH records.

I had begun to hope that Dr. Nepvue was a psychiatrist who might actually help me and not make me regret I'd ever met her. I had seen her in an outpatient setting for months and her approach was something I had never experienced before. The woman was actually trying to help me learn what was wrong.

Debby strode into my hospital room and demanded that I pack my things and leave with her. I began to cry. Debby continued to rant and rave, which brought the head nurse into my room. She told Debby that Dr. Nepvue felt I needed to be in the hospital, which only made Debby angrier. She was rushing around the room trying to stuff my clothes into my suitcase when Dr. Nepvue came in.

Dr. Nepvue asked Debby to leave my room so that they could talk privately. Later, I learned that Debby had been told that she could not take me out of the hospital against doctor's orders and no such scenes occurred again. My condition continued to spiral out of control and my fears only grew as I watched myself fall apart.

I regressed into childlike states where I could barely take care of my daily needs. I then became suspicious and fearful and at other times I fell into almost catatonic states where I couldn't wake myself out of the strange captivity, and I couldn't communicate.

One of these episodes involved descending into a strange twilight where I felt trapped in a frightening nether world. I saw a desert-like landscape filled with structures I had never seen anywhere before. They appeared to be shaped in designs so foreign to me that I was later unable to even come close to describing them. I seemed to be alone in the desert but I was fearful that I would encounter something very terrible there. I don't know how long I was in this strange place and I have no explanation for it.

One weekend the nurses brought a man dressed in a suit and tie into the day room to talk with me. He introduced himself to the weekend nursing staff and to me as a member of the hospital administration. I had been experiencing an unusual preoccupation with God and the Devil and I was very disturbed by the thoughts and feelings that I was having. Dr. Nepvue was out of town for the weekend and I agreed to talk to the man.

He asked me what was troubling me and I tried to explain. He sat quietly listening and then began to talk to me about other dimensions. He described how a person living in a one-dimensional world would never be able to comprehend what it was like to live in a three-dimensional world. He asked me if I understood the point he was trying to make and I said that yes, I understood. I don't remember if we talked about anything else and I don't remember him leaving.

When I told Dr. Nepvue about the rather strange conversation I'd had with the man from the hospital administration, she seemed surprised. She went to the nurses' station and learned that the man who claimed to be from the hospital administration had actually visited me and when she sat back down to talk with me, she seemed even more perplexed. Whoever the man was, he was not a member of the hospital administration and to my knowledge his actual identity was never discovered.

In 1981, Dr. Nepvue scheduled me for a biofeedback session at Lamoille County Mental Health Clinic. She wanted to try to help me stop smoking. I was hooked up to a machine with various leads attached to my body. The man running the biofeedback machine asked me to shut off the persistent beeping the machine made in response to tension in my body. He explained to me that shutting off the beeping was a matter of concentrating and that he couldn't tell me how to do it. Within moments, I shut off the beeping by merely concentrating. The man was obviously surprised and excited and I was a little unnerved by the fact that he ran out into the hallway of the clinic and asked the people there to be quiet.

He asked me to shut off the beeping again and I did so within moments. When Dr. Nepvue talked to me about the report from the biofeedback session, she told me that I had an unusual ability to raise and lower my body temperature, and raise and lower my heart rate and blood pressure, merely by concentrating and that I clearly had an ability to go in and out of trance. She called it "auto-hypnosis" and asked me if I had ever been hypnotized. I had no memory of ever being hypnotized.

In his book, *The C.I.A. Doctors: Human Right Violations by American Psychiatrists*, Dr. Colin Ross quotes from an MKULTRA Subproject 49 document that discuses the CIA's interest in auto-hypnosis:

"In order to investigate the possibility of hypnotic induction of non-willing subjects. . . an investigation should be made into non-verbal induction techniques...can auto-hypnosis be taught so as to be as effective as hetero-hypnosis in the canceling out of pain or other stress conditions; if this can be done a person could create his own world and be happy in it even though he were actually confined in a very small place which was extremely filthy."

Was MKULTRA Subproject 49, conducted by Alden Sears at the University of Denver, linked to the experiment I was subjected to at VSH, where I was held in seclusion and restraint for nearly seven months? Unfortunately, because of the many missing medical records, and because state and federal agencies and officials who know the answers refuse either to provide me the information or acknowledge the CIA Vermont experiments, I will never know.

Shawn, the teenage boy I taught how to play the guitar brought my acoustic guitar to the hospital. I woke up one day to find it in my room. I tried to play it but I couldn't seem to. Later during the hospital stay I was able to play again.

I was accustomed to periods of time when I couldn't do things I usually did, like play the guitar or draw. It was simply the way my life had always been. I was also familiar with being accused of doing things that I swore I did not do. Since childhood, I had felt that I was different somehow and I believed that difference was a bad thing that I tried to hide from people.

When I was in early elementary school and on summer vacation, I asked my cousins to go to my house to play. It took some effort to convince my aunt that day for whatever reasons. While my cousins finished their chores, I went back home where my mother confronted me about doing something that I had no memory of doing.

When my cousins finally came to the door, I greeted them with, "I've found something better to do."

They went back home, confused and angry I'm sure. I knew when my mother accused me of doing something that I had no memory of, that I needed to cover. As a young child I must have figured out that it was easier to let people think whatever they wanted to about me as long as they never were allowed to suspect that I was somehow different. I had no idea what the difference was, but whatever it was, I protected myself from everyone.

Dr. Nepvue decided to schedule an EEG in Burlington and she phoned Debby and asked her to drive me to the appointment. The EEG required that I remain awake the night before and as Debby and I drove to Burlington, all I wanted was to sleep. Debby promised that we would stop and get something to eat after the EEG and then she'd take me back to Copley.

I walked into the office for the EEG and I was almost immediately swept into a deeply disturbing panic. I struggled not to let anyone see how upset I was and as each moment passed, I grew more and more frightened. I knew that these people were preparing to do something dreadful to me and I felt helpless to leave or to refuse to allow them to harm me.

By the time I was led downstairs into the basement-level EEG lab, my mind was screaming at me to run. The feelings of impending doom and hopelessness overwhelmed me as I waited to be tortured. The technician who was going to conduct the EEG began to prepare me for the EEG lead wires to be attached to my head, when she started a conversation with me. Much to my shock, the moment I began to talk with her, all of the panic and feelings of impending doom disappeared. I felt very confused, but very thankful that nothing terrible happened.

After reading my medical records and learning about the Metrazol activation in 1971, I'm convinced that I had the panic reaction about the 1981 EEG because of the excruciating physical and emotional effect of Metrazol. Although I have never recovered any memory of the Metrazol activation, the information I have read about its effects tells me why I reacted the way I did in 1981 and according to Baird 6 records, the way I also reacted to an EEG while in Baird 6.

Debby drove me back to Copley after a meal and after initially trying to bring me back to the Waterbury Center house for a few hours. I was so exhausted that all I wanted was to go back to the hospital and sleep. I saw the anger in her face when she dropped me off in front of the hospital and I just didn't care.

Dr. Nepvue told me that she was going to start me on a drug called Mysoline. I learned after I obtained my medical records that I had been prescribed Mysoline in VSH. The drug hit me hard. My entire body felt numb. My brain didn't seem to want to work. I felt very detached. Slowly, I adapted to the drug.

Dr. Nepvue told me that the first time she met me she knew almost immediately that I was not a deteriorating schizophrenic. She told me that I was a multiple personality. The diagnosis meant little to me. She asked me questions about other names I may have used before but I had no memory of other names.

I learned years later in therapy that my mother remembered me referring to myself by other names and I too would remember some of those names. But in 1981, I had no such information available to me. I was relieved that whatever was wrong with me had a name and was something that was recognized and, from what Dr. Nepvue said, it was treatable. Maybe I wasn't hopeless after all.

I'd grown close to the nursing staff at Copley. They weren't psychiatric nurses but their kindness and compassion made a difference for me. It had been a very long time since people around me encouraged me and supported me. I began to let myself believe that I might actually have a life.

In the early summer of 1981, I was discharged and went back to the Waterbury Center house with Debby. I didn't think that I had any other choice. I knew from previous experiences that I couldn't live at my parents' home. Every time I tried, I ended up back in VSH. I had no place else to go and I didn't believe that I could make it out there in the world on my own. I told myself that Debby had saved my life by taking me out of VSH and I had stayed out because of her. I tried to make the best of things.

One afternoon Debby and I came home to find a young man sitting on the hood of his car parked in the driveway. It was Phil Fass. When I was living in Baltimore, my mother called to tell me that Phil had been looking for me. I got out of the car and hugged him.

Phil and I sat on the back steps and talked for a long time. It was so good to see him again. He wanted me to go with him and he told me that all I had to do was get in the car and we could have a life together. I remember feeling conflicted. I wanted to go with him and I was afraid to go with him. I told him I needed to think about it and we agreed that he would come back the next day. I still had feelings for Phil and it was clear that he still had feelings for me.

The next day I waited for Phil to come. I was going to leave with him, and as I paced the floor waiting, Debby confronted me. She had been eavesdropping on Phil and my conversation and she was angry.

"Either you tell him to get back into his car and never come back again or I will tell him that you are gay. I'll have him arrested if he comes back here."

I was filled with fear and with shame. I knew I wasn't gay and Debby knew I wasn't gay, but we had engaged in sexual activities. I could not allow her to tell Phil. When Phil came to the door, Debby was standing behind me. I told him that I wasn't going with him and that if he didn't leave, never to come back, he would be arrested.

Phil looked devastated. I watched him drive away and I hated myself for not having the courage to be sitting next to him in the car. I never saw Phil again. I realized how far I would go to remain free, yet deep down, I knew I was not free. Living with Debby had become another form of captivity and I couldn't seem to find the strength to just walk away.

I was admitted to Copley Hospital shortly after the incident with Phil. I was seriously depressed and Dr. Nepvue continued to try to get me to open up to her about my relationship with Debby, but the shame I felt was too great. I spent several weeks in the hospital and then one evening Dr. Nepvue told me that she would discharge me the next day.

I phoned Debby and told her I was coming home and would she come and pick me up.

"Find another way home. You left me alone. Do you know how many bills I have and with you in the hospital all the time I have to do the housework on top of everything else. Find your own ride."

My reaction was immediate and powerful, although I said nothing in reply to Debby. I hung up the phone furious at Debby and frightened by the prospect of being on my own. The nurses were aware that something was wrong but I refused to talk to them about it. How could I tell them about all the awful things I had been willing to do just to remain free? I was filled with self-hatred and disgust. I didn't want them to feel those things about me.

My mind raced as I tried to figure out what to do and where I would go. I didn't have much money and I didn't have a car. During the middle of that night, I fell into a suicidal despair. I couldn't see a way out.

Anna, one of the nurses I had grown close to, tried to talk with me. She kept reassuring me that whatever I said to her would not change how she felt about me and it wouldn't change how the rest of the staff felt either. Finally, I took the risk and told her everything about Debby and me, about all I was willing to do to stay out of VSH and how I just wanted a normal life for myself.

The next morning, Dr. Nepvue and I talked about my remaining in the hospital until a place for me to live could be found. One by one, the Copley nurses told me that they were relieved that I had finally been able to trust them enough to tell them the truth. They had suspected all along that Debby was abusive and that the relationship was sexual. I couldn't believe that they still supported me, but it was very clear that they did.

Anna and her husband, Harold, owned a huge house in Johnson and rented rooms to Johnson college students. The college was within walking distance of their home. Anna offered to have me rent a room from them and they would include me in their meals and in their lives. I was excited about the idea, but Dr. Nepvue had reservations about allowing me to leave with a staff member. Anna and Harold met with Dr. Nepvue and the decision was made that I would go with Anna and Harold to Johnson. Dr. Nepvue told me that I had to either get a job or go to college. I jumped at the chance to go to college.

I struggled with how to tell Debby that I wasn't coming back. One of the nurses told me that her daughter knew me. Deanna had been a friend of Debby's and I had known her for years. She worked at VSH and frequently spent the night at the Waterbury Center house rather than make the long drive to her own home. Deanna came to Copley to talk with me.

"Debby saved my life when she took me out of VSH," I told Deanna. "It's because of her that I've stayed out of that place."

"You don't have to pay with your life, Karen," Deanna replied.

Deanna's words immediately settled my conflicts about leaving Debby. She agreed to be at the Waterbury Center house when Harold and I went to pick up my things. That way Debby couldn't try to bully me into staying with her. Harold and I loaded my belongings into his truck and we drove away. I never returned to the Waterbury Center house again.

Decades later, I began to question many things about Debby. I thought about how quickly she singled me out in VSH and how George Brooks never hesitated to discharge me to live with Debby. I thought about how adamant Debby was that I be seen at Johns Hopkins and how her mother couldn't understand why Debby insisted on taking me downtown to Hopkins when Saint Agnes Hospital was only moments away from where we lived in Baltimore. I also wondered about Debby seeming to regularly come into large quantities of money. She tried in vain to have me return to the Waterbury Center house. I wondered if it was possible that VSH paid her to live with me. I doubt I will ever be able to answer these questions, but after finding the Vermont CIA experiments and not being able to fully know what happened to me during those experiments, questions remain.

I felt liberated living in Johnson and for the first time in years, I wasn't dependent on Debby or subject to her whims and abuse. Copley nurses gave me clothes to wear and visited me at Anna's home. I studied for the upcoming entrance into Johnson College, where I planned to take two courses. I helped with chores around the sixteen-room house and began to try to get to know a couple of the college students who also rented rooms from Anna and Harold.

One weekend day I walked down into Johnson village where I ran into Sharon and her daughter Becky. Sharon asked me to have coffee with her and we began to talk. I told her about leaving the Waterbury Center house and how I planned to attend Johnson College. Sharon was happy for me. She told me about her suspicions about Debby and about her concerns that I was being abused. I thanked her for helping me. It was good to sit in a diner and share a cup of coffee with a friend without worrying how Debby would feel about it.

It hadn't occurred to me before that anyone saw that Debby was cruel and overbearing. After talking with Sharon, I began to think about how locked in my own world I had been. My world was severely limited to my own subjective judgments about other people and the resulting determinations I made were shaped by my fears of returning to VSH and by Debby's almost constant proclamations about how stupid and worthless I was. Debby frequently reminded me over the years I was with her that VSH was still there. I understood the underlying threat in her words and she knew I did.

There were a few incidents when I was with Debby when she put my life in danger. I can't explain how I managed to push the incidents out of my mind and continue to stay with her.

Debby and I canoed across the Waterbury Dam one afternoon and it was a good distance from one shore to the next. On the way back across the Dam I decided to try to swim the distance. There was a canoe beside me and I felt safe enough to try.

In the middle of the Dam, Debby shouted at me that I was on my own and I watched in disbelief as she quickly paddled away, leaving me to swim without the safety of a boat nearby. I struggled not to panic in the deep water and kept swimming. When I finally reached the shore, I was completely exhausted. Several people who had been swimming and witnessed Debby leaving me in the middle of the Dam swam out to help me back to the shore.

The people on the shore were outraged and a few of them openly and angrily confronted Debby. One woman told me that they were afraid I was going to drown. I don't remember leaving the lake that day and I don't remember driving back home after this incident.

Another incident involved riding in a Jeep Debby borrowed. She drove to the dirt roads around the Waterbury Dam and began driving fast up and over steep hills. Several times I almost lost my grip and the faster and more wildly she drove, the closer I came to being thrown from the Jeep. I asked her to stop but she ignored me. I somehow managed to stay seated in the topless Jeep and I had a sickening feeling that she was trying to get me thrown from the Jeep. When she dropped me off at the house and drove away I felt very alone.

Debby liked to ridicule me, especially when I said that I was good at something. I often talked about the fact that I could ride horses and she loved to taunt me with remarks about how I made it all up. When we lived in the Stowe apartment, a neighborhood girl was taking care of a friend's horse and invited Debby and I to go along with her.

The horse wore a halter and on that chilly autumn day, Debby began taunting me to go ahead and prove that I really could ride a horse. She ridiculed me to the point where I decided to prove to her that I could ride a horse and ride it well. The young girl hitched a rope to the halter and I swung onto the horse's back.

The horse bolted and bucked and whirled in an effort to throw me from its back. I dug my legs into the body of the horse and as the horse raced wildly, I looked down at the ground. The dirt was solidly frozen in ruts and craters. I knew that if I were thrown, I would be seriously injured.

The horse finally gave up and began to walk under my control back to the fence where Debby and the girl stood. I was furious to learn that the horse hadn't been ridden by anyone for a long time and that Debby had set the whole thing up beforehand with the girl. I knew deep inside myself that Debby thought I would be thrown and very likely hoped that I would be thrown. After this incident, she never taunted me again about whether or not I could really ride a horse. The insides of my legs were black and blue for days, bruised from clutching the sides of the horse to hang on.

Many years later, in my therapy with Kathy, I learned that Debby had very likely targeted me while I was on 1A and that her good-natured generosity was merely a façade. Kathy helped me understand that Debby used me for her own needs and used my fear of returning to VSH to control me. Kathy also helped me understand that my illness as a multiple personality would have limited the choices I was able to envision for myself.

I later learned that Debby had been repeatedly fired from several area stores where she worked for stealing. There were also allegations that she was selling drugs. The information came as a shock to me and I never found out for sure if the allegations were true. The allegations did, however seem to explain why Debby suddenly had money she hadn't had only days before. She would come home with a three hundred dollar bicycle or an expensive camera and she never explained where the money came from.

When Debby realized that I wasn't going to go back to the Waterbury Center house, she repeatedly called my parents and tried to get them to talk me into returning. She tried to convince me to come back during a phone call I made to her. I called to ask her to allow my parents to drive to the house and take my dog back to Brandon with them. Debby pleaded with me to come back and offered me a room in her house where she said I could do as I pleased. I refused her offers.

I will never know Debby's true motive in taking me out of VSH and despite everything that happened while I was with her, I still believe that she saved my life when she took me out of VSH. After years of therapy I no longer blame myself for being willing to endure Debby's demands. I'm just thankful that I was able to find the courage to leave.

Dr. Nepvue and the Copley nurses supported me, encouraged me and helped me eventually find the courage to leave the Waterbury Center situation and I will always remember their kindness, their caring and their belief in me at a time when I had no belief in myself.

I began taking classes at Johnson State College in August, 1981 and the first day I was nervous and excited to begin a new chapter in my life. The campus was only a few minutes walk across a field from Anna and Harold's house and as I walked across the beautiful campus, I began to entertain dreams for myself of a college degree.

Studying was difficult for me and sitting in a classroom for the first time since I was thirteen years old was even more challenging, but I kept working at my class assignments. Each day I went to class and turned in the homework assignments and each day Anna and Harold were there to support me when I returned home. The Copley nurses always showed an interest in my classes when I went to the hospital with Anna. They cheered me on and it felt good.

I woke up one night in Anna's home to see my grandmother standing at the foot of my bed. I was confused. My grandmother lived in Brandon. What was she doing standing in my room in Johnson in the middle of the night?

"Gram, what are you doing here?" I asked her as I sat up in bed.

"Everything is going to be okay," she replied.

"Gram, what are you doing here?" I felt even more confused.

My grandmother vanished before my eyes. Stunned, I looked at the clock on the table next to my bed. It was 2:45 A.M.

The next morning I checked the newspapers to see if my grandmother had died, but I couldn't find any news. I told Dr. Nepvue about my experience and she suggested that I phone my parents. I hadn't much contact with my parents during this time but I finally decided to call.

My cousin answered the phone and put my mother on to talk to me. I told her what happened and told her the time on the clock when Gram vanished. My mother began to cry. My grandmother died the night I had the strange visit from her. She died at 2:45 A.M.

After my grandfather died, my grandmother shared with me that she had been visited by him the day after he died.

He told her, "Everything is going to be okay."

I have no explanation for what happened that night in Johnson except that my grandmother wanted to make sure that she visited me on her way to somewhere better.

By October, I began to slip into a deep depression and although I tried to fight my way out of it, the depression only seemed to deepen. I tried to hide the depression from everyone and the worse it got, the less I understood what was happening. I began to wonder if Debby had been right. Maybe it really didn't matter where I was or what I did. Maybe the problem was me.

I felt guilty that I was depressed. Anna and Harold had opened their home to me. I was attending college and I was freed of Debby, but there I was, descending into depression again. I couldn't understand what was wrong with me.

I sat on the grass that October day and watched the Johnson College students walk across the campus. The sky was a brilliant blue and the sun shone brightly. I began to feel strangely detached and I became aware of how separated I suddenly felt from everyone and everything. I stared at the college students and realized that no matter what I did, I would never fit in.

Anna tried to talk with me but I brushed off her concerns. I was numb. There was simply no way I could tell Anna that all that she had done for me had been wasted. I knew what I was going to do and once I decided to commit suicide, the eerie relief that settled over me convinced me that I had made the right decision.

That evening I walked across the campus, unsure of the reason I was there. I passed by the auditorium and heard the sound of music coming from inside. I quietly slipped into the darkened auditorium to find a young man on the stage playing beautiful music on the piano.

The young man finished playing and called out, “Who is there?”

“Just an anonymous music lover,” I replied.

He wasn’t able to see me sitting in the darkened auditorium and I sat for a few minutes longer to listen to his music. I left the building and began walking aimlessly.

I walked down into Johnson village where I bought four bottles of sleeping pills and a six-pack of beer. I purchased the pills in two different stores so as not to raise any questions about the amount of pills I bought. I stood on Route 15 and tried to decide which direction to go when a car offered me a ride to Morrisville.

Once in Morrisville, I was still not sure where to go to take the pills. I opened one bottle and took the contents, washing the pills down with beer. I walked in the darkness along the neighborhood streets and stared at each one of the houses as I passed by. I thought about the families inside and wondered what kind of life I might have had if only things had been different. When a dog began barking I told myself that only the dog knew I was there.

I realized quite suddenly as I approached the cemetery that this was the perfect place to take the pills. I climbed up a steep hill and entered the graveyard. There was a full moon and as I searched for the right spot to die, the light of the moon illuminated the gravestones and the cemetery.

I chose a spot toward the backside of the cemetery, sat down and leaned back against a headstone. I swallowed the other bottles of pills, throwing each bottle into the bushes. I didn't want to take the chance that someone might find me and know by the pill bottles what I had taken. I sat back and waited to die. There was no pain, and no second thoughts. I began to feel sleepy and I called out to Phil to let him know that I would be with him soon.

I woke up. My body felt numb and I couldn't believe that I was still alive. I tried to get up, but my legs didn't work right. I tried again and managed to get to my feet. I looked around trying to decide what to do next when suddenly I felt overcome by sheer terror. I looked around again, certain that there was someone or something terrible lurking in the moonlit cemetery. I felt I had to get out of there as quickly as I could because I could not let whatever the frightening presence was catch me.

I tried to run but my legs wouldn't obey and when I reached the steep hill I had climbed to enter the cemetery, I was afraid that my legs would buckle beneath me as I stumbled down the hill. I made it out of the cemetery and found myself standing in the middle of the road. I couldn't raise my head up. I don't know how long I stood in the middle of the road.

The voices of the men seemed unreal and I had difficulty answering their questions. The two police officers placed me in their cruiser and drove me to the emergency room where the nursing staff immediately recognized me. I remember being asked if I took any pills and then I recall Anna standing in front of me. My vision was blurry and I had a hard time seeing her.

My next memory is sitting on an exam table with a nurse standing in front of me. Without warning, I began to vomit and began choking. I clutched the arm of the nurse and my memory ends there. My memories after this are vague and scattered.

I learned later that Cheryl, my friend who had known me in VSH, offered to work an extra shift to sit with me on the ward. I was taken to intensive care. The doctors believed that I had been in the cemetery for hours and because of the below freezing temperatures, hypothermia had probably saved my life. Anna and Harold had been looking for me that night, after discovering I was not in my room.

I felt trapped between two worlds. I wasn't alive and I wasn't dead. I was angry that my suicide attempt failed. I tried to get out of bed to get dressed, but my body wouldn't obey. I raged at people I couldn't see who taunted me to get up and leave the hospital, when suddenly I realized that I could hear two men talking about me. I pulled back the curtain next to my bed to see two men in hospital beds. I thought it was strange that one of the men had a saxophone in the hospital bed with him.

"You need to stop causing all this fuss and stop fighting or they will send you back to VSH," one of the men said to me while the other played the saxophone.

The man who spoke to me smiled. I wondered how he knew I had been in VSH but I decided to take his advice. I resigned myself to the fact that I had failed to die.

I'm not sure how much time passed when Dr. Nepvue came in ICU and sat on the edge of my bed.

She hugged me and said, "We almost lost you."

I told her that I was sorry. She let me know that the nurses had gone together to ask the hospital administrator not to send me back to VSH. They assured him that they could keep me safe and offered to stay with me 24 hours a day until I was okay. I was moved by the news.

I told Dr. Nepvue that the two men in ICU had helped me quiet down. Dr. Nepvue looked confused by my statement.

"What two men are you talking about?"

"The two men in those beds," I replied and pulled back the curtain between us.

I was shocked. My bed was only inches from the wall and there were no beds on that side of the room. Dr. Nepvue told me that I was the only patient in ICU. I have no explanation for this incident except to say that I am thankful for the advice I was given that night in ICU by the two men who apparently had a message for me.

Anna visited me and I apologized to her. I told her that nothing she had done factored into my suicide attempt. I made sure that she understood how much I appreciated all that she and Harold had done for me. I couldn't really explain to Anna why I did it, except to say that once the strange numbness settled over me and the pain left, I wanted to die. The last thing in the world I was able to do was tell anyone what was happening to me.

I spent several days in ICU and slowly the nurses began to bring me out onto the general ward. The transition from the quiet of ICU to the noises of the ward affected me and I felt overwhelmed and fragile for the first few days.

When I was stronger, the nurses asked me to meet with them. These women and I had become close over the time that I had been a patient in the small Morrisville hospital and they were angry that I attempted suicide. I couldn't really explain why I did it and my inability to answer that question frustrated the nurses.

"If you wanted to die, why didn't you just go and buy a gun?"

The words hit me hard and I felt myself instantly go cold inside. I had no feeling for the nurses and no emotions about myself or about them. I stopped answering their questions and walked out of the room, leaving my fondness and my attachment to the nurses behind. I felt very strange, yet at the same time the lack of feelings seemed to liberate me.

Over the next few days, I didn't talk with anyone except Dr. Nepvue.

The nurses tried to talk with me, but I had nothing to say. I spent my time reading and thinking about what to do next. I decided to rent a car and leave Lamoille County. Dr. Nepvue and I talked about my plan after I phoned a car rental agency in Montpelier to check on the availability of a small station wagon. I had enough money in the bank due to a small loan I had obtained for college costs. One of the weekend nurses offered to drive me to Montpelier to pick up the car.

I told Dr. Nepvue that I had reached a turning point and that deep down inside I feared that I was losing my will to survive. I didn't want to die and I certainly didn't want to go back to VSH. I needed something that would bring me bring me back in touch with the strong desire to live I had always drawn upon before.

Dr. Nepvue explained that if she let me leave and I did any harm to myself, she would be the person who would be held responsible.

"If I let you go, you have to promise me that you will not do anything to harm yourself," she said.

I promised her that I would not do anything to myself and stressed again that this was not about dying, it was about living again. Dr. Nepvue agreed to let me go. I made arrangements to withdraw from college.

Earlier that day, I had phoned my mother and asked her if I could come home for a while. I told her what had happened and she cried. She and my father wanted me to come home. After years of problems between my mother and me, we both just wanted everything to be okay. Neither my mother nor I were yet able to comprehend the reasons why things had become so bad between us beginning when I was thirteen years old. It wouldn't be until I obtained my medical records and learned the details of my early childhood trauma that we would even begin to mend our relationship. But in November, 1981, we were ready to try.

I got a ride to the car rental agency in Montpelier and the man behind the counter remembered me from the phone call I made to him the day before. The man held a big cigar between his teeth and squinted intently at me as we talked. I'm sure that I didn't look well and he knew that I called him from the hospital. I had no credit card but he was willing to take cash. After I filled out the paperwork, he showed me to the nearly brand new Chevy station wagon.

I sat in the idling Chevy and felt a rush of excitement at the prospect that I could go anywhere I wanted anytime I wanted to go. I drove out of Montpelier onto Route 2, choosing not to go onto the Interstate until I was more familiar with the car. I went onto the Interstate in Middlesex, turned up the FM radio, lit a cigarette and let each mile that I drove sooth me. I stopped for a six-pack of Coke, a carton of cigarettes and a deli sandwich in Waterbury Center and even the simple act of tossing the carton of cigarettes on the passenger seat seemed to symbolize my newly found sense of independence. I was on my own and it felt fantastic. The car rental was paid for one week and those seven days ahead of me felt like forever. I drove to Johnson and spent my last night at Anna and Harold's home.

Anna didn't want me to leave and after I packed my things into the car, I tried to say goodbye to her but she wouldn't come out of her bedroom. I drove to Stowe and bought a pair of jeans and a sweater at the second-hand shop. The new clothes seemed to symbolize my transformation even more and when I pulled onto the Interstate and headed toward Brandon, I knew I was leaving this part of my life behind. The physical and emotional strain of the last sixteen years had taken its toll on me. I was twenty-nine years old and I was tired.

5
GOD, KING AND BEGINNING, 1981-1988

I drove fast down Route 7 and the closer I got to old, familiar territory, the more I wanted to see my parents. I neared the village of Brandon and I was unexpectedly overcome by emotion. I pulled the car off from the road and called my mother from a pay phone to tell her that I'd be home in a few minutes. After I gathered myself I drove down Maple Street and pulled up in front of my parents' house.

My parents were at the car before I even got out of it. We hugged and we cried and we went inside and talked for a while. The dog that my parents rescued from the Waterbury Center house wagged her tail and lapped my face with her tongue. I looked around the living room of the house I hadn't been able to live in since I was thirteen years old and hoped that this time, I could stay.

I could see that my parents were genuinely happy that I was with them. I'd always known that they loved me, in fact I never doubted for one moment that they loved me and I loved them. I just was never able to explain why I couldn't remain in their home or why my mother seemed to elicit such unexplained and disturbing behavior from me. I looked at my father, who was becoming more and more crippled by arthritis. Dad was a quiet man but he was a good man who worked hard all of his life, paid his bills and loved his family. I saw the emotion in his blue eyes as we sat at the kitchen table talking. Dad was happy to have his little girl home again.

Mom could see that I was exhausted. I saw the concern in her face. I told her that I needed some time to rest and some good home cooking and that I'd be okay. My mother carried a deep sense of guilt about the VSH years and it appears from the medical records that VSH doctors like Havas did everything that they could to make sure that she did blame herself. I too blamed her and my family for abandoning me, and it would take over fifteen more years before she or I would know the truth about what happened in VSH.

My nephews came to see me. Jeff was born when I was fifteen and after 1970, I rarely saw him. Chris was born when I was on 1A and I saw him for the first time when he was three years old. I hadn't seen much of my brother and sister-in-law since 1970 and it felt awkward trying to reestablish the close relationship Kip and I had before I was first hospitalized.

Before I left Johnson, I met with Cheryl, the Copley nurse I had been friends with in VSH. We sat in the hospital cafeteria and I told her my plans. Cheryl had been so supportive during my months in Copley and nothing I told her changed that. She wanted only the best for me. In the 1990's, Cheryl was found murdered in Morrisville. To my knowledge no one has ever been arrested for the crime and although the police had a suspect they were never able to make a case against him.

One of the Copley nurses told me before I left that she would be attending Castleton State College and she gave me her phone number so that we could arrange to meet. That November night I drove along the winding road that parallels the Otter Creek from Brandon to Castleton. I'd been on this stretch of road many times but because of the winding curves and the ever-present deep waters of Otter Creek, I exercised caution as I made my way through the sharp turns in the road.

I was suddenly startled when the field on my right became illuminated in the otherwise pitch-black darkness. A huge deer raced toward my car and all I could think was that I was driving a rented car and it was going to be wrecked when the deer hit. My mind raced to try and make sense out of what was happening and right before my eyes the charging deer transformed into a huge hawk that flew directly over my car.

Everything was happening so fast and none of it made any kind of logical sense. The field was dark again and I was driving along the road.

My heart was beating fast as I tried to comprehend what had just taken place. Only moments had passed but the scene that played out in front of me seemed to have gone on longer than a few moments. When I first saw the field illuminated it was as if I was no longer even in the car. Everything around me except the deer and the hawk had vanished. It was as if I wasn't physically present in the car, yet I managed to keep the car on the road. I told myself I saw what I saw but I knew the entire incident simply made no sense. As I continued to drive I wondered if I had hallucinated, yet deep down I really didn't think so.

I met with my friend in Castleton and told her about the strange incident on the highway. She suggested that I see a psychiatrist and I couldn't blame her for coming to that conclusion. The entire incident sounded crazy and it was crazy, yet I didn't believe that I was crazy enough to hallucinate. On the drive home I wondered what it all meant

My mother and father listened as I told them what had happened. I said that it made no rational sense yet I saw what I saw. I told them that I did not want to see another psychiatrist and they agreed with me. My parents had experienced the destruction psychiatrists had brought into our lives and they were not eager to go down that road again.

I tried to shake off the incident but it troubled me. My mother gently suggested that I talk with the new, young Congregational church minister. My brother and his wife thought highly of the minister and his wife.

"Why don't you let me phone him and go and talk to him? What can it hurt?" my mother asked as my father nodded his head in agreement.

When Reverend Peter Anderson opened the door and invited me into the parsonage I noticed how intently he was looking at me. We sat and talked for quite a while and I told him about being in VSH and problems with my mother. I told him about my recent suicide attempt and the frightening presence that drove me out of the cemetery that night. I talked about losing Phil and Reverend Anderson remarked that he had recently learned about Phil's death through Phil's mother Helen, who was a member of the Congregational church.

I attended Sunday School beginning in kindergarten and Kip also grew up attending the Brandon Congregational church. Mom stopped going to Sunday services around the time I first went into VSH but she remained a member. In the two or three years leading up to my 1965 breakdown, I began openly challenging the Sunday school lessons, which caused somewhat of an uproar among the Sunday school teachers. I was trying to settle my own questions about religion and I didn't hesitate to give voice to the questions I had, but the teachers usually couldn't give me answers that satisfied me.

I tried to read the Bible when I was still in early elementary school but I couldn't understand the things I was reading. I asked my mother for a white covered Bible when I was seven years old and felt frustrated that the words on the pages still made little sense to me. Mom tried to tell me that when I got older I would be better able to understand what I was reading. By the time I got my first horse in 1960, most of my preoccupation with religion had faded into the background.

Peter asked me if I objected to having his wife, Sharon sit in on our conversation. He said he didn't usually ask Sharon to join in but that he felt that Sharon might be able to help. I agreed and Sharon joined the conversation.

Sharon was only a few years older than I was and she seemed calm and gentle. She listened as Peter filled her in on our conversation and she asked me several questions. After a few hours Peter began to explain what he believed was behind my problems and as he spoke, my heart began beating rapidly.

Peter explained how "demonic oppression," as opposed to demonic possession could be responsible for both my emotional upheavals and the strange, unexplained events that had frequently occurred in my life. He said that sometimes unwitting contact can be made with forces better left alone and that exposure to evil people, evil places and evil things all contributed to spiritual oppression of a vulnerable person.

I tried to think of anything that I might have been exposed to that would cause such a problem, but I couldn't think of anything. I felt shaken by the things Peter and Sharon were telling me but, at this point in my life, I figured anything was possible. I certainly hadn't found any other answer for the things that had happened to me. Maybe Peter and Sharon were right. I asked Peter what could be done about such a thing and he asked me if I would agree to bring Kip and Sue into the conversation. He thought they could help.

My brother and his wife joined us and after they were filled in on the problem, we all agreed to meet the following night so that Peter could lay hands on me. I left the parsonage that November night and as I walked to the rented car, my brother hugged me.

"Everything will be okay. You'll see," Kip said as we walked to our cars.

"I'll stop at Mom and Dad's and talk to them with you."

My parents listened as Kip and I filled them in on Peter's belief that I was "oppressed." My father seemed to accept the possibility easier than my mother. She was very disturbed by the idea. She wasn't the only one.

When I was finally alone that night in my bedroom, I thought about all that had taken place over the last several hours. The strange incident on the highway with the deer transforming into a hawk, being told that I might have come in contact with something "evil" and being faced with a "laying on of hands." Could this all be true and if it was true could this be why my life had been so insane?

My 1971, Baird 6 records contain a curious description of my reaction to a man who was visiting the unit. For some unexplained reason I was convinced that he was "Satan." According to the records I was very

frightened by this man and absolutely convinced that he was evil and that he would harm me and others
on the unit. I have no memory of this and, in retrospect, I find it to be out of the ordinary for me during the hospital years. The records contain no other references to spiritual preoccupations in the 1960's and 1970's, with the exception of Copley Hospital in 1981. I had definitely had several unexplained events in my life but the idea that I might be oppressed was very disturbing.

Peter, Sharon, Kip, and Sue stood in the parsonage preparing to lay hands upon me. I had no idea what to expect. Peter said prayers and asked me if I accepted Jesus Christ as my Savior and I said that I did. The four people in the room to help me placed their hands on my body as Peter said a prayer and in moments, the ceremony was over.

I'm not sure what if anything I expected to happen but what did happen was that I felt a huge physical and emotional surge of relief, as if I were suddenly unburdened. I told those gathered with me how I felt and they smiled. Peter explained to me that I would need to immerse myself in the Bible and that by doing so, I would have much better protection from potential "evil."

I felt that I might have a new beginning. I wanted to understand about God and I spent hours reading the Bible. Sharon and I began to spend a lot of time together and it was nice to have a friend. She had a beautiful soprano singing voice and I often brought my acoustic guitar to accompany her when she sang. We spent many hours talking, laughing and sharing our deepest hopes and dreams with each other.

Peter counseled me and answered my questions. I attended church services every Sunday, except for the very first Sunday after the laying on of hands. I learned that Kip stood up in front of the congregation and talked about how thankful he was that his sister had come home, met Peter and found God again. People who knew my brother well were very surprised that he stood and spoke that morning. Kip was a quiet, unassuming guy and a little on the shy side. When I heard about him addressing the congregation I began to understand the significance of all that had happened. Kip, who was temporarily laid off from his job as a truck driver, spent time with me talking about the Bible. He told me how his own life had been changed when he became an active member of the church. It was so good to have my brother in my life again.

I immersed myself in study, sometimes getting up at four in the morning to read the Bible. Peter warned me about how important it was to stay grounded in the Bible. He told me that the oppression could come back a full seven times as strong without a firm foundation in God's word.

Sharon and I became closer and we spent much of our time together. Peter and Sharon had three young children and I enjoyed watching them play. Mom sometimes babysat for the children and both she and my father grew very fond of the entire family.

Peter's Sunday services were recorded and played back later on a local radio station and Sharon suggested that she and I work up a musical number to play for the congregation. She found a song and I set my own arrangement to it. We performed the song for the congregation and we both felt pleased and satisfied. Several parishioners came up to us after the song to tell us how much they enjoyed our song.

Sharon believed that my presence in she and Peter's life was not an accident and that something spiritually driven had led me to them. It was hard for me to take it all in and to try to comprehend what it all meant. I began to feel frightened by the enormity of the situation. The idea that God might be using me in His plans seemed to place a huge responsibility on my shoulders and I wasn't convinced that I was in any way up to the responsibility. Once again, depression settled in.

My preoccupation with religion caused me to experience fear and increasingly unsettling conflict. I wrote poetry about God and the Devil and described terrible scenes of destruction. I began to envision a battle between Good and Evil that would take place right in Brandon. Sharon had her own vision of God's plan for Peter's congregation and I seemed to be a part of her vision. I was growing uneasy with the intensity of my religious experience but I could not leave it. I couldn't walk away from God and I didn't want to walk away from God. I just wanted to be a normal, regular person who went to church every Sunday, believed in God and tried to live a good life. What was happening to me was far from normal and I feared that I might be trapped in the middle of something I couldn't defend myself against.

I went to see Peter and Sharon one night when I felt ready to pack up and flee Brandon. They showed me into their living room where I sat on the carpeted floor listening while Peter tried to reassure me. Nothing he said seemed to help. The only thing I could think of to do was to run as fast as I could and leave all of it behind. Yet, this time, there was no place to run. I was caught in a spiritual dilemma.

Peter reached for the Bible and turned to a Psalm I was unfamiliar with. Then in what I can only describe as the most profound and disturbing incident I have ever experienced, Peter's voice was no longer Peter's voice. I couldn't see Peter sitting directly in front of me and I couldn't actually see who it was sitting in front of me. Everything in the room had disappeared in a way similar to when I saw the deer turn into the hawk on the highway. There was nothing except the voice speaking directly to me, reciting the words of the Psalm.

With each and every word spoken, I felt incredibly frightened. I wanted to hide myself from the power of that voice and at the same time I felt drawn to the power of the words it spoke. Then it was all over. The room around me returned. Peter was sitting directly in front of me again. Sharon was there. I looked at them, trying to read their faces. Had they too experienced something? I asked Sharon what had just happened and she asked me to tell them what I had experienced.

I described what happened and Sharon smiled at me in a way that made me feel that whatever she and Peter also experienced, it was something good. Again I asked if they experienced something strange. Sharon said that Peter was led to read me the 91st Psalm. Peter agreed and said that it was important for me to understand that the 91st Psalm was my Psalm and that God wanted me to know it.

I left Peter and Sharon that night profoundly affected by the strange event and despite the fact that to this day I can still visualize what took place that night, I simply cannot explain it. It remains the most powerful and profound event of my life.

It's interesting to me that this incident with Peter and Sharon was the last of these strange incidents I had. Why I had them and why this one was the last one, I still don't understand. I do know that the 91st Psalm remains special to me.

Peter and Sharon suggested that I spend some time at a religious retreat in Massachusetts, and after talking with them about it, I decided to go. I wrote a poem shortly before I left for the retreat in which I described a large white building with large marble columns. It was surrounded by cedar trees.

When Kip and I arrived at the religious retreat, I was surprised by what I saw. The building was made of marble, it had huge marble columns and there were numerous cedar trees surrounding the property. I mentioned my poem to Kip before he drove back to Vermont. I took the coincidence of my poem as a sign that being at the retreat was a good thing.

I was shown around the huge estate by a staff member and then introduced to three women who would be sharing a dorm room with me. We talked to each other about the reasons we had come to the retreat. One woman told us that the staff had brought her to the retreat from New Orleans where she had been mixed up in a scenario that included crime figures. The retreat staff was hiding her. Another girl told about being accused of being "demonically oppressed." The girl was only in her late teens and seemed to feel that the label of oppression was misplaced. I kept information about my own circumstances to myself.

The daily routine of the retreat revolved around religious instruction. Almost immediately, I was uncomfortable with this instruction. The dinner meal was an odd mixture of ingredients we were told were vegetable based. It was like a thick paste. I found this somewhat strange. There was no actual food like meat, potatoes or vegetables and I was never sure exactly what we were being fed.

We sat around a table listening to a red-haired woman staff member instruct us on the Bible and when she made an obvious inflammatory remark about Jewish people, I bristled and looked around the table to see if anyone else had the same reaction that I did. No one seemed to object. One of the people sitting at the table was a young Jewish man named David and when the staff member made a second negative remark about the Jewish people, I couldn't sit silently any longer.

"David, you're Jewish, aren't you?" I asked turning my attention toward him.

He looked startled by my comment.

I then directed my anger and my comments at the woman staff member and said that in my opinion this was not religious instruction, it was religious bigotry. The woman was caught off guard and she became even more rattled when others in the group joined me with their own objections. When the class was over David came up to me and thanked me. He said he couldn't explain why he hadn't spoken up sooner. I began to watch the staff very closely. Something wasn't right.

One night several of us walked the long distance from the retreat into town to have a pizza at a little café. The owner of the café greeted us warmly until he learned that we were from the retreat. Upon hearing where we were from, his attitude toward us drastically changed and he became hostile. This did not go unnoticed by any of us and we talked about it all the way back to the estate. That night I phoned Peter and voiced my concerns but he urged me to stay. I then phoned my parents and filled my mother in on what was taking place. She encouraged me to come home.

The staff was not pleased to hear that I was disenchanted enough to leave, but agreed to drive me to the bus. In the dark of the night, the red-haired woman staff member dropped me off on the street in Worcester. I sat with three duffle bags and an acoustic guitar in a case on a city bus stop bench and waited for the bus. The bus driver nearly drove past me and I had to run to catch the bus. A sole passenger aboard the bus helped me get my duffle bags and guitar on the bus and bought me a cup of hot coffee when we pulled into the bus stop. After hearing that I had been dropped off at night by the staff at the retreat the bus driver commented that in his opinion this was not Christian behavior.

I bought a bus ticket to Vermont and waited in the small bus station. Much to my alarm, the attendant closed the bus station at eleven that night, forcing me to stand alone outside in the dark to wait for the bus. I was very uneasy waiting in the dark, alone in the city. A man and woman came after about twenty or so minutes to wait for the bus with me and I felt somewhat more at ease not having to wait all alone. When I finally boarded the bus I realized that I would have to stay awake all night because I had to change buses several times. I looked out at the street lamps along the Charles River and thought to myself how incredible it was to be sitting on a bus in Boston.

During my investigation, I learned that Robert Hyde and Dr. Hudson Hoagland conducted extensive CIA experiments at the Worcester Foundation for Experimental Biology and that MKULTRA Subproject 8, conducted at Worcester, was Hyde's Subproject. Whether it was the four Vermont CIA research sites or the two Baltimore hospital CIA sites, it seemed that I had been in the same city or in the same hospitals again and again, where the CIA experiments were conducted. It seemed an incredible coincidence that I ended up in Worcester when at the time I had no idea that I had ever been used in CIA experiments. I never identified the religious retreat in Worcester as a CIA site, but the fact that CIA was very interested in using religion to control people, makes me suspicious. CIA was particularly interested in religious conversion (MKULTRA Subproject 98 dealt with individual and mass conversion) and the location of the retreat was in the same city as a well-known CIA front where Hyde had conducted MKULTRA research.

After learning about the Vermont CIA experiments and realizing I had been in two CIA sites in Baltimore, I took a closer look at the retreat experience in Worcester. Because the CIA, UVM and the two Burlington hospitals continue to refuse to provide me with the full record of the CIA experiments I was subjected to, I am forced to be suspicious about my experiences in the retreat. I had been at a total of seven CIA sites in three states and given the fact that the CIA was operating in Worcester, my suspicions only grew.

The first night I was at the retreat, I learned that one of the women was apparently being hidden by the retreat from organized crime in New Orleans. She wasn't there for religious instruction. I've recently wondered if what sounded like a witness protection program was in effect with this woman and if that was the case, as far as I know, the federal government runs the witness protection program.

I thought about the reaction of the man in the little café when he discovered that a group of us were from the retreat. His immediate reaction was clearly an indication that he had some type of strong negative feelings or knowledge about the retreat.

I attempted an internet search for the retreat after learning about the CIA experiments. I knew that a branch of the religious retreat was located in Switzerland, but I was unable to find the retreat. I found this unusual, having conducted many previous internet searches. It seemed to me that even if the organization no longer existed, I still should have been able to locate information on it. I never succeeded. It's as if it never existed.

The Rockland Project, which I have determined was a CIA project, is another instance where, to quote former Governor Phil Hoff, "It's just as if it never existed."

The actual location of the retreat was in a hamlet of Worcester called Shrewsbury. The Worcester Foundation for Experimental Biology was also based in Shrewsbury. It's a stretch for me to believe this was a coincidence.

The religious instruction offered at the retreat was troubling from the start and I was always perplexed that the other people at the retreat seemed willing to be taught what was so clearly religious bigotry until someone spoke up and challenged the teaching. It was as if they were asleep or dulled somehow. In addition, I was essentially dumped on the city streets of Worcester, alone at night, in the cold of February to get a bus and get back to Vermont. CIA operated out of Worcester and when I look closely at the night I left the retreat, it was a run from the retreat. I had a long history of running and CIA knew this from the VSH experiments. Was that night in Worcester another experiment? Was the estate where the retreat operated a CIA site? I don't know the answer to these questions and I do not like the fact that I have to ask myself these kinds of questions. It's not knowing the full story of the CIA experiments I was subjected to that is so disturbing all these years later.

All of the others at the retreat with me were young people. I recall no middle-aged or elderly people. They were from all over the country. In retrospect, given what I've learned over the last fifteen years, I wonder if it's possible that all the people there were former CIA unwitting subjects like I was. I will very likely never know the answer but even the possibility that this could have been the case is very disturbing.

A few days after I left the retreat I got a phone call from one of the women who shared a dorm room with me. She told me that when the people staying at the retreat learned that I had been dropped off alone in the city they were not pleased. Apparently seven or eight of the people who were there openly challenged the retreat staff about how I was handled and about the religious instruction. She told me that the seven or eight people, including her, packed up and left the retreat right after I left. She was back home in Texas. She thanked me for waking everyone up. I'm left to conclude that my objections to how the retreat behaved were shared by many others staying there.

My experience at the retreat was a game changer for me. Peter and Sharon didn't seem to understand or believe the things I told them happened at the retreat. I plunged into a severe depression. My parents tried to support me and they were concerned as I sunk deeper and deeper into despair. In an effort to try to ease the situation, my arthritic father climbed the stairs to my bedroom one afternoon with my mother. They sat in my room describing how my room could be turned into an apartment and that they would do everything they could to help me. They wanted me to be home with them and my father said they didn't care if I went to church or not. He just wanted me to be home with them and safe.

I struggled with a terrible conflict. If I left the church and Peter and Sharon would I be surrendering my soul to the Devil? I didn't know what to do. I went to Pater and asked him for the key to the church. I wanted to go inside the church and try to decide what to do.

I was resistant to the idea that I had been exposed to a demonic force from the beginning when Peter first suggested that this had been the case. It frightened me and I was even more frightened at the thought of pulling back from Peter and Sharon. Would I find myself at the mercy of far more oppression than I had when I first came to them for help? I felt doomed.

I stood in the church looking at the stained glass windows and prayed for God to help me decide what to do. It was an almost eerie experience to be alone in the big church. The emotional conflict I was caught in felt threatening to my survival. I couldn't even kill myself because whether alive or dead, I felt that I was caught directly in the middle of God and the Devil. If I pulled away from the church, would I open the door for seven times the torment? Dying wouldn't protect me. I had no escape and it terrified me. I believed in God and it wasn't God I was trying to escape.

When I walked into Peter and Sharon's house that night in November, 1981, I didn't yet know about the violent childhood trauma I suffered and I didn't yet have the documents to prove that I had been experimented on by the CIA. It took me over twenty years after my experiences with Peter and Sharon to even begin to comprehend and to accept that Peter's determination that I had been "oppressed by evil" was true.

I would eventually realize that I was so afraid of the idea that I might have been influenced by something or someone evil that I had to distance myself from the intensity of my relationship with Peter and Sharon. For many years I was able to tell myself that they were wrong. Peter and Sharon weren't wrong but, in 1982, I was trying once again to survive.

In 1981, I wasn't able to recognize or accept the idea that I had been exposed to evil. After fifteen years of obtaining information on the Vermont CIA experiments, I clearly recognize that I was surrounded by evil. There is simply no other word that accurately describes and explains the CIA experiments. There was no ethical, moral or medical explanation for the experiments and the intent of the doctors who conducted the experiments is very clear in their research project documents.

I left the church that snowy day in March, 1982, and told my parents that I needed help. They were understandably concerned when I said I needed psychiatric help. They knew all too well what my previous attempts to get help from psychiatrists had brought me. I phoned my family doctor and told him that I needed help. He quickly arranged for me to be admitted to the Rutland Regional Medical Center psychiatric unit. I held my breath and prayed that I had made the right decision.

I don't have clear memories of being admitted to the Rutland psychiatric unit but I am sure I was afraid. The first person I recall talking with came into my hospital room and introduced herself as the occupational therapist, Mary Patten. Mary wore a bandana over her hair and was non-judgmental in her approach. I talked to her about the frightening spiritual crisis I was caught in and she reassured me that I would find help on the unit.

Dr. Bob Ross, a senior psychiatrist, visited me and we talked in more depth about my crisis. He told me that the unit staff had experience with situations like mine and asked me to hang in with them. He asked me for permission to contact Dr. Nepvue. I didn't talk to him about Dr. Nepvue's diagnosis, but Dr. Ross learned of it when he and Dr. Nepvue spoke on the phone.

Sharon and my sister-in-law visited me and Sharon, who was very frightened that harm would come to me while I was on the unit, tried to convince me to leave the hospital and enter a Christian-based psychiatric hospital. I felt torn. I was already uneasy about being in another psychiatric clinic and I was still deeply connected to Sharon. I followed Sharon and Sue to the door of the unit, still not sure if I was going to stay or leave with them.

A nurse standing at the desk stopped us and asked me, "What do I have to gain from you staying here Karen? What's in it for me?"

It was the perfect challenge and I stopped at the door. Sharon and Sue left without me.

Days became weeks on the unit. My family doctor visited me every day and promised me that before he allowed anyone to send me anywhere, he would discharge me.

He stressed, "Just don't do anything that will take the decision out of my hands."

He remained my doctor of record during the entire hospital stay.

The nursing staff on the unit was all psychiatric registered nurses. The difference between highly trained psychiatric nurses and the untrained and uneducated aides at VSH was markedly apparent. I sought out Mary Patten to talk with and time and time again, she seemed to provide me with information and insight I felt was extremely helpful.

Rosemary Johnson, the mental health clinic worker I first met after Phil Cram died in 1969, was one of the unit staff. I'd always liked Rosemary and she too became a person I went to for insight and help. The head nurse, Lynne Colville became another person I felt safe with. Lynne became a person I would turn to in times of crisis for many years to come. Hiding my strange condition was for me self-protection and although I was aware of the diagnosis, I didn't have much information about it. Rosemary, Mary and Lynne approached the subject numerous times, but for me, it was still something buried in my unconscious mind.

My family doctor ordered blood tests to check the status of the immune disorder and much to my surprise the L-cell, which was the cell that positively confirmed the diagnosis of systemic lupus, was found. I was shaken by the diagnosis. Mary had been diagnosed with lupus many years earlier and she helped me through the initial stages of acceptance and understanding of the disease. Mary and I would share a bond that would last for many years, but not only because of our shared illness.

Mary seemed to just "get it." She had a depth of understanding about the human condition I hadn't encountered before. Mary was a quiet, unassuming person who was very clearly motivated to help other people. She would go on to obtain her Master's Degree in Psychology and work on the unit as a therapist and she told me later that it was when she met me that she discovered her ability to counsel, not to just do occupational therapy.

She became a highly sought out counselor by patients on the unit.

After a couple of months on the unit, Dr. Bob Ross retired, and filling his position as head of Psychiatric Services was Dr. Tom Fox. I'd seen Dr. Fox come in and out of the unit to speak with patients and the day that he officially took over remains a memorable day for me. Many years later he told me it was a memorable day for him as well.

I watched as Dr. Fox came into the dayroom to get patients to talk with. He had officially been my doctor for several days, yet he had never introduced himself to me and I was irritated. He asked me to come with him so that we could talk.

"You've been my doctor for days now but you haven't bothered to introduce yourself. So now you finally say something to me and I'm supposed to jump up and act like it's okay that you totally dismissed me for days?"

Dr. Fox smiled at me and said he'd be back a little later. He continued to see patients on the unit and when he finished, he came over to me one more time.

"You want to talk now?" he asked me.

I noticed a twinkle in his eye, but I still had reservations about this new psychiatrist. I went with him to talk.

"I apologize for not introducing myself before now," Dr. Fox began, "You've done hard time, haven't you?"

"So, you read my chart and saw I'd been in VSH," I fired back.

Dr. Fox smiled at me.

"I have to tell you, I haven't had a patient talk to me like that and I love it. Too many patients don't stand up for themselves. But I also recognize that you have done hard time. Pretty bad, huh?"

I was surprised by Dr. Fox's attitude. We talked and at the end of our first meeting, I felt that he might actually be someone who might help. It was worth a try. Over our next several meetings, he impressed me as being fair, open and willing to work with me. He didn't push me about my diagnosis of MPD but he said he hoped that he could help me make progress in dealing with the disorder. He seemed to appreciate the spiritual crisis I was struggling with and as the weeks went by, the intensity of my spiritual conflict diminished.

My condition was erratic and my behavior was unpredictable. Mary sat down with me and tried to learn about the other personalities, but I wasn't able to provide much information. It was frustrating for me to be so shut off from my own mind.

I fled the hospital for reasons I have never really understood. I wandered around Rutland city, where, apparently, I was struck by a bicycle. I was found by an ambulance crew, bleeding from my nose. Although the episode is fuzzy for me, I recall having a great deal of difficulty speaking. Dr. Fox met me in the emergency room and I went back to the unit on a stretcher.

Dr. Fox suggested that I consider attending the "day hospital" program. Day hospital was an intensive group therapy-based program run by Rutland Regional Hospital. There were several groups a day and Dr. Fox wanted me to remain on the unit while I attended. I agreed to give it a try.

Group therapy was grueling. Seven or eight patients sat in a circle discussing topics that ranged from personal situations to plans for discharge. I entered the group feeling that time was not something that I could afford to waste. The first day I began to talk in the group, which clearly angered one of the members.

"People who come into this group don't talk until they have been here awhile. I am the most senior member of this group and I've been here longer than anyone," the petite young woman announced, staring straight at me.

"Really? You've been here longer than anyone and if I've heard you right, you take some kind of pride in that?" I asked, staring right back at her.

She was caught off guard and shuffled around in her chair.

"Seniority or not, I'm here to work on my own issues and I'm not going to hang back just because you think I should," I said, looking around the entire circle.

A staff member later told me that I reminded him of a line from the song, *Me and Bobby McGee*: "Freedom's just another word for nothing left to lose."

He was right.

Group therapy was an interesting mixture of revelations by others whose issues more often than not set off the issues of many others in the circle. There were times when one person talking about how they felt or about whatever they were struggling with set off a chain reaction of emotion and identification among the other people. There were other times when days went by and we all sat there managing to accomplish nothing except to irritate each other.

There were days when I returned to the unit exhausted and emotionally fragile. The unit staff helped those of us in the group deal with the aftermath of a day in therapy. Despite the urging of Dr. Fox, I didn't talk about my MPD in the group. I was still protective and secretive about the disorder and only a few of the unit staff actually knew my diagnosis

By the end of June, I had gone as far as I could in the group and I talked with Dr. Fox about leaving the hospital. He voiced concern about my returning to live with my parents, but I didn't have other options at that point. The night before my discharge, Rosemary Johnson sat down with me.

"I want to you to know that Kathy Judge is in private practice now. If you ever decide to go into therapy and deal with the MPD, give Kathy a call."

Dr. Fox suggested that I see a therapist as an outpatient and it's clear to me in retrospect that, in 1982, I was not yet ready to deal with my disorder. I saw a psychologist after discharge and it was clear to me almost immediately that he and I were not a good match. He dismissed my diagnosis and told me he didn't believe in MPD. I remember looking at him that day and thinking to myself that there was simply no way I was going to get into a struggle about whether or not I was multiple with this guy.

"Whether or not you believe in my diagnosis doesn't change the way I have to live my life. I think me coming here is a mistake."

I didn't return to therapy with him.

Tensions between my mother and me were escalating again and the day I ended therapy, I boarded a bus to Morrisville where I secured a loan from the bank. I decided to buy a horse.

I think that I decided to buy another horse in an attempt to recreate a time in my life when having a horse helped me hold myself together. My parents were not altogether pleased by my news, but they agreed to go with me to look for a horse. Mom and Dad only wanted me to be okay and they hoped that maybe having a horse would help me.

I walked through three huge horse barns looking at each of the many horses stabled. When I reached the third barn I saw King. He was a beautiful red chestnut thoroughbred with a blond mane and tail and a white blaze down his face. King nickered softly to me when I approached him in the stall.

It would take twenty years for me to be aware of the possible connection between King, the red chestnut horse with the white blaze down his face and the other red chestnut horse with a white blaze that Curlin brought out behind the VSH back ward for me to see in 1970. I would learn during my investigation that CIA used horse imagery as hypnotic symbols in the drug and mind control experiments.

The ranch owner tried to discourage me from buying King. He was a high-strung former three-day eventer and only an experienced rider could manage him. As I rode him around the large ring I was nearly breathless with excitement. If there was one thing I could do well, it was ride a horse and riding King was akin to riding a bolt of lightening. King was magnificent and I needed to feel the ways in which he made me feel. I was alive again.

My cousins, Sally and Gene, had pastureland and barns at their home in Brandon and they agreed to let me keep King there. I did chores in their small stable and my mother joined me. She enjoyed being around the horses and has said many times over the years that for her it was one of the best times. My father and I began spending time together as well. It was nice to not only have time with my father but also to have the chance to get to know him all over again. Dad was frustrated that his arthritis prevented him from helping me do some of the heavy work required with a horse, but his quiet, constant presence was invaluable, as was the time we were fortunate enough to be able to spend together.

King's health problems began almost immediately. He was diagnosed with shipping fever and required a veterinarian. I was shaken by King's illness but the vet pulled him through the disease. The horse barn at my parent's home was repaired and the backyard was fenced in. I leased an adjoining piece of pasture from the neighbor who had allowed me to pasture my first horse on her property in 1960. I remember riding King down through the streets of Brandon the day I moved him to Maple Street. King had elegance in his movement and sitting atop the high-strung animal made me feel alive, free and in control.

The backyard soon was regularly filled with neighborhood kids who ranged in age from six to sixteen. King loved the attention the kids gave him and many of them helped me load hay bales and eventually joined in to build King a new barn. I grew close to these kids and they confided in me regularly about their problems and concerns. When the school bus passed by King's corral every afternoon, the kids on the bus could be heard calling King's name.

My father loved to sit in his chair in the backyard and listen to the kids. Dad's two brothers began to be regular visitors, as did my sister-in-law's father, Bob. I think Dad missed talking to people as he had always done when he worked and now that I was home and the back yard was almost always filled with people, he was content.

It's still difficult for me to find the words to explain my relationship with King. I know the terms that have been used, like anthropomorphism and dissociation and I agree that I did experience a form of both. In retrospect I realize that unconsciously I was King and he was me. King was a dissociated externalized self in animal form. I would later learn that things I did for him, I was on another level, doing for myself. I almost constantly worried that someone would harm him and that I would not be able to protect him. I got up out of bed many nights to stand and look out the window at the barn because I was so fearful. It got so I rarely left his side. I was constantly on alert for a threat from nameless, faceless people.

I realize now that the longer I had King, the less I was in touch with my own emotions or my own self. I recall standing beside him, stroking his neck and looking into his huge brown eyes. It was almost hypnotic. Every breath he took breathed life into me. King was a fiery, powerful animal who in the wrong hands could have actually been dangerous. He required an experienced rider and knowledgeable handling.

King foundered in 1986. Founder is a painful, potentially fatal disease of the hoof. The vet saved him and after a long recuperation I was even more cautious with him. No matter the weather, I remained by his side, all day every day. My parents worried about me in the freezing winter and in the heat of the summer. After King's illness, I began to have trouble with my stomach and my family doctor prescribed a drug to help.

I decided to build a new barn and the neighborhood kids eagerly pitched in to help. My uncle was instrumental in the construction of the barn, as was Dad. The kids learned carpentry from my uncle and father and they were proud when the barn was finished.

King began to have problems again and the vet diagnosed the condition as navicular disease, a serious and painful nerve disease in the feet and legs, usually found in horses that have been used for jumping. The vet suggested King be fitted with special shoes. It was only a matter of weeks before King's condition dramatically worsened.

I felt like I was trapped in a nightmare. I watched King as he took painful steps and inside of myself, I knew. On a cold, sunny November morning I looked out the window at the barn as I had done every morning for five years. This morning, King didn't have his head out the top dutch door of the barn as he always had every morning before.

When I opened the barn door I saw King lying down. I stared into his huge soft brown eyes and suddenly I felt sickened. I knew I had to put him down. I kneeled down next to him and cradled his head in my arms. For me, putting King down was committing suicide. I went inside and called the vet.

The vet refused to allow me to stay while he put King down. My father and uncle remained at the barn and my mother and I drove to my aunt's house to wait. When King first foundered, Sally and Gene gave me a Morgan mare that I kept in King's old barn. She was a sweet mare but she wasn't King. I hated to have her there when King was put down.

I sat in my aunt's house and listened while military jets conducted maneuvers overhead. The roar of the jets was at times deafening. At the time I had no way of knowing that the thundering roar of the jets flying overhead was a trigger to a childhood trauma. I learned years later that when I was eighteen months old my mother rushed outside to the fenced-in play area I was in after several low flying jets caused me to become hysterical. She couldn't calm me and had to call a doctor because of my hysterical reaction. My mother explained that when she couldn't help me calm down, she too became hysterical. I have no memory of the low flying jets and in retrospect I find it ironic that on the day King was put down, the jets flew over my aunt's house.

Returning to King's empty barn felt surreal, but I tried to push ahead and take care of the Morgan mare. I felt sick. The anti-nausea drugs my doctor had given me months before didn't seem to be working and he once again increased the dose. The neighborhood kids came to offer their condolences and they all had tears in their eyes. I stood in the shower that night and sobbed. Why did God take the only thing I really cared about away from me?

Over the days that followed, I took care of the mare and rode her a few times. My depression was steadily worsening. I watched rats scurry around under the bird feeders that were hung around the corral. For years, many birds came to the feeders, along with squirrels who liked to sit atop the board fence of the corral with their babies. When King was alive I refused to fire a gun near him and risk frightening him, but as I watched the rats eat the birdseed, I was repulsed.

I borrowed a rifle from a neighbor and Bob, my sister-in-law's father, gave me handmade bullets to use. I'd fired a rifle when I was in elementary school, target shooting with my brother, and I knew enough about a rifle to be able to shoot a rat. I loaded the gun and waited for the rats to show themselves.

I pulled the trigger and saw the rat stagger and fall. Suddenly I felt myself racing backwards, as if I was spinning through a tunnel at a hundred miles an hour. I felt disoriented and frightened by the strange sensations I felt. As if on automatic pilot, with no conscious thought or decision, I placed the barrel of the rifle under my chin and pulled the trigger. Nothing happened. I pulled the trigger a second time. Nothing happened.

My father and uncle rushed into the backyard. My father later told me that I was as white as a sheet. They asked me if I was okay and I said, yes. I still wasn't sure what had just happened. I had never killed anything before but even this didn't explain what I had done when I placed the barrel of the rifle under my chin. I took the rifle to Bob who ran a rod down the barrel of the gun to dislodge the bullets. The handmade bullets saved my life. I told no one about my suicide attempt.

I stared at the dead rat for hours. I couldn't bring myself to bury it and each time I tried, something inside of me prevented me from placing the rat's body in the hole I dug. One of the kids buried the rat for me. I tried to pull myself out of what felt like a quicksand of despair by getting up every morning and tending to the mare. I saddled her and rode a few miles each day but nothing seemed to matter. I kept seeing King's eyes as I knelt next to him in the barn. It was like I was looking into my own eyes.

The teenage boys next door were down behind the barn target shooting at a plastic Coke bottle and they invited me to shoot. I stood a considerable distance from the plastic bottle, aimed and fired. The bottle didn't move.

One of the boys ran up to check the bottle and turned around and shouted, "You hit it dead center!"

I laughed as the kids teased me to try again and I aimed and fired. The bottle didn't move. This time the boys were excited by the fact that I hit it dead center again.

"Where did you learn to shoot like that?" they asked.

I had no answer and in the back of my mind, I felt uneasiness. One time might have been a fluke but when I shot dead center twice without even moving the plastic bottle, it bothered me. It would not be the last time I had disturbing questions about guns

The dark, dreary skies of November only seemed to make the depression I felt worse and as each day passed, I became more overwhelmed. I knew I was in real trouble. I sat down with my parents and told them I had to get help and that I knew who to call. Rosemary Johnson told me when I left the hospital that Kathy Judge was in private practice and

I knew that she was the person to contact.

When I spoke with Kathy on the phone, I told her that we had known each other at Rutland County Mental Health in 1969. Kathy was booked solid with patients until January and couldn't see me. Kathy would tell me years later that during this phone conversation she was struck by the fact that I talked as though she and I had just recently seen each other. I decided to try to hang on until January when she could fit me in, but things only got worse for me.

I visited Lynne Colville, the head nurse on the Rutland unit and after we talked Lynne asked my permission for her to speak with my family doctor. Lynne told me that she thought I should come back onto the unit. I knew she was right. Something was very wrong and I knew that my life was on the line. Arrangements were made by my family doctor for me to be admitted to the unit.

My family was fearful and tried to discourage me from going back into the hospital. My brother couldn't understand why losing King had affected me to the degree it had and I had no way of explaining to him what was going on. I didn't understand either. It was about King, but it was about something else too. I just didn't know what that something else was.

Dr. Fox immediately zeroed in on my relationship with King and told me that when he learned that King had died, he knew I would have problems. Dr. Fox asked me to explain to him how and why I constructed the new barn and the corral fence the way I had. I told him how important it was that the new barn had several windows in it and that it be big enough that King wouldn't feel closed in. The rear window had a screen across it so no one could reach into the barn.

I explained how when I built the board fence for the corral, each board had to be six inches apart and that the handle and lock on the gate was on the inside of the gate. I told him that the gate was very heavy and that my uncle rigged it with what's called a "dead man." A wire attached to the gate is fixed to a weight buried in a hole and this keeps the gate opening and closing properly. I explained that for some reason the dead man bothered me.

"The handle and lock on the gate were on the inside of the gate?" Dr. Fox asked me.

"Why do you suppose you put the handle and lock on the inside of the gate?"

I asked him to check my left leg. I was having pain and I wondered if he thought I foundered. He replied that he wasn't a foot doctor. Then he asked me to listen to a story:

"There was a young horse kept in a canyon with many other horses. The man, who had been searching for just the right horse for a long time, surveyed all of the horses and chose one particular horse because it was very special. He began to groom and train this horse for a very important occasion. The young horse was easily excited and the man instructed the horse about a very special carnival that was coming to town. All of the grooming and training was going to pay off when the horse heard the sound of fireworks at the carnival. The horse needed to recognize that the fireworks would signal the exodus."

I was stunned. I thought the word exodus meant exit and that Dr. Fox was telling me to kill myself. I didn't say a word to him. My condition rapidly deteriorated and my mind began producing frightening images, some of which I realized were hallucinations. I didn't tell anyone what was happening as fear and increasing paranoia over took me.

I entered the day room to find a doctor standing in front of a terminally ill patient. I saw the doctor transform in front of me into a priest and tell the woman that she was going to die. I was outraged and as he left the room and went into the hall, I chased after him. He disappeared.

I went to the nurse's station where I saw the patient charts hanging in the metal container they were kept in. Beside each patient's name was another name. I was enraged when I realized that every person on the unit was an imposter. These people were playing a strange game with me and my head spun in confusion. I grabbed the Bible and slid it down the hall toward where Dr. Fox was sitting with a patient. He came up the hall.

I told him that he needed the Bible more than I did. He agreed. I described seeing the doctor who was pretending to be a priest. He agreed that it was a terrible thing to do. He asked me if I had stopped taking the Xanax he prescribed and I told him there was something wrong with the pills. I returned to my room and when I lay on the bed, a crazy-looking woman in the other bed suddenly pulled the curtain between us back and snatched the pillow from under my head. When I got out of bed to confront her, she had disappeared.

I began to hide food under my bed. I couldn't eat because of nausea and I listened as the nurses in the hall talked about me as if I were already dead. I recounted to Mary the story Dr. Fox had told me. I didn't see him standing behind the curtain, listening and I only learned of his presence later. Dr. Fox diagnosed me as suffering a psychotic break.

The church sent me a can of Christmas cookies. The coffee can was wrapped in Christmas paper. I brought the cookies up to the nurse's station to share them with the night shift. When I returned to my room I tore the paper off from the can and to my horror read on the coffee can: Poison - Do Not Eat.

I was panic-stricken. I thought that I had just given the nurses poison. I couldn't handle it and despite the efforts of the night nurse, Marlene, to stop me, I put on my jacket and fled the unit. I ran to the elevator.

I wandered around the basement of the hospital while security searched for me. There was a blizzard that night and they feared that I had gone out into the storm. I found myself curled up on the floor in the stairwell.

I have no idea how much time passed until I returned to the unit. The sound of the elevator going up and down remained in my head for a long time. I couldn't get the mechanical noise out of my mind as it replayed again and again. The stairwell where I woke up was near the elevator shaft. Walking into the unit I passed by a nurse and watched her sneer at me. I realized I could only see her in profile and I told myself that she wasn't real.

Because my jacket was dry, the unit staff knew that I hadn't left the hospital. Dr. Fox ordered a shot of Haldol. I remember sitting in front of him at the nurses' station and suddenly feeling very sleepy. I put my head down on the counter for what felt like only a few moments and when I raised my head, I knew I had to get out of there. I knew that for some reason I was hallucinating and I wasn't sure that I could trust anyone on the unit. I was convinced that there had been something in the drugs they gave me.

The 1971 Metrazol chart shows that I recognized that I was hallucinating and I accurately attributed the cause of the hallucinations and the severe physical and emotional distress to the drugs the doctors were giving me. The incident in Rutland is the second time I was able to realize that I was having hallucinations. Apparently I didn't recognize that I was hallucinating all of the time.

Dr. Fox reluctantly let me go against medical advice and my parents drove me back home. I started shivering when I got into bed but it didn't take long before it was clear that I was having an adverse drug reaction. My muscles began to spasm severely. Mom called the family doctor. My facial muscles were in spasm and the spasms distorted my face.

The doctor gave me Benadryl and I pleaded with him, "I'm not crazy!"

"I know you're not crazy. You're having a bad drug reaction. I'll contact Dr. Fox and find out what he gave you. Don't worry. You will be okay," the doctor tried to reassure me.

My mother sat in the front of the ambulance and the ambulance attendant took my blood pressure. I knew the attendant. We had grown up together. I remember feeling very strange and very far away. I heard him call my name. My mother later told me the ambulance driver closed the window between us so that my mother couldn't see what was happening.

I was no longer in the ambulance. I had no body and no form. There was no physical or emotional distress. Wherever I was didn't seem to be a physical place. I felt a surge of exhilaration in that I had never felt anything as freeing and spectacular in my life. I realized that I was dying and I didn't mind. I clearly remember thinking if this is what dying is, I'm okay with it.

Suddenly and without audible words I "heard" a voice.

"This is not the right time."

I was immediately back on the stretcher in the ambulance. The emergency room doctors told me that I had a severe allergic reaction to Haldol. I learned later that the anti-nausea drug that I had been on since before King died had a phenothiazine drug in it. The two drugs collided. Dr. Fox later told me that very likely the psychotic break I had was drug-induced. In the ambulance my blood pressure dropped to a potentially life-threatening level. I think I was close to dying and the experience I had in those moments remains almost impossible for me to adequately describe. I do know that since that strange experience, I have never again feared dying

I recuperated at home and took Benadryl for several days. I had a very distressing incident after I got home. I tried to read the TV Guide and felt my mind mix into the words on the pages. It was a very frightening. My mind had lost the ability to separate itself from the words I tried to read. It was as if the boundaries of my mind had been breached. The experience passed after about twenty-four hours.

After I learned that I had been used in CIA experiments, I was able to reexamine the strange events during the unit hospitalization. Kathy and I talked about the things that happened during the unit stay many times.

Even before I obtained my medical records, I couldn't stop returning to those incidents on the unit. They troubled me.

I looked closely at the "story" I thought Dr. Fox told me and came to a conclusion, based on information both from my VSH records and from documents about MKULTRA. Special interrogations utilized hallucinogens, hypnosis, isolation, chemical shock and ECT. I read several declassified CIA documents detailing CIA use of SI with unwitting subjects and CIA interest in dissociation, particularly in children between the ages of thirteen and eighteen.

I believe the "story" I thought Dr. Fox told me was actually a flashback to the experimentation. Because of the memory loss I have for those almost seven months in seclusion, I do not have memory of what happened during the experiments in 1970-1971 to fall back on. The fact that I was having an adverse drug reaction in 1987 may have made me more vulnerable for the flashback to occur.

The man selected the horse to groom and train for an upcoming occasion. This would fit with having been selected by those experimenting on me. I believe hypnosis was used, as was LSD. The use of a horse is also key, and information about my love of horses was available to the researchers when I was thirteen years old. CIA used imagery of horses in their experiments with selected subjects. The carnival may have signified a pre-selected event. The symbolism of fireworks might have been used in place of a gunshot. CIA special interrogations tested hypnosis by instructing a subject to pick up and fire a gun and have no memory of the event. The fireworks signaled the exodus. At the time I thought exodus meant exit and believed Dr. Fox told me to kill myself. I believe the word exodus had a double meaning in the hypnotic set-up: to move from one place to the other or to flee the scene and also to kill myself after the special occasion.

Much of the MKULTRA research is thought to have been done so that CIA agents could be protected if captured by enemy agents. If an agent could hold information in a dissociated state, he would be unable to give the information up even under torture. CIA interest in dissociation led the researchers to use special interrogation methods as well as other methods to intentionally further dissociate the subject. CIA wanted to explore the possibility that under hypnotic command, a subject might obey previously implanted hypnotic commands. Memory for the event and for the set-up would be lost.

The after-effects of the adverse drug reaction indicate an LSD flashback. I couldn't read without the words mixing into my mind; LSD is known to break down the normal barriers in the mind and leads to an inability to separate the internal from the external. I spoke with Tom Fox before he died and he believed that I was given LSD. Kathy agrees.

In the book, *A Father, A Son and the CIA*, author Harvey Weinstein quotes an excerpt from the book, *Battle For The Mind: A Physiology of Conversion and Brainwashing*, by William Sargent: "If a complete, sudden collapse can be produced by prolonging and intensifying emotional stress, the cortical slate may be wiped clean temporarily of its recently implanted patterns of behavior, perhaps allowing others to be substituted more easily."

Weinstein summarizes the research objectives stated in a 1950 CIA BLUEBIRD memorandum:

1. Discover means of conditioning personnel to prevent unauthorized extraction of information by known means.
2. Investigate the possibility of control of an individual by application of special interrogation.
3. To study memory enhancement.
4. Establish defensive means for preventing hostile control of Agency personnel.
5. To evaluate offensive uses of unconventional interrogation

techniques including hypnosis and drugs.

A 1952 CIA Project ARTICJOKE memorandum maps out further objectives:

"The evaluation and development of any method by which we can get information from a person against his will and without his knowledge. Can we get control of a person to the point where he will do our bidding against his will and even against such fundamental laws of nature as self preservation?"

Robert Hyde conducted CIA experiments in Projects BLUEBIRD, ARTICHOKE and MKULTRA. After years of investigation and consults with experts, I believe LSD, hypnosis and other forms of brainwashing were used on me while I was a patient in the Burlington hospitals and in VSH. I would have one more disturbing incident during therapy with Kathy that once would once again raise the question of implanted hypnotic suggestion.

After I recuperated from the adverse drug reaction I returned to the unit in December, 1987. All signs of the drug-induced "psychotic break" were gone and I tried to settle into the routine of the unit again. There were new patients on the unit and I became friends with two. Peggy was a young mother struggling with her own issues from childhood. She and I shared a hospital room and quickly became friends. Andrea joined in with Peggy and I and the three of us spent most of our time together.

It was still almost impossible for me to openly discuss the MPD although I did talk more freely with Mary and Lynne. I was still struggling to understand my illness and to be able to access information buried in my unconscious mind. The unit staff watched as I cycled through one personality after the other. There were child alters and intensely protective alters. It still amazes me how consciously removed I was from my own self.

Dr. Fox wanted me to deal with the MPD in private outpatient therapy and I was adamant that the only therapist I would see was Kathy Judge.

Kathy didn't have an opening in her schedule until January. The unit staff brought me the names of numerous local therapists and I rejected all of them. Kathy was the only therapist I would consider. Rosemary Johnson, who worked with Kathy in 1969 at Rutland County Mental Health, phoned Kathy. Rosemary reminded Kathy that she had known me in 1969 and told Kathy that she was the only therapist I would see. Dr. Fox also contacted Kathy to ask her to see me in therapy.

Kathy later told me that during the phone call with Tom Fox, he told her my diagnosis. Kathy told Tom that although she had experience in dissociation, she hadn't taken on a full-fledged multiple before and that she wasn't even sure that she believed in the disorder. Tom replied that she would believe.

"Why me?" Kathy asked Tom.

"Because she believes that it's you," Tom answered.

In January, 1988 Kathy Judge came to see me on the unit.

6

THERAPY, CHAOS AND INTEGRATION, 1988-1997

Kathy came to meet with me on the unit. I don't recall the details of our conversation except that I did acknowledge the MPD. I found it easy to talk with her and at the end of our meeting she agreed to see me in outpatient therapy. I remember feeling hopeful.

In 1969, when I attended the outpatient clinic where Rosemary and Kathy both worked, I never sought out Kathy to talk with. I watched her but I never approached her. She drove me home from the clinic one day and on an outing for the outpatient clinic, I recall swimming with her. In 1988, seeing Kathy again was just as if 1969 was yesterday.

Many years after that first meeting with Kathy, she told me that I presented one of my child alters during the meeting. Kathy would teach me in the years to come that despite what appeared to be self-destructive behavior or inexplicable behavior, that my personality system was organized to always insure my survival. MPD is the province of childhood trauma, as it usually develops in early childhood as a result of trauma. My expectations and assessments of the world and of people around me were based on a child's interpretations. In 1988, I was thirty-six years old, and I wasn't even close to understanding the illness that created such chaos in my life.

Although the MPD served its purpose by protecting my mind from unbearable early childhood trauma, the older I became, the more life-threatening the disorder became. My alter personalities were stuck back in a time long since passed and a great deal of the logic I used in my adult life was dictated by what Kathy described as " trance logic." I had frequent episodes of a cross-over in time where something in the present triggered off an emotional reaction that had much more to do with something that had happened in childhood. It didn't take Kathy long to realize that I had memory loss, but the extent of the memory loss wouldn't be discovered for several years.

In addition, despite the fact that I knew I was multiple, I was not consciously aware of the dissociations or what set them off. At times I heard conversations in my head and at other times I became aware of seeing and talking with my alters. I wasn't yet able to comprehend that the alters were actually all me.

On the unit Peggy and I had grown to be good friends. We supported each other, laughed together and cried together. I couldn't handle seeing my family and I didn't think returning to my parent's home would turn out any better than it ever had. I carried a deep-seated sense of shame about being sick and when I was with my family it only seemed to intensify. I desperately wanted to be normal and to not be the way I was. I knew that they didn't understand. I didn't understand either. Dr Fox and Kathy agreed that it would be okay for me to live temporarily with Peggy and her family. Peggy and her husband agreed that the arrangement might be good for both Peggy and me. Although Peggy was aware of my diagnosis, she didn't really understand what I was going through and I didn't expect her to. Peggy was my friend and in February, 1988, I was discharged from the unit and moved in with Peggy and her family.

Peggy had four beautiful children ranging in age from nine to two years old. The kids accepted me into their home and we all got along well. I slept in one of the bunk beds in their room. I always loved kids and enjoyed being around them.

Kathy had her hands full. Over the years Kathy has described herself as a "plain vanilla" therapist. She wasn't prone to over-reaction and her solid, sane approach to therapy began to prove to me that she was someone I could lean on without fear that she would suddenly step aside and allow me to fall. She didn't have a secret agenda. The Kathy I saw one week would be the Kathy I found the following week.

I was at times defensive, aloof and fearful about trusting her too much. I tested her frequently and many times in the beginning of therapy I contemplated leaving therapy. But in 1988, I was out of options and I knew that my life could not continue the way it had.

Kathy began to seek out experts in MPD. She attended a conference given by Dr. Colin Ross early on in our therapy, as well as other well-known psychiatrists like Dr. Richard Kluft.

During the first few months of therapy I began to dissociate more often and my personalities became more separate. Kathy later told me that I actually didn't become more floridly multiple in therapy. She said that I had been floridly multiple for a very long time before she began seeing me. I began to feel safe enough in therapy to allow the alters to emerge and be acknowledged by Kathy. It was a very frightening time for me.

For reasons that I cannot recall, I arranged to take out a loan at the bank in Morrisville to buy a car. The bank required me to sign the papers in person. Peggy cashed a check for me and dropped me off at the car rental agency. Once again I felt liberated and free behind the wheel of a rented car. I was no longer vulnerable and needy. I was capable and independent. As I drove along Route 100 toward Morrisville and listened to the FM radio, I felt transformed in every fiber of my being.

I signed the papers at the bank and returned to Rutland. I became increasingly uneasy at Peggy's for reasons I couldn't understand and I began to drive around in the rented car for hours at a stretch. My goal of buying a car had vanished.

I ate meals in diners and fast food restaurants and almost continuously drove. I began to feel a mounting and disturbing compulsion that I was at a loss to either explain or resist. Although I had no suicidal thoughts or feelings and no thoughts or feelings about harming anyone else, the strange compulsion overwhelmed my ability to resist. I purchased a pistol.

I drove away from the sporting goods store with the unloaded gun on the passenger seat. I began driving aimlessly searching for the place I was supposed to go. I wasn't sure where that place was or what I was supposed to do with the gun once I got there. I grew more confused as I drove, trying in vain to find the place I was supposed to go.

The compulsion was frightening. Whatever it was I was supposed to do was lost somewhere inside of me. I drove for hours until for the first time in my life I checked into a motel. I kept the pistol, now loaded, next to me on the bed in the motel room. For reasons I couldn't explain, being in a motel seemed to be a piece of the strange compulsion that was driving me. I waited, but I wasn't sure who or what I was waiting for.

My ease with the pistol both captivated and frightened me. I instinctively knew how to handle the gun. I loaded and unloaded it. I knew where the safety was and how to use it. The pistol felt natural in my hands. My mind raced to make sense of the situation.

The bed in the motel directly faced a large mirror and I sat on the bed and stared at myself in the mirror. I raised the loaded gun and placed it to my temple. I didn't feel suicidal but as I stared at my image in the mirror, I suddenly felt very frightened. I phoned Kathy.

Kathy later told me how frightened she was on the phone with me, fearing that I would either intentionally or accidently kill myself. Kathy made a decision when she first began therapy with me that she would never be a participant in having me sent to VSH and that night she hoped that I would safely unload the gun while we were on the phone.

After I unloaded the gun we talked for a long time. I tried to explain to her that I was not suicidal and did not have thoughts or feelings of harming anyone else. I was at a complete loss to explain the strange compulsion. Kathy instructed me to get rid of the gun before I came to her office. She would not see me while I remained in possession of the gun.

The next morning I checked out of the motel and contacted friends of mine who I knew would be safe with the gun and who would keep the entire situation quiet. The gun was eventually returned to the sporting goods store. I drove around for a long time, trying to understand what was happening to me. Eventually I drove to Kathy's office.

After learning that I had been used in experiments, this incident and the other episodes with guns, whether it was my familiarity with a gun or my accuracy when I fired a gun, came under close scrutiny. Kathy and I discussed the gun episodes many times and when I obtained declassified CIA documents and documents related to CIA Special Interrogations, I realized that my seemingly inexplicable knowledge and behavior related to guns may have come out of the experiments I was subjected to.

Declassified CIA documents describe Special Interrogation methods using unwitting subjects in hypnosis experiments. In one experiment a woman was placed in a hypnotic trance and instructed to pick up a gun and to fire it at another person. The woman did not know that the gun wasn't loaded. She was instructed that she would have amnesia for the event. The woman, who had expressed a fear of guns, picked the gun up and fired it at another person. She had no memory of the event. CIA use of guns in its mind control experiments has been written about in several well-known books.

I asked my brother if he had ever taught me to handle a pistol and he said no. He took me target shooting two or three times but a pistol was never used. Several people, including Kathy have told me that they would not have known how to load, unload or operate the safety of a pistol without prior instruction or experience with firearms. Yet I knew how to handle the pistol and I demonstrated an ability for accuracy when I fired the rifle at the plastic Coke bottle.

The question of whether or not I was subjected to the use of a gun during the Special Interrogations conducted on me is a valid and disturbing question that remains unanswered by CIA, UVM and the State of Vermont. The medical records that I was able to obtain were incomplete and contain large sections where records are missing. The records I have contain no references to the use of guns. They do contain references to UVM Psychologist Patrick Sullivan visiting me once a week while I was in seclusion on 1A. Yet there are no notes about these visits and no notes about what he was doing when he visited me.

I have no idea how many times he visited me, or who asked him to visit me. I have one brief memory of him entering my seclusion room and telling me that I could not be hypnotized. My memory of Patrick Sullivan permanently ends with his statement. Until CIA, UVM and the State of Vermont acknowledge the CIA experiments and provide me with the answers by turning over the documents I am certain they are in possession of, I will be forced to continue to have to wonder exactly what they did to me.

When I parked my car at Kathy's office I found that I couldn't seem to open the car door. My mind felt numb and I struggled for several minutes to try and open the car door. I sat in the car feeling dazed by all that was happening to me. Kathy would later explain to me that the reason I couldn't seem to make my mind and body cooperate was that my mind shut down in an effort to protect me.

I was admitted to the unit. I couldn't explain to Dr. Fox why I bought the gun and it was difficult to explain the compulsion that drove me to purchase the weapon. I had as many questions as everyone else.

Dr. Fox and Kathy convinced me to go to a residential treatment facility called Spring Lake Ranch. The condition I was in required a protective environment and the Ranch seemed to be the appropriate place for me to be for a while. Mary was familiar with the Ranch and she and her husband Joe had worked there years earlier. I remained on the unit for several weeks before moving to the Ranch

I was in pretty bad shape. Everything seemed to overwhelm me to the point of having my mind shut down on me again and again. I was frequently reduced to tears by my inability to do even simple everyday tasks. Noises bothered me terribly and seemed to add to the fog that had enveloped my mind. I repeatedly asked Kathy if what I was going through was expected during treatment for MPD and she tried to reassure me that it was.

Spring Lake Ranch was a unique residential treatment center for the mentally ill, located in rural Rutland County. Nestled at the top of a mountain, the Ranch had acres and acres of scenic pasturelands, woodlands and breath-taking views. Several houses were spread out over the property where several residents lived with house parents. The staff came to the Ranch from countries all over the world.

Based on the theory of work therapy, the Ranch had a working farm with livestock, a small chicken farm, huge vegetable gardens, hay fields and a thriving maple syrup business. Meals were eaten in a large dining room in the main house where residents had rooms upstairs and staff had offices downstairs. Residents were transported into Rutland to see their own therapists. The Ranch gave me an opportunity to live in a supportive and protected atmosphere while I tried to work through the MPD with Kathy.

Dr. Fox and Kathy decided to reveal my diagnosis to only a select few staff at the Ranch. I was floridly multiple and easily triggered into dissociation and as the weeks passed, the stress of dealing with dozens of people everyday began to take its toll. The amnesia I had made it impossible to figure out what had triggered me or why certain situations seemed to cause sudden dissociations. I wanted things to work out for me at the Ranch but I began to frequently go back and forth between the Ranch and the unit. I was at a loss to explain my behavior.

In child alter states I was vulnerable and dependent. When protective alters took over I became aggressive and more often than not,

I ran from the Ranch. I often found myself miles from the Ranch, having hitchhiked away in an attempt to flee some unconsciously perceived threat. I could rarely explain my actions to anyone including myself. It was easier to let the people around me be angry with me than it was to try to explain myself.

I was increasingly afraid of my own mind. I didn't yet know what was driving me or what was triggering the dissociations and the longer I remained in therapy with Kathy, the more my life felt like it was spiraling out of control.

At the Ranch I became friends with a British woman who worked as staff. Jane was a horse lover and kept her horse at the Ranch. My roommate at the Ranch, Marianne and I became good friends, Marianne was struggling with the chaotic effects of bipolar disorder. Jane, the British staff person came to me one day and told me that I was required to be seen by the psychiatrist working at the Ranch. I was not pleased about this. Dr. Fox was my doctor and I made sure my feelings were known.

Jane accompanied me up the stairs to see the Ranch psychiatrist, Dr. Hans Huessy. I made sure he knew that I was not pleased to have to see him and that I had no intention of talking to him about anything. Jane was noticeably uncomfortable.

"You spent quite a bit of time in VSH in the 60's and early 70's," Huessy began.

"Things were rough for you there. You and I don't have to talk about anything you don't want to talk about. I understand that you are a horse lover. I too have a love of horses."

Dr. Huessy and I talked about horses and nothing more. He told me that I did not have to see him again. I would see him one more time when a drug Dr. Fox had placed me on, began to build up in my system and cause me severe problems including throwing me into a manic state. Dr. Huessy stood in the hallway of the main house and pleaded with me to trust him when he assured me that Benadryl would help ease my symptoms. I was suspicious of what might be in the capsules. Huessy was gentle in his approach and stayed with me until I agreed to take the Benadryl

In 1989, I had no way of knowing that Dr. Hans Huessy had played a pivotal role in preventing me from being returned to the care of Dr. Otto Havas when I was transferred from Baird 6 to VSH in October, 1971. At the Ranch Huessy was, in retrospect, very aware of who I was and what he had done for me in 1971. After the meeting with Huessy at the Ranch, Jane remarked both about my defensive attitude toward Huessy and about his reactions toward me.

In my investigation into the CIA experiments, Dr. Hans Huessy appears to have had at least some degree of knowledge about my treatment by Havas at VSH. The specifics of what Huessy may or may not have known, I will very likely never learn. I never found him in any way associated with the CIA experiments. I will always be thankful that he stepped in and prevented Havas from having contact with me again. But I will always wonder exactly what he knew about my treatment at VSH.

After the adverse reaction to the drug, Dr Fox admitted me to the unit. My blood pressure was very high as a result of the adverse drug reaction. He discontinued the drug. I was extremely depressed after the drug left my system and I felt increasingly overwhelmed by the increasingly chaotic state of my condition and by what I perceived as my failure to be able to live anywhere. Nothing seemed to help and while Kathy continued to try to reassure me that the process that was unfolding would lead me to be able to integrate my personalities, I was feeling more and more hopeless.

When I returned to the Ranch, I secluded myself from the residents and staff. Jane and Marianne tried to talk with me but I retreated inside of myself. On a weekend day I left the main house to walk up the hill to the house I lived in. As I turned the corner and walked across the driveway to my house, I suddenly realized what I had to do. It was as if one moment I was simply walking along and the next moment, seemingly out of nowhere, I was suicidal.

Marianne had plans that would take her out of the house for the rest of the day. I recall sitting on my bed as she called out goodbye to me. Without any emotion, I broke a bottle, sat down on my bed and began slicing my arm with vertical slashes. I have no idea how long I sat there before Marianne returned. Marianne had forgotten something and came back early.

Marianne called Jane and arrangements were made to drive me to the emergency room where I had over fifty stitches. I hadn't harmed myself since 1972 and I was very disturbed by the awakening of my self-destructive behavior. At the emergency room a mental health crisis worker spoke with me and I made it clear to her that I was not suicidal.

"If I had wanted to die, I assure you I would be dead," I looked her directly in the eyes when I spoke.

She believed me and I was allowed to return to the Ranch. Within days, I was returned to the unit. Dr. Fox and Kathy were concerned that I had harmed myself. Years later Kathy told me that she and Dr. Fox, as well as the staff at the unit and at the Ranch were all worried that I would commit suicide. I didn't want to die. I just wanted the pain to stop.

I understood that my life was at stake and that integration was my only hope. I had tried everything else over the years to try to survive and all that was left was to try to survive long enough to integrate. Kathy stood by me during extremely challenging times for me and for her as my therapist. There were times when I left her office when she was not sure I would be alive the next day. But we soldiered on and I remained in therapy.

Again I went back to the Ranch but I was unable to tolerate the stimulation produced by my interaction with all of the people at the Ranch. Kathy later explained to me that because of my florid dissociations I was too susceptible to unconscious triggers from the other people at the Ranch.

I wanted things to work out at the Ranch but it was not to be. After returning to the unit, I began to rethink my options.

When I revealed my plan to Kathy and Dr. Fox, they received the news that I wanted to try to live in my own apartment with trepidation. They agreed to allow me to contact my bank for a loan so that I could rent a car and have enough money to rent an apartment. Dr. Fox and Kathy later told me that neither of them believed that I would secure a loan, but I did. I rented a car, drove to Morrisville to sign the papers at the bank and returned to the unit. Dr. Fox wanted me to remain on the unit until I found an apartment and during the day I went out looking for a place to live.

I found a very small efficiency apartment. I bought a sleeping bag and slept on the floor until I was able to get a bed. I was able to find an old lamp and some other necessities. I picked up my belongings from the Ranch and was finally discharged from the unit. Kathy was supportive of my trying to live on my own and Peggy, Jane and Marianne also tried to show me support. I was thirty-six years old and I was living on my own, in my own apartment for the first time in my life.

Therapy continued to push me to the edge. Numerous alters came forward during therapy and Kathy tried to understand why they had been created. Several of my alters were children, stuck in a time long ago. Several more alters were teenagers, aggressive and defiant. Kathy slowly built a trusting therapeutic relationship with as many of the alters as she could.

Looking back I appreciate how dedicated Kathy was. Many therapists would have thrown up their hands and walked away but Kathy stayed and worked with me. We spent many hours on the phone in between scheduled sessions. I seemed to be going from one crisis to another. Several times Kathy found me in near catatonic states and other times I found myself in other cities and towns, unsure of how I got there or how long I'd been gone.

In 1989, my father died of leukemia. It was painful to see him so terribly thin and sick. The night he died I couldn't sleep all night and I sat alone in my apartment and cried. My father was a sweet, gentle man who only wanted his children to have good lives. I know that my illness and my hospitalizations tore him up. I will always be grateful for the time we had together when I had King.

There were times when I lost almost all hope that I would survive, much less integrate. During those low points, Kathy was able to maintain hope until I was once again able to begin to hope for myself. There is absolutely no doubt in my mind that without Kathy Judge, I would not have survived.

In 1990, I moved into a larger apartment. I immediately felt that the new apartment was a place I might call home. My landlords, Jules and Mary, who owned the house were easy-going and helpful. I lived a very quiet life in the apartment. I rarely had visitors and paid all my bills on time. The apartment upstairs in Jules and Mary's house has been my home for twenty-two years.

My last stay on the unit when Dr. Tom Fox was the Clinical Director of the Rutland psychiatric unit in 1989 was sobering for me. Dr. Fox told me that he had taken another job in New Hampshire. I was devastated by the news. Tom had been an important and a safe presence in my life for seven years. Dr. Tom Fox, like Dr. Judy Nepvue had shown me that not every psychiatrist was to be feared. Tom told me that if a time came when I really needed him I could phone him. He gave me his new phone number and a warm hug goodbye.

For me, the loss of Dr. Fox meant that the unit was no longer a safe place for me. Lynne Colville tried to explain to me that I would be safe on the unit. I wasn't buying it. I managed to stay off the unit for quite a while until another crisis put me back in the hospital. Every time I was readmitted, I felt ashamed that I couldn't seem to pull myself together and get on with my life. I felt that no matter how hard I tried or how hard people who were trying to help me tried, I continued to spiral out of control again and again. The unit staff continued to support me and they gave me all that they had learned as registered psychiatric nurses. More importantly for me, they gave to me of themselves. The unit nurses became fond of me and I definitely became fond of them. I could see in their faces the emotion that they felt when I was struggling through one crisis after the other. They gave me the best of themselves as well as the best possible care.

In all of my stays on the unit I always avoided the group therapy sessions until I stabilized. I was usually in crisis when I first arrived and the stress and stimulation of the groups only served to make things worse for me. After the initial crisis had calmed, group therapy was more often than not very helpful.

The new psychiatrist on the unit came into my hospital room and introduced himself as Dr. Alan Shirks. He insisted that I attend the group meetings and my attempts to explain why I needed to delay attending the groups for a little while fell on deaf ears. It didn't take me long to decide that I would be safer weathering the storm alone in my own apartment. I left the unit against medical advice and didn't return for nearly seven years.

Therapy with Kathy continued to be excruciating. Many of my memories of therapy during this time are sketchy at best. As Kathy and I worked toward integration I rarely left my apartment and with very few exceptions I had little contact with other people. Peggy and I had drifted apart as I worked toward integration and she tried to get on with her own life. I saw less and less of Jane as I withdrew from practically everyone.

Around 1994, I began to have terrible repetitive dreams filled with nightmarish images and scenarios. Night after night for months on end the dreams haunted me for hours after I was awake. Kathy tried to help me understand the dreams that were filled with images of the piece of land my parents bought for me to ride my horse on in 1963. I dreamed about guns and many of the dreams contained graphic sexual images. I couldn't seem to escape the dreams and the longer they went on the more distressed I became.

When I was a small child I spent a good deal of time with my older next-door neighbor, Janet. She was in her early twenties when I was about four years old. I always recalled her taking me across the river onto the land my parents eventually bought from her parents. The repetitive dreams continued and I finally decided to phone Janet.

I felt ridiculous asking Janet if anything out of the ordinary or traumatic had ever happened on the land when she was with me.

"Yes, traumatic things did happen there," Janet began.

I was so shocked when Janet confirmed that something traumatic had actually happened when I was with her on the land, that I backed up against the wall in my kitchen and slowly slid down and sat on the floor. I listened as Janet described two incidents when someone fired a gun over our heads as we walked on the land. She told me that the bullets were so close that she heard them fly past her head. She claimed not to know the identity of the shooter. She said I was four years old and that I ran away from the gunshots and from her. In disbelief I questioned her about the shooting happening a second time and she confirmed that a second shooting incident did happen.

It's difficult to explain what it was like to hear someone describe events like these and realize that I had no memory. My head spun listening to Janet, but I realized that I had just learned something important. I phoned Kathy.

Kathy arranged for Janet to come to the office and talk with her and me. Kathy later told me that Janet called a few times and tried to back out of the meeting but she finally came to Kathy's office. I hadn't seen Janet in many years and I was pleased to see her again but I also had questions about why she remained silent about these incidents for years.

Janet talked for four hours. She described the two shooting

incidents for Kathy and noted that some of the bullets remained lodged in the side of her father's barn for years. This was the same barn where I kept my first horse in 1960. When Janet began talking about her husband Willy's sexual relationships with his own daughters, I was absolutely shocked beyond belief. I knew him when I was a small child and in later years. He was frequently with Janet when I was a child.

It took me hours after Janet left Kathy's office to realize that Janet might have identified the person who sexually molested me as a child. Dr. Judy Nepvue had raised the issue of early childhood sexual molestation with me in 1981, but I had no memory of any such activity. I had scattered images and body sensations that went with sexual molestation but there was nothing else. Kathy also determined that I had the symptoms of childhood sexual molestation and she, unlike me, immediately recognized what Janet was telling us. Kathy also recognized, as I would later, that the piece of land that my parents bought in 1960 was not only the site of childhood trauma, but that in the dissociated world of a small child, I incorporated this piece of land into my MPD.

In therapy, as Kathy and I tried to understand the layout of my internal world, numerous alters had frequently referred to the place where the alters existed internally. This place was called "the land." Until Janet provided the information, neither Kathy nor I realized that "the land" was a literal place.

I phoned Janet a second time and directly asked her if her husband had sexually molested me. She said yes. I was stunned. I asked her why she had remained silent about this even after I was hospitalized at age thirteen. She knew that I had been committed to VSH and she knew that no one seemed to have a clue as to why I suffered such a severe breakdown. She didn't answer.

Traumatic amnesia is a very frustrating and disturbing condition to have. No amount of effort spent trying to remember works to free up the blocked memories. The only glimpses into my early childhood trauma came from the repetitive dreams and they continued. I had flashes of images in my mind of the gunshots, of running away and of hiding under the wooden bridge.

I began to have dreams about a yellow cat. The cat sat on Janet's parents' lawn looking sick. In the dreams I felt terrified and I wanted to protect the yellow cat. The dream came over and over, night after night and I awakened feeling horrified and helpless.

After learning that Janet had information I decided to phone one of my cousins who lived close by when I was small. I asked her if there was ever a yellow cat that could in any way figure into a traumatic experience when I was a child.

June described a horrific incident. The yellow cat belonged to Janet's parents and the cat had been very sick. Janet's father shot the cat and buried it. Janet's mother became hysterical upon realizing that the cat that had been buried was not dead. Janet's father immediately dug the cat up and repeatedly fired bullets into it. June said I would have been about three years old.

When I told Kathy about my conversation with June I realized that I witnessed the entire event. As the images flooded my mind in Kathy's office I began to feel panicked. I was overcome with fear and no matter how I tried to push the images and the feelings away from me, they just kept coming. I never recovered the full memory of this horrific event but the fragmented images and gut-wrenching emotion that had begun with the repetitive dreams spilled out of me.

I began asking my mother if there was ever anything traumatic that might have happened when I was a small child and I was stunned by her reply. Mom told me that when I was nine months old and just beginning to stand up, I pulled a coffee table over onto myself. The table cut my mouth badly and I bled heavily. Mom became hysterical and phoned the doctor.

Apparently I too became hysterical.

Mom also told me about the incident with the low flying jets when I was eighteen months old, which produced hysteria in me. She told me that when I was two years old my father took me with him to a house fire in town. When the windows blew out of the house, I became hysterical. My aunt was at the fire and convinced my father to leave and take me home. One of my cousins also remembered this event.

I learned that when I was three years old Dad took me to a fire. He stood near the old railroad station in town and held me because my feet were bare and there was broken glass all around the railroad tracks. When the people in the crowd who had come to watch the fire were told that a woman was trapped in the burning house, a wave of horror swept through the crowd. Apparently I struggled to get away from my father but he wouldn't let me down onto the railroad tracks. This fatal fire was confirmed by a cousin, by Janet who was present at the fire that day, and by a 1955 *Rutland Herald* newspaper article.

Kathy helped me understand the implications of the information. My inability to bury the rat I shot after King died and my unexplained aversion to the "dead man" set up on King's gate were attached to the yellow cat being buried alive when I was three or four years old. The very first flashback I had when I lived in Waterbury Center when I had images of railroad tracks and my own bare feet was about the fatal fire when I was three years old. This flashback had been set off by a chimney fire.

Guns played a role in my early childhood trauma. My brother had been shot during deer hunting when I was two years old and although I never recovered any memories of seeing him after he came home to recover or of the incident when his wound hemorrhaged, there is a likelihood that some portion of my mind retained the memory. Kathy tried to help me deal with the information about Willy but it remained out of reach for me.

During this time, I spoke regularly with Kathy on the phone and we discussed the emerging information and talked about the repetitive dreams I continued to have. It was about this time that I began to receive hang-up phone calls at three o'clock in the morning. Night after night the phone would ring and when I got out of bed to answer, whoever was on the phone hung up. This led to my contacting the phone company. They placed a trap on my phone twice and the calls started again after the second trap was removed, I was informed that the phone company believed my phone was wiretapped.

It wouldn't be until after 1997 that I learned that the tap was extremely sophisticated and was very likely placed on my line by the government - specifically by the CIA. Of course I cannot definitely prove that the CIA has wire tapped my phone. They are too good at what they do to allow themselves to be identified, but information I have been given by phone technicians and by security officials at the phone company leaves little doubt about the identity of who wiretapped my phone. Who else not only has the sophistication to wiretap in this manner but who else would be even remotely interested in the content of my phone conversations? Perhaps the NSA did the taps on behalf of the CIA.

The timing of the 3 A.M. phone calls coincides with my emerging memory and after fifteen years of investigation into the Vermont CIA experiments, it's clear to me why CIA might be interested. Inducing permanent memory loss was at the top of the list for MKULTRA experiments. CIA spent a lot of time, money and man hours researching whether or not they could produce a permanent state of amnesia. The wiretap, along with stolen certified mail and harassment by strangers began only after I filed the lawsuit and began filing FOIA requests with the federal government. My phone may have been wiretapped in other places I lived but I have no way of knowing for sure.

Kathy spent years preparing me for integration and as we worked in therapy I was repeatedly shocked to learn about the previously hidden world my mind had constructed to defend and protect me from the impact of the childhood trauma. I began to understand why I felt such anger toward my mother and why the anger started after my parents bought the piece of land.

Kathy explained that a small child believes that the mother is all-knowing and can see and is aware of everything that happens. Kathy called this "magical thinking." She explained that when I was being shot at or when Willy was molesting me, my four-year old mind absolutely believed that my mother would know and rescue me. Because I had amnesia for the trauma, I was unable to go home and tell my mother what had happened to me, but as a small child I believed that the mother not only knew what had happened but that she didn't rescue me.

My mother was in the crowd the day of the fatal fire and when the crowd realized that a woman was trapped inside of the burning house, she and my aunt moved a considerable distance from where my father stood holding me. My mother later said that she was so horrified by the news that a woman was trapped in the building that she had to get away. She believed that I was okay with my father. Kathy also explained that when I had the two episodes of hysteria at nine months and again at eighteen months, the fact that my mother also had a hysterical reaction would have compounded the impact on me.

The onset of my suicidal feelings when I was eleven years old coincides with both the purchase of the piece of land by my parents and of the beginning of puberty. The changes in my body as an adolescent would have set off an onslaught of disturbing emotions and sensations. Despite the amnesia for the trauma, my unconscious mind was reacting.

For the first time since I was hospitalized at the age of thirteen, things began to make sense. Kathy said that my reactions and behavior made a lot of sense once we understood the basis of the dissociations. One of the biggest challenges for me was to be able to understand and accept that my personalities were aspects of me. They were me and I was them. There was a "disconnect" in this logic for me and although on a conceptual basis I understood what Kathy was saying, I couldn't "own" it. Even when I knew that the other personalities were indeed aspects of me, they still seemed like other people to me

I was also very concerned that if I integrated the personalities that had protected me for forty years, I would be left totally vulnerable and unable to function. Despite Kathy's assurances that this would not be the case, I continued to fear integration would render me helpless.

I heard the voices of my personalities inside of my head. They urged me to run. They warned me that I was going to die. At times they talked about me among themselves as if I wasn't there. They woke me up at night calling my name. One night as I sat watching television, I heard coming from outside my window a child screaming in pain and fear. I rushed to the window but I couldn't see anything. I crouched under the window so that no one would be able to see me as the screams of the child grew louder. I looked out the window again to see what was happening and to see if anyone else heard the child's cries. It took me several minutes to calm down and to realize that the likelihood was that the screams and cries that I heard were not coming from outside my window in 1996 but that they were part of a flashback to 1956. Flashbacks or abreactions, as Kathy described them, were so real and involved so many physical and emotional components that while they were happening, I couldn't tell until after the fact that they came from my mind.

I couldn't sleep. Night after night I sat in my living room struggling with feelings of doom and the effects of nightmares. I felt trapped by my own mind. I had powerful physical sensations in which nothing I tried to do to alleviate the constant pull at me relieved the pressure. I told Kathy it was almost like being hungry or wanting a cigarette. I couldn't satisfy the terrible mounting pressure no matter what I did.

I began to feel suicidal and I worried that in trying to integrate I would become so ravaged by my own mind that I would either successfully kill myself or even worse, that I would be sent back to VSH. I felt as if I were staring into an abyss.

I had a strange, compelling dream filled with images of a cat and kittens. Although I don't recall all the content of the dream, I do know that it set off dangerous suicidal feelings. I told Kathy about the dream. There was something about the dream that made me feel desperate and I sat for hours with a rope in my hands. I had thoughts of hanging myself and the conflict over whether to live or die tormented me.

Kathy recognized that I was in serious trouble and made arrangements to have me placed on the unit. I heard her talking with Lynne Colville as I sat in her office.

"If she isn't admitted, I don't think she will be alive tomorrow," Kathy told Lynne.

I knew that Kathy was right and I was afraid.

Kathy drove me to the hospital. I remember walking with her as we approached the doors of the unit and I hesitated. Kathy took my arm and guided me through the doors of the unit where Tammy, a nurse I had known and trusted showed me to my room. Much of the next few days are a blur to me. I knew the staff and they knew me and we all knew that I was truly in a fight for my life.

I met with Dr. Alan Shirks, the same psychiatrist I walked away from a few years earlier. This time Dr. Shirks was very different. He seemed to understand what I was going through and his kindness and the degree to which he appeared to be resonating with the powerful emotions I was struggling with showed me a very different approach than I had experienced the first time I met him.

I was repeatedly overcome by anguish and I couldn't shut off the pain, the fear or the grief that racked my body and my mind. The staff helped me understand that the grief that I felt was coming to the surface after forty years of being repressed. Marlene, my primary nurse helped guide me through intense episodes of grief in which the pain and my inability to shut it off frightened me so much that I thought I was losing my mind. Marlene told me that some of the grief was related to my recognition of all that I had lost to the forty years as a multiple.

Other staff including Lynne, Tammy, Lesa, Susan, Rosemary and Mary literally held me in their arms at times, helping me to hold myself together. I saw the emotion in their faces and at times I saw tears in their eyes as they sat with me. If they could have willed me to survive the onslaught of emotions they would have done so.

Mary took a job in Maine shortly after I integrated and she and her husband Joe and I have remained in contact. Susan died a few years ago after being diagnosed with a brain tumor. Rosemary passed away last year. Lesa, who I first met in 1982 when she was still a nursing student, is now head nurse on the unit. Tammy and her husband moved to Arizona a couple of years ago. Lynne retired as the unit's head nurse and continues to work in Rutland county counseling patients. The last time I saw Marlene was the night I was admitted to intensive care with a heart attack.

Kathy and I talked about these nurses after I successfully integrated and we both agreed that without the support and caring they demonstrated to me, I very likely would not have survived the integration. I needed what they were able to give to me. Back when I was in Copley hospital, one nurse named Debbie G. told me that when Dr. Nepvue asked her to sit with me on her shift, Debbie G. was afraid. She said that she wasn't a psychiatric nurse and that she was afraid that she would say or do something to make me worse. Debbie G. told me that what she discovered that day she spent with me was that all she needed to do was be a human being.

I was exposed to the worst of psychiatric care in VSH and I was exposed to the worst of human nature there as well. Yet I was also fortunate enough to have been exposed to the very best in psychiatric care from nurses in Baird 6, Copley and in the Rutland Regional Medical Center psychiatric unit, where the very best of human nature was given to me. Although the doctors on Baird 6 were apparently involved in the experiment, the nurses, for the most part, tried to help me. All of the dedicated nurses on the Rutland Regional Medical Center Psychiatric unit played a key role in helping me survive the integration process and I will always be grateful to them.

I felt fragile and very much younger than my actual age of forty. As the days passed, I began to realize that, as Kathy told me, I had experienced a spontaneous abreaction that set off the integration. The terrible physical sensations of pain and choking along with the sheer terror that overtook me were all parts of the trauma from early childhood that led to the MPD and the amnesia. Much of the content of the actual events from my childhood never returned in actual memory, but enough did so that the integration process could continue. Kathy reminded me often that it was a process and that it would take time for me to complete the integration.

Dr. Shirks explained to me that during the second shooting when I ran from the gunshots and hid beneath the wooden bridge, my four-year old mind believed that I was about to suffer the same fate as the yellow cat I had earlier seen shot and buried alive. Dr. Shirks told me that it was when I was hiding under the bridge that I suffered the dissociative trauma that made me multiple. He told me that as a small child I identified with the cat and that identification set me up to have the anthropomorphic and dissociative experience I had with King.

By April 1996, I had been on the unit nearly two months. Kathy and the staff helped me understand that the rage I felt about my mother was displaced rage and was a result of both the trauma and the amnesia. I understood that when as an eleven-year old child I once again began to walk on the piece of land where the trauma had taken place years before, a whole range of emotions overtook me. The amnesia prevented me from being able to attach my feelings to those events and my rage was displaced onto my mother. Many of my personalities were children who were trapped in 1956 forever. For the next forty years, much of how I interpreted the world around me and how I interpreted my own emotional responses to people and to events was driven by a child's perceptions about life.

In therapy I learned about my personalities and that they were created to protect me. I had child alters who constructed an elaborate internal world where good always triumphed over evil. I had a personality who played guitar. I had a personality who was an artist and another personality who was obsessed with horses. One personality was consumed with spiritual matters, while several others were protective personalities who ran away and escaped dangerous situations. Several of the personalities appeared to have endured the brunt of the VSH years. Over the years to come in therapy, Kathy and I would not learn much at all about those several personalities. I remain blocked from knowing why the alters existed and what their roles were.

It took five years after integration before I played the guitar again. The mechanics were there but there was no motivation. The experience was empty. When I began playing guitar again, I discovered that my ability had improved a great deal. The same was true for drawing and it took over a decade before I was able to draw again. After the heartbreaking loss of King, I found it nearly impossible to be near horses. To this day I stay away from them.

After I learned that I had been used in drug and mind control experiments, the possibility that this group of personalities had been created during the research I was subjected to was discussed by Kathy and me. Before Dr. Tom Fox died in 2002, he advised Kathy to never explore this group of alters because the possibility that they were created in the covert research was a valid concern.

I was discharged from the unit in April, 1996 and I returned to my apartment to try to live my life as an integrated multiple. At the time I didn't realize that I still had the capacity to dissociate under certain conditions and it would take me a long time to actually accept this as a part of my life.

I struggled with painful realizations about my life. Kathy and I talked about the series of childhood traumas and I had difficulty understanding why all of those things had happened to me at such a young age. It was as if I never had a chance at a normal life because of the trauma that began when I was only nine months old. Kathy said she believed that if the shootings and the molestation had not occurred, the chances of my becoming multiple would have been much less.

The MPD protected me from what could have been a psychosis but I also understood all that I had lost because of the disorder. I fell into a deep depression. Kathy tried to help me understand that grief was a part of the healing process and that feeling the grief and the sense of loss about my life was a necessary part of healing. My therapy continued and I tried to adjust to actually feeling my own emotions, which was at times an overwhelming experience.

In the fall of 1997, I tried to explain to Kathy that something I didn't understand was happening to me and I found it very hard to describe. It was as if some other world was descending on me and that this world was a very terrible place that I felt was drawing me into it. It was as if I were trapped between this world and some other dreadful existence that I couldn't fully comprehend. It was during this time that Kathy suggested that I try to write a narrative of my life, which led me to pick up the phone and request my medical records from the State of Vermont. I would soon learn that this terrible world that was drawing me in and tormenting me was a world I had lived in many years before.

In 1997, I thought that I knew what had happened to me but when the VSH records revealed that I had been used in covert drug and mind control experiments, I would spend the next fifteen years obtaining documents and investigating the CIA MKULTRA research conducted in Vermont.

I doubt that anyone could be prepared to learn that they had been covertly experimented on by hospitals, doctors and the CIA and in this respect I was no different. The realization was profoundly shocking and disturbing for me, my family and for Kathy. Tom Fox reacted with anger and disgust that so much information had been intentionally kept from me and from all subsequent caregivers.

In the years after the lawsuit was over I continued to investigate and to obtain original source documents. I felt a deep-seated sense of anger and rage over the experimentation and all that my medical records revealed that I had been subjected to. I felt betrayed by the doctors, by the hospitals, by the State of Vermont and by the CIA. I think that I, like many other VSH patients confined in the state mental hospital, was considered to be expendable, but as my investigation continued over the years I began to wonder if VSH and the CIA took the concept of expendable people to its ultimate conclusion.

7
AFTERMATH

I taught myself how to investigate the Vermont CIA Experiments beginning with the name of Hyde and the names and information in the VSH book, *The Vermont Story*. Over the next fifteen years, as I obtained original source documents and purchased books by authors like John Marks, Martin Lee and Dr. Colin Ross, I learned about the CIA drug and mind control programs generally referred to as MKULTRA. The fifteen-year search for the truth about what happened to me and thousands of other VSH patients changed me forever.

I was repeatedly lied to by my State, by the federal government, by CIA and by agencies that funded VSH-UVM experiments. I learned that my elected officials in the State and in the federal government did not want to hear about the Vermont CIA experiments and I learned first-hand that almost without exception, no United States Senator, Congressman, or other official was willing to assist me in finding the proof about the Vermont CIA experiments. When confronted with original source documents, no State of federal official would respond, with the exception of Senator Bernie Sanders. Even Sanders was not willing to go public with the information.

There is very little published material about Robert Hyde. Despite the major role he played in the CIA programs, he still appears to be the CIA researcher who remains most closely guarded by CIA. The 1977 newspaper article on CIA MKULTRA mentioned his name in passing but spent more time focusing on Hyde's defenders. H.P. Albarelli's book, *A Terrible Mistake*, notes that Hyde has been pretty much overlooked in the CIA MKULTRA programs. I do know that obtaining information and documentation on Hyde is extremely difficult and that thirty-five years after Hyde's death, CIA continues to classify many of his research projects and, as Dr. Colin Ross and I discovered, CIA refuses to acknowledge Hyde's projects or allow FOIA requests to be fulfilled.

In a November 30, 2008, *Rutland Herald-Barre Times Argus* front-page newspaper article, by Associated Press reporter Louis Porter, entitled "Evidence Suggests CIA Experiments at State Hospital," Vermonters and the rest of the country were exposed to the first information about VSH CIA experiments. The article was primarily based on my medical records and on Hyde and the VSH CIA experiments. Eighteen months earlier I had walked into *Rutland Herald* Editor Randal Smathers' office after we spoke on the phone. I presented Smathers with original source documents about VSH-UVM and showed him portions of my medical records.

Randal Smathers remarked that many people had come into his office in the past and demanded that he investigate their concerns on various subjects, but that I was the very first person to come to him with documented proof. Smathers contacted Louis Porter and Louis spent eighteen months investigating the Vermont CIA experiments. When the article came out, no Vermont local news programs on television mentioned the Vermont CIA experiments. *Rutland Herald* Editorial Page Editor, David Moats wrote in the editorial that ran in the issue about the VSH CIA experiments that although there had been opportunities for the CIA experiments at VSH to be made public, including my lawsuit in 1998, information had not been made public. Since the 2008 article, I have obtained much more evidence and the 2008 article did not contain information about the VSH patient deaths.

I attempted to contact the national news media several times over the last fifteen years, but none of the outlets I contacted were interested. I contacted CNN, ABC, NBC, FOX, CBS, and the *New York Times*. They were not interested. I found this to be curious at best. News organizations seem to like to get a story that involves government cover-ups but in this case, they were not even willing to hear me out. Fortunately for me, I don't give up easily.

In 2009, Dr. Colin Ross, who I had remained in contact with after the lawsuit ended in 2002, asked me if I would be interested in speaking to a London-based documentary film producer about possibly appearing in a documentary about the CIA programs. I agreed to speak with the producer.

I was filmed for a documentary in August, 2009. It was an experience I never thought I'd have in my life. The film, *The Real Bourne Identity*, also had Matt Damon in it as well as many former CIA agents. Dr. Colin Ross held up my medical records and stated that because of the types of drugs in my records and the methods employed by VSH, he believed I had been a subject of experimentation.

The London, England film crew, Blink Films spent four hours with me and stopped on the way to film VSH. The documentary was shown on the Smithsonian Channel in 2010.

I still deal with the effects of both my illness and with the knowledge that I was a CIA research subject and that CIA, VSH, UVM, the State of Vermont and the federal government refuse to provide me with the information about the CIA experiments I was subjected to. I have bouts of severe depression, anxiety, insomnia, PTSD and I still dissociate in certain circumstances. The autoimmune disorders haven't been active for a while now, but they remain a concern. I am sixty years old now. Practically my entire life has been caught up in one way or another in trying to understand and learn what really happened to me in VSH and I still do not know.

The last fifteen years have been filled with anger, frustration, disillusionment, disgust and a deep sadness about the behavior of the State of Vermont and the federal government. Not only have I been lied to and deceived, but my family has been lied to and deceived. Vermonter's have been lied to, deceived, manipulated, used, abused and possibly died as a result of the VSH-UVM CIA experiments. It is clear when reading the Report on the 1977 Senate Hearings that the Senators were far more interested in protecting the rights of universities, hospitals, the individual researchers and the United States government than they were interested in safeguarding the rights of those who were used in the CIA experiments. It appears as if in America there are expendable people and in Vermont, they are the mentally ill.

There were no consequences for the CIA. There were no consequences for the universities and hospitals. The actions of all involved in the covert experiments were criminal. The actions of VSH-UVM, as evidenced in their own research project documents were, if not criminal (and they may indeed have been criminal), violations of internationally accepted methods of conducting research, violations of the civil and Constitutional rights of every unwitting subject used in the experiments and violations of each physician's Hippocratic Oath.

The CIA drug and mind control programs were done, according to the CIA, to protect America from enemy threats. The experiments were inspired by the content of the medical records found in the Nazi concentration camps. What was done to me and to thousands of others in VSH did nothing to protect me or them - quite the contrary. The CIA experiments served only the interests of the CIA and their stated reasons for conducting the experiments were to gain control of human beings. The experiments used unwitting American citizens because these experiments were unethical, immoral and illegal as stated in the declassified CIA documents. These experiments harmed all of us as Americans and the cover-up continues even now.

Every time I contacted an elected official and requested assistance, I got another lesson in how my government works to protect my rights. I learned that my Senators and Congressmen and others in positions of power were not interested in my rights as an American citizen nor were they interested in the fact that almost 3000 VSH patients died during the twenty years the experiments were conducted. CIA chose its unwitting subjects carefully and usually chose them based on the fact that they were vulnerable Americans. I certainly was vulnerable when they chose me at age thirteen. Thousands of VSH patients were vulnerable when CIA chose them as well. Sadly, I've learned much about who my government really values.

My father died in 1989 and he never had the chance to know what happened to his daughter. My mother just turned eighty-eight years old and she often tells me that she prays that she will live long enough to find out the rest of what was done to me in VSH. I've been investigating the Vermont CIA experiments for fifteen years now and with very few exceptions, no one in the State or federal government has been willing either to acknowledge the Vermont CIA experiments or conduct any type of investigation into the experiments.

CIA defenders like to point out that the drug and mind control programs have already been investigated and that nothing new would be learned. I beg to differ. If I have been able to document the massive presence of CIA in Vermont institutions, what might the government with all its resources be able to learn? The lack of interest in an investigation has everything to do with making sure that the CIA activities in Vermont remain covered up. Protecting the CIA appears to be the government's priority, not protecting the rights of American citizens.

I had my memory stolen, my physical health ruined, and my emotional health almost destroyed. I was tortured, as the records demonstrate. I had my freedom taken away from me and I will never know what my life might have been if not for the secret activities of the CIA and UVM-VSH. Nothing will give me back what they took from me.

There is a massive, coordinated State and federal cover-up ongoing in Vermont. Every Vermont citizen has been lied to and deceived. Every American citizen has been lied to and deceived. I am certain that the CIA, VSH-UVM and the federal government never anticipated that anyone would uncover the Vermont CIA experiments, but I did. It is time for those responsible for the Vermont CIA experiments and for the massive, coordinated State and federal cover-up to acknowledge both what happened in Vermont institutions and to acknowledge the cover-up.

I have a right to know what happened to me. Many of my medical records are missing and those missing records very likely hold the answers to the questions that remain concerning what was done to me during the experiments. Vermonters have a right to know what happened in their State. American citizens have the right to know that the country as a whole was lied to and deceived by the CIA experiments and by the actions of all concerned in covering up the Vermont CIA experiments.

I will never stop trying to learn the full extent of what happened to me and to thousands of other VSH patients. I will never know what my life might have been if only I had been admitted to a hospital at the age of thirteen that was not conducting CIA research. But what I am certain of is that the research conducted at VSH-UVM had nothing to do with medical science. It had everything to do with evil. There simply isn't another word that better describes what happened in the VSH-UVM CIA experiments.

I survived the Vermont CIA experiments. Many other VSH patients did not survive and their voices are silenced forever. I have a voice and I am using it for all of us who were unwitting subjects of the Vermont CIA experiments.

November, 2013

During the first week of September, 2013, I found a package of documents from the CIA at my door. Much to my surprise, the documents were Hyde's more fully declassified MKULTRA Subprojects 8, 10, 63 and 66. These documents were the Hyde Subprojects that CIA refused to make any determination on after I filed a FOIA and an appeal in 2003, which led me to go to the Executive Secretary Interagency Security Classification

Panel (ISCAP). ISCAP informed me at the time that CIA refused to make any determination, and that essentially kept ISCAP from making any determination and kept my request in limbo. For reasons known only to CIA, ten years later I received the documents.

Although the Hyde documents are still not fully declassified, the new declassification sheds important light on his activities for the CIA. One of the most startling new pieces of information in Hyde's Subprojects is the name of a previously unknown CIA subproject.

Hyde's MKULTRA Subproject 63 involved the use of LSD, LAE, alcohol and the mapping of "social personality" types. MKULTRA Subproject 63 was renamed MKCOTTON in 1961 and it was funded through Human Ecology. The funding for Hyde's Subproject is signed for by Sidney Gottlieb and addressed to payee John Gittinger - dated December, 1961. Under the heading for charge allotment number M125-1390-3902 is the date - stamped in two separate places - August 25 and August 26, 1964.

Another document dated April 8, 1964 shows funding invoices received by Human Ecology in 1962. The certification date for the expenditures is April 22, 1964.

MKULTRA Subproject 63 was closed in December 1961 and was "integrated into the total research effort of Human Ecology," and renamed MKCOTTON.

In 1964, Robert Hyde was the Assistant Commissioner of Mental Health in Vermont. Rupert Chittuck, Superintendent of VSH, was Commissioner of Mental Health in Vermont. In 1964, UVM-VSH had research contracts involving the use of Gittinger's PAS and sent the results of the CIA psychological test directly to Gittinger at CIA headquarters in Washington, DC. UVM-VSH contracts with Psychological Assessment Associates and the use of Gittinger's PAS are noted in UVM-VSH documents and cited by Richard York as beginning in 1958.

On October 7, 2013, I filed a Vermont Records Act request with the Vermont Department of Mental Health requesting, "Research contracts, invoices, funding sources and applicable financial documents, excluding USPHS, NIH, NIMH, HEW, VOC REHAB for VSH-UVM projects OM-372, 1958, NO.1-1-R11-MH 01076, 1963, MH-10176, 1966, funded in 1958, 1963 and 1966 by The Society For The Investigation For Human Ecology, 201 East 57th Street, N.Y., N.Y, and Psychological Assessment Associates, 1834 Connecticut Avenue, NW, Washington DC."

A response from the State of Vermont dated October 16, 2013 reads:

"The records you requested in your letter dated October 7, 2013, are not available because they were discarded pursuant to a public records retention schedule, effective March 3, 2010, on file with the State Archives and Records Administration."

"Under the records retention schedule, contracts are retained for three years past the expiration date of the contract. Generally, financial files, (invoices, payment information, etc.) are kept for five years beyond the end of the fiscal year they were relevant to."

"Since the records you requested are about 50 years old, they were discarded pursuant to the record schedule approved by the State Archivist. See 1 V.S.A. 317a."

I knew that contracts had to exist between Psychological Assessment Associates, Human Ecology and UVM-VSH. The State of Vermont did not respond that no documents were located. The response was that the documents I requested had indeed been located and that they had been destroyed. Therefore it is clear that research contracts existed between CIA and UVM-VSH.

On October 24, 2013 I filed a Freedom of Information request with CIA for photocopies of:

"Research project documents including subprojects for research conducted and or funded by CIA at the University of Vermont College of Medicine (UVM) and the Vermont State Hospital (VSH) during the years 1959, 1962, 1965 and 1966."

"Please include the names of all drugs, research procedures and methods used as well as the name of the CIA Subproject relevant to the Vermont research. Also include the names and titles of all research personnel as well as the identities and location of all other institutions and or agencies that participated."

"I filed a Vermont Records Act Request on October 7, 2013 for research contracts that existed between UVM-VSH and Psychological Assessment Associates and the Society for the Investigation of Human Ecology during the years noted."

"The response from the State was that the records I requested had been destroyed. Therefore a contractual relationship existed between CIA and UVM-VSH."

"I obtained UVM-VSH research documents MH-01076 that show that the psychological test known as PAS, created by CIA psychologist John Gittinger, was given to VSH patients and that according to the documents the results of those tests were sent directly to Gittinger at 1834 Connecticut Avenue, NW, Washington, DC. Also noted in the UVM-VSH documents are plans to expand and continue research with Gittinger."

On November 21, 2013 I received a response from CIA that reads:

"This is a final response to your 24 October 2013 Freedom of Information Act (FOIA) request, received in the Office of the Information and Privacy Coordinator on 7 September, 2013, for photocopies of the following documents: Research project documents including subprojects for research conducted and or funded by CIA at the Vermont State Hospital (VSH), Waterbury, Vermont and the University of Vermont College of Medicine (UVM) during the years 1959, 1962, 1965 and 1966...In accordance with section 3.6 (a) of Executive Order 13526, the CIA can neither confirm nor deny the existence or nonexistence of records responsive to your request. The fact of the existence or nonexistence of requested records is currently and properly classified and is intelligence sources and methods information that is protected from disclosure by section 6 of the CIA Act of 1949, as amended, and section 102A(i) (l) of the National Security Act of 1947, as amended. Therefore, your request is denied pursuant to FOIA exemptions (b) (1) and (b) (3)."

"FOIA Explanation of Exemptions: (b) (1) exempts from disclosure information currently and properly classified, pursuant to Executive Order."

"(b) (3) exempts from disclosure information that another federal statute protects, provided that the other federal statute either requires that the matters be withheld, or establishes particular criteria for withholding or refers to particular types of matters to be withheld. The (b) (3) statutes upon which the CIA relies include but are not limited to, the CIA ACT of 1949."

This is the very first time CIA has ever acknowledged that UVM-VSH research was classified and remains classified. It is interesting to note that the response to my Vermont Records Act Request did not state that no records were located. The response was that the documents I requested had been destroyed. Additionally, I obtained the UVM-VSH research project documents that clearly detail UVM-VSH research relationship with John Gittinger at CIA headquarters, 1834 Connecticut Avenue, NW, Washington, DC. The research documents MH-01076 are publicly available and they contain descriptions of the UVM-VSH research relationship with Gittinger at CIA's Psychological Assessment Associates and describe methods, i.e. the use of Gittinger's PAS.

CIA made a mistake noting the date they received my FOIA, noting the date as 7 September, 2013. I filed the request on October 24, 2013. Curiously, CIA did not note that I had very specifically asked them for documents relating to Psychological Assessment Associates and the Society for the Investigation of Human Ecology.

Although I could file an appeal with CIA, given the classified status of the material I am seeking, my appeal would very likely be denied. I am not filing an appeal. I am actually quite pleased by the State of Vermont's response, which confirms the existence of a contractual relationship between CIA and UVM-VSH and by CIA's response that the records I sought regarding CIA-UVM-VSH research are classified. These responses tell me both what I want to know and what I have long suspected to be true.

In July, 2013 I received information that the Vermont State Archives and Records Administration released documents relating to VSH research activities. I obtained a listing of these documents. In series VSH-003, under VSH-0011-2 and VSH-0011-3 it reads as follows: Director of Research, Vermont State Hospital - 1940-1975 Dr. Robert W. Hyde and 1943-1975, Dr. Robert W. Hyde.

I always suspected that Hyde maintained an active presence at VSH throughout the years that he was at Boston Psychopathic Hospital and Butler Hospital. The new documents clearly support my theory.

Back in 1998 when I obtained CIA MKULTRA documents from the National Security Archives, Hyde's MKULTRA Subprojects 8, 10, 10a, 63 and 66 were heavily redacted; I had a growing suspicion that under the redactions were UVM and VSH. Over the years I collected UVM-VSH research documents and identified more and more CIA researchers involved in UVM-VSH experiments and identified procedures, pharmaceutical companies and covert CIA funding sources; it became clear to me as I read Hyde's CIA Subprojects that my initial suspicions were very likely accurate.

The newly more fully declassified CIA subprojects 8, 10, 63 and 66 not only identify a previously unknown CIA project named MKCOTTON, but place Hyde in Vermont during the time when MKCOTTON was operational. Gittinger's name on these documents in 1961-1964 also matches UVM-VSH research projects in 1958, 1963 and 1965 - the same projects that sent the results of the PAS directly to Gittinger at CIA headquarters in Washington, DC.

MKCOTTON documents note that Hyde made regular trips to Washington as part of his CIA duties and made trips for "special projects" at a site that remains redacted. In 1962, Gittinger moved Psychological Assessment Associates to the Washington address. It is also noted that he traveled abroad as part of his regular duties for CIA.

An April 8, 1962 MKCOTTON document shows funding invoices received by Human Ecology. The certification date for the Hyde expenditures is April 22, 1964.

Where was Robert Hyde during the years after he graduated from UVM College of Medicine in 1935? He did an internship at the Marine Hospital in New Orleans, 1935-1936. In 1936-1940, he was in general practice in Fairfax, Vermont. In 1940-1945 Hyde was a Lt. Col. In the U.S. Army. Recently released VSH documents show that Hyde is identified as Director of Research at VSH, 1940-1975.

In 1945-1957, Hyde was Assistant Superintendent at Boston Psychopathic Hospital. Hyde was Superintendent at Butler in 1957-1962. He was Acting Director Division of Legal Medical Liaison Office, 1st Service Command, Massachusetts Department of Mental Health, 1958-1959.

In 1959-1964 Hyde was Assistant to the Commissioner (the declassified CIA documents don't specify where he was Assistant to the Commissioner) and in 1964 Hyde became Assistant Commissioner of Mental Health in Vermont. He was a Professor of Psychiatry, teaching at

UVM in 1967.

Where was Robert Hyde in 1964 during MKCOTTON?

What is known about UVM-VSH research activities during this time frame -1955-1964? In 1955, UVM secured a contract with the Air Force School of Aviation Medicine and through funding by the Department of Energy, human radiation experiments and behavioral experiments were conducted at UVM. Hyde is identified in the Department of Energy Human Radiation Experiments list of participants. It is known that CIA was involved in these experiments.

At VSH, research is noted in documents to have begun in 1955 - becoming "schizophrenia" studies in 1957. One UVM-VSH research document notes that research had actually begun at VSH as early as 1944. Recently released VSH documents place Hyde as Director of Research 1940-1975.

In 1958, UVM-VSH were administering Gittinger's PAS to child patients and this research and affiliation with Gittinger extended at least until 1968 - possibly longer. In 1957, UVM-VSH began using unwitting VSH patients in experimental drug research. The drugs were obtained from CIBA. Milton Greenblatt of Boston Psychopathic Hospital (where CIA LSD research was well underway) acted as a "Consultant" to UVM-VSH research and VSH was visited by John Bockoven and Richard York who also acted as "Consultants."

Both Bockoven and York conducted CIA LSD experiments with Hyde. York worked out of Gittinger's Psychological Assessment Associates. Hyde's MKULTRA Subprojects note that Gittinger's PAS was used extensively in Hyde's research. Gittinger is noted as the "payee" for funds in Hyde's MKULTRA Subproject 63.

Harold Wolff was President of Human Ecology and the Executive Director of Human Ecology was Lt. Col. James Monroe, United States Air Force. Wolff was interested in brainwashing and the Air Force ran parallel experiments to those done by the CIA. UVM conducted Special Interrogation experiments that involved the use of LSD, mescaline, isolation, electric shock, chemical shock and induced amnesia - essentially these experiments were brainwashing experiments. UVM had research contracts with the Air Force starting in 1955. UVM and VSH began their joint research projects in 1955.

Dr. Ewen Cameron at McGill conducted CIA-funded experiments beginning in 1957, the same year UVM-VSH officially began "schizophrenia" experiments. UVM-VSH documents state that the schizophrenia research actually began in 1955 with more formal experiments that began in 1957. Cameron conducted depatterning and brainwashing experiments and he expressed a desire to conduct terminal experiments, according to John Marks. In 1959, VSH's Dr. George Brooks presented a paper at McGill on VSH experiences with schizophrenics.

Human Ecology was gone in 1965 but, as John Marks notes, Gittinger's PAS continued after Human Ecology stopped funding the research and Psychological Assessment Associates continued the funding.

I have a PAS that was conducted on me as a thirteen-year old child in VSH dated December, 1965. UVM-VSH documents show that the PAS was conducted on VSH child patients beginning in 1958 and continued at least until 1968 - possibly longer.

CIA BLUEBIRD methods included the use of heroin, morphine, electric shock, lobotomies, hypnotism, fatigue, isolation, sensory deprivation and torture according to H.P. Albarelli, Jr. By 1953, BLUEBIRD became ARTICHOKE, funded in part by U.S. Department of Agriculture, FDA, HEW, NIH, and Army, Navy, and Air Force intelligence. ARTICHOKE and MKULTRA ran alongside each other.

ARTICHOKE experimented with chemical lobotomies and employed radioactive tracers in its studies of the brain, according to Albarelli. One ARTICHOKE document states that, "A non-toxic drug may be found by radioactive tracer techniques that will be attracted to such an area of the brain as so to produce a taming that can last for some time."

The Department of Energy Human Radiation Experiments included UVM and Robert Hyde in the list of participants. UVM is known to have conducted Special Interrogations well into the early 1970's. Hyde conducted radioactive isotope tracer experiments in his LSD research for CIA and documents from the DOE Radiation Experiments show that UVM installed a cobalt source onsite after securing the contract with the Air Force School of Aviation Medicine.

Based on numerous UVM-VSH documents, CIA declassified documents, DOE documents and known methods of experimentation conducted at UVM-VSH, it appears as if UVM-VSH research included BLUEBIRD, ARTICHOKE and MKULTRA. Considering the fact that UVM-VSH were research affiliates of Boston Psychopathic Hospital, Butler and McGill (all three were MKULTRA sites), this should not come as any surprise. It is, however, more than curious that UVM-VSH have never been publicly identified in any government hearing. CIA continues to remain silent on UVM-VSH

The newly declassified MKULTRA Robert Hyde Subprojects that I requested using FOIA still redact Hyde's name from each page, despite the fact that I asked for Hyde by name and the CIA cover letter included in the package of documents delivered to me states that my request for Dr. Robert W. Hyde subprojects 8, 10, 10a, 63 and 66 are included in the package of documents. It's like a game played for reasons I simply cannot understand. I strongly suspect that hidden under the remaining redactions are research sites UVM-VSH and the content of Hyde's Subprojects support my suspicion.

Hyde's MKULTRA Subproject 8 was conducted at The Worcester Foundation for Experimental Biology and the newly declassified documents seem to suggest that another hospital site was also involved in the research.

My best guess is that Boston Psychopathic Hospital is the second site, yet the Boston hospital remains hidden behind redactions despite the fact that it is widely known that the hospital was a primary CIA LSD experimental site. John Marks writes extensively about Boston Psychopathic Hospital's CIA LSD research in his book, as does H.P. Albarelli, Jr.

On the other hand, Butler is named in both Subprojects 63 and 66. References to additional sites that conducted the research remain redacted.

Hyde's MKULTRA Subproject 8 documents read:

"(Redacted) of (Redacted) has just been given a grant to study human subjects. (Redacted) at the (Redacted) (now collaborating with (Redacted) hospital, 2 laboratories to study chronically mentally ill patients response to award conditioning in terms of their ability to develop desired behavior and to continue such behavior over long periods of time."

"As soon as this human laboratory is set up and reliable curves of behavior developed in humans in collaboration with (Redacted) we plan to test the effects of lysergic acid on behavior curves."

Where was Hyde in 1953-1955 during MKULTRA Subproject 8? He was at Boston Psychopathic Hospital, a research affiliate of VSH and UVM.

The content of Hyde's more fully declassified CIA Subprojects bears more than a little resemblance to the content of UVM-VSH research project documents. While Hyde was at Boston Psychopathic Hospital, at Butler or at Worcester, he was conducting CIA experiments. LSD was a primary interest, along with other drugs that acted as LSD antagonists. Hyde's research for CIA in personality types was also a hallmark of his research, as was his use of Gittinger's PAS.

In Subproject 63, Hyde notes in a 1960 document that he began pilot studies in 1956, with more organized studies in 1957, 1958 and 1959. Hyde began his research with LSD in 1949 but CIA sponsorship didn't begin until 1953. It is highly likely that Hyde's sponsor prior to CIA was the Department of Energy, since it is documented that he conducted LSD and radioactive isotope experiments during the DOE Human Radiation Experiments. The DOE experiments began in the 1940's and continued into the 1970's. UVM College of Medicine has been identified as a participant in the DOE experiments. UVM Department of Pharmacology secured a research contract with the Air Force School of Aviation Medicine in 1955 - the same year VSH launched its "schizophrenia" research with UVM.

Hyde's MKULTRA Subproject 10 notes an intent to experiment with the drug Serpasil, also known as Reserpine, a new drug discovered in 1954 and distributed by CIBA Pharmaceuticals. In 1954, Dr. George Brooks negotiated a contract with CIBA to purchase the new drugs, Reserpine and Thorazine; these drugs were used extensively by staff at VSH. Brooks also secured a contract with Smith, Kline and French that same year. Both pharmaceutical companies are identified in declassified CIA documents as having supplied experimental drugs to CIA. Both drugs are known to have been used in LSD experiments.

In 1956, Brooks spent six months at Boston Psychopathic Hospital, on a Smith, Kline and French Fellowship for "special drug studies." Boston Psychopathic doctors Hyde, Rinkel, Solomon and other CIA researchers were well underway experimenting with LSD for the CIA at Boston Psychopathic when Brooks was there.

Hyde's MKULTRA Subproject 66 notes that in LSD research, "different observers use different methods of assessment closely related to the observers' values."

UVM-VSH research projects beginning in 1955 were all conducted under the guise of "rehabilitation of chronic schizophrenics." Brooks and other VSH staff psychiatrists published papers under the title of "The

Rehabilitation of the Hospitalized Mentally Ill."

Based on an overwhelming amount of documentation drawn mostly from the content of UVM-VSH research documents and from Hyde's MKULTRA Subprojects, as well as highly respected published books on the CIA and LSD, there is very little doubt that the University of Vermont College of Medicine and the Vermont State Hospital were conducting CIA LSD research and were funded by CIA cover groups and agencies.

A tremendous number of documented CIA researchers are identified in UVM-VSH research project documents along with cover groups, funding conduits, pharmaceutical companies known to have supplied CIA with experimental drugs and CIA LSD methods of research. UVM-VSH affiliate hospitals were Boston Psychopathic, Butler and McGill - all MKULTRA research sites.

The November, 2013 response from CIA to my FOIA, and the response from the State of Vermont to my Vermont Records Act request also confirm what I suspected for many years: the research conducted at UVM-VSH for CIA is classified. Still classified after all of these years.

Why CIA had a change in policy and finally admitted that the UVM-VSH research is classified, after I spent years peppering CIA with FOIA requests regarding its UVM-VSH research in drugs and mind control, and after CIA denied every request, and never admitted that the research was classified, is anyone's guess.

Why after ten years did CIA finally send me Hyde's more fully declassified MKULTRA Subprojects in September, 2013? I hadn't communicated with CIA about the Hyde subprojects since 2009. Why now?

Several people I have spoken with raise the question as to whether or not the recent revelations by former NSA employee, Edward Snowden, and the resulting scrutiny the intelligence agencies are under, played any role in CIA's apparent change in policy as it relates to the Vermont experiments. Again, I will probably never know the answer.

"One can safely predict techniques for controlling behavior and modifying personality will grow more effective by the year 2000. Thousands of experts at conditioning are now trying out their behavior changing techniques on tens of thousands of people in classrooms, prisons, mental hospitals, day care centers and nursing homes."

American Academy of Arts and Sciences, 1967

The covert CIA research that was conducted in the State of Vermont and all across the country, matters to every American in every walk of life - maybe more now than it ever did.

December, 2013

Memory loss is such a strange and difficult thing to live with. No amount of conscious effort or strength of will brings about any additional memory. I have found that when bits and pieces of memory return they are almost always only small expansions of memory I already had. More often than not, when I regain a portion of memory it isn't a new memory, it's a broader view of a memory I previously had. It's as if for some reason I was unable to incorporate the information in the memory and to fully appreciate the information in the memory.

In late December, 2013, I had just gone to bed for the night and I wasn't thinking about anything in particular when I began to think about and picture in my mind the memory I have always had about Curlin removing me from a seclusion room on the locked ward 1A in October, 1970.

This memory is one of only three instances I have ever been able to recall about Curlin, and Kathy and I have talked about this particular memory for years.

I have a faint memory of a man peering into the seclusion room. A nurse opened the door and Curlin was standing there with her. I don't recall ever meeting him before, yet the VSH record shows that he and Brooks were my doctors of record on the medical ward where I had been only days before I was transferred to the locked ward. The records show I had been kept in seclusion and in leather wristlets while on 1A. I was naked and I was lying on the seclusion room floor.

Curlin told the nurse to get me dressed and he began to lead me toward the exit door. The nurse screamed at him that he could not take me off the ward.

He yelled back at her, "The hell I can't!"

My memory ends at the door.

My next memory, which is supported by the records, is of standing in the Weeks 3 nurses' office as Curlin sat in a chair and told me that Dr. O'Shea would take good care of me.

In late December, 2013 this memory became fuller. I realized that there was only one nurse on the ward when Curlin took me out of seclusion and that there were no patients in the hallway. This would have been very unusual. Patients were always milling around the halls, propped up against the walls and standing around. 1A always had a nursing staff of between five and eight nurses. Curlin and I would have had to pass directly by two nurses' stations on the way to the exit door, the second one being only feet from the exit. They were both empty.

I realized that Curlin had to have taken me off the locked ward at night - after eleven when the night shift, which would have been only one nurse, was working. This would be why there were no patients in the hallways. They were in bed in their rooms.

This memory is the same as I have always had except I wasn't able to fully understand the information available in it. I always knew there was only one nurse and I always knew there were no patients in the hallways. It never occurred to me what this meant.

When Curlin brought me to Weeks 3, it was daytime. There was a full nursing staff when he sat in the office and told me that Dr. O'Shea would take good care of me. This raises the very disturbing question: where did Curlin take me in the middle of the night and for what reason? Given the information I learned was in the closing of the lawsuit regarding Curlin's admission of "sexual misconduct," I can imagine why he removed me from the locked ward in the middle of the night and why I showed up with him in the daytime on Weeks 3.

Apparently no one at VSH - not the nursing staff, not the hospital administration - no one, did anything except keep the situation covered up. This is an example of the total lack of integrity and the total lack of human compassion that was at work at VSH during the years I was there and during the years that UVM-VSH were conducting CIA experiments.

Having substantial memory loss is a difficult thing to live with and an even more difficult thing to understand. Why it took me so long to realize that Curlin had to have taken me off the locked ward at night is a question I don't know how to answer. I've told and retold this memory in therapy for years, yet the details in the memory didn't come together until December, 2013. Those details were always there. I was just unable to incorporate them into an understanding of what actually took place that night in October, 1970.

VERMONT STATE HOSPITAL DEATHS, 1952-1973

While investigating CIA experiments at VHS, I continued to have mail stolen. In 2009, I sent a letter to Senator Bernie Sanders at his Burlington office. The letter was sent using Certified Mail, and it never arrived at Senator Sanders' office. I contacted my Postmaster who tracked the Certified Mail to a mail facility in New Jersey, where the letter had been signed for. I checked with Senator Sanders' staff only to learn that the person who signed for the letter was not a person known to Senator Sanders' staff. My Postmaster contacted Sanders' office and verified that the name of the person who signed for the letter was not a person known to Sanders' office.

Another Certified letter sent by me to CIA Director Leon Panetta was also stolen. Despite the evidence held by the Postmaster and by the Postal Inspectors that two letters mailed using Certified Mail were stolen, I was never contacted by the Postal Service and to this day, to my knowledge, no action taken by them has resulted in the discovery of the identity of the perpetrator. How the Postal Inspectors were able to ignore the verified thefts of Certified mail to a United States Senator and to the CIA Director, is a question I cannot answer. Senator Sanders' Certified mail theft also involved someone who signed for the letter who was not known to Sanders' staff. Why and how my letter addressed to Sanders in Burlington, Vermont, mailed from Rutland, Vermont, ended up stolen in a New Jersey mail facility remains unknown, unanswered and apparently not investigated.

I also had mail sent to the Department of Justice stolen and mail DOJ sent in reply to me stolen. Numerous FOIA requests and requests for assistance to elected officials were stolen. I have no way of knowing the true extent of my stolen mail, but I was able to find information that might help explain the lack of an investigation by Postal Inspectors.

In Dr. Colin Ross's book, *The C.I.A. Doctors: Human Rights Violations by American Psychiatrists,* a CIA cover-up of its operations involving mail tampering on American soil are documented by a quotation from an internal CIA memo:

"In 1952, the CIA began to survey mail...in 1953 it began to open and read mail...the program was approved by the Director of CIA and at least three Postmaster Generals...and Attorney General John Mitchell."

"Unless the charge is supported by the presentation of interior items from the project, it should be relatively easy to "hush up" the entire affair or to explain that it consists of legal mail cover activities conducted by the Post Office at the request of federal agencies. Under the most favorable circumstances including the support of charges with interior items from the project, it might become necessary, after the matter has cooled off during an extended period of investigation, to find a scapegoat to blame for unauthorized tampering with the mails."

I thought about how my Postmaster began to stop returning my phone calls and how he finally refused to contact me. I wasn't able to learn anything more from my Postmaster, and I was never contacted by the Postal Inspectors.

After the Patriot Act became law, the intelligence agencies no longer had to obtain a warrant to wiretap phones and after years of dealing with a wiretapped phone, I wondered if the intelligence agencies had returned to mail tampering. I also wondered if the explanation as to why the Postal Inspectors and the Post Office apparently didn't find the theft of Certified Mail to a United States Senator worth investigating was that mail was routinely being opened, read and in some cases, stolen and that the Postal Service was well aware of this matter. I doubt that too many American citizens have to deal with stolen mail or have experienced a lack of interest or investigation by proper authorities.

As far as I know, my mail is no longer being stolen but it is noteworthy that I no longer send FOIA requests and no longer write letters to elected officials requesting their assistance. In addition, I have no way of knowing if any investigation by the Postal Inspectors was ever done.

After years of being followed and harassed by strangers I did not know, and after being able to identify at least one of the strangers who followed me as a federal agent, I attempted on several occasions to speak with the local office of the FBI. Not only would the two agents who worked in the office not return my phone calls, but they also refused to meet with me. I found this to be curious at best.

It took a phone call to Senator Sanders' office with an angry complaint by me about being followed and harassed, after which Senator Sanders sent a Congressional Liaison Officer to CIA to complain, and a phone conversation with the Albany office of the FBI, before these strangers finally stopped following and harassing me.

After being followed around stores, approached on the street, harassed and bumped in traffic, and after watching strangers pull their vehicles next to mine and sit and stare at me, flash their car lights at me after they pulled into parking spaces directly in front of me, after all of this nonsense, as of the writing of this book, it appears as if these strangers have stopped following me. I've grown accustomed to watching who is near me and I notice if any vehicle appears to be following me, but things seem to have quieted down. It would seem to me that the amount of time and personnel that was involved in the harassment must have cost quite a bit of taxpayer dollars. These were wasted taxpayer dollars.

I had been troubled for a long time about why the government would go to the lengths they have gone to keep tabs on my phone and my mail, and to follow me. It became clear early on that whoever was conducting the harassment had to have a high level of sophistication in order to pull off the types of surveillance they used. It made no sense to me and the more I witnessed the surveillance the more questions I had as to the reason.

I wondered why, decades after the drug and mind control program ended, would CIA be interested in my activities? The details of the CIA experiments that came under scrutiny in 1977 were extremely disturbing and it seemed to me that whatever CIA was concerned about my discovering must be even worse than the details of research that were already known.

The book, *Empty Beds*, lists VSH patient death rates over the same time when VSH-UVM conducted the CIA experiments. I began to study the death rates. Vermont Department of Mental Health Biennial reports contain yearly death rates and as I read the statistics I began to realize that the death rates at VSH during the time experiments were being conducted were extremely high and seemed to be way out of proportion.

For a twenty-year period, 1952-1973, VSH death rates when matched with the yearly patient population. I noticed that in 1973, the same year CIA halted MKULTRA and the federal funding to VSH for active patient research ended, the death rates dropped significantly and continued to drop over the following several years. An average high patient population over the twenty-year time frame was about 1200 and the average low patient population was about 600. In 1958, 186 VSH patients died in one year. This would be the equivalent of one body being removed from VSH every other day for the year 1958. I knew that something was dreadfully wrong.

During the years 1952-1960, 1233 VSH patients died.

By 1969, an additional 1210 VSH patients had died.

During the years 1970-1973, 392 VSH patients died.

1952 - pop: 1260 - deaths: 144

1953 - pop: 1280 - deaths: 126

1954 - pop: 1270 - deaths: 105

1955 - pop: 1280 - deaths: 125

1956 - pop: 1280 - deaths: 147

1957 - pop: 1240 - deaths: 154

1958 - pop: 1240 - deaths: 186

1959 - pop: 1145 - deaths: 131

1960 - pop: 1150 - deaths: 115

1961 - pop: 1200 - deaths: 124

1962 - pop: 1228 - deaths: 116

1963 - pop: 1240 - deaths: 134

1964 - pop: 1224 - deaths: 119

1965 - pop: 1243 - deaths: 137

1966 - pop: 1172 - deaths: 145

1967 - pop: 1163 - deaths: 125

1968 - pop: 1058 - deaths: 167

1969 - pop: 1025 - deaths: 159

1970 - pop: 940 - deaths 126

1971 - pop: 880 - deaths: 130

1972 - pop: 608 - deaths: 90

1973 - pop: 604 - deaths: 46

VSH death rate statistics in the years 1974 through 1978 are "unavailable" according to the Vermont Department of Statistics. Do these death rates from 1952 to 1973 hide terminal experiments done on patients at VSH? Does anyone care, or want to investigate?

On June 19, 1972, CIA Director Richard Helms ordered the destruction of MKULTRA files. I was discharged from VSH on June 19, 1972. Helms knew that the CIA drug and mind control programs were under scrutiny. The files were actually destroyed on June 30, 1972.

By 1973, Helms ordered a halt to the MKULTRA programs and ended funding. In 1973, VSH halted active patient research and the federal funding sources dried up.

In 1973, VSH patient death rates plunged and continued to plunge over the next few years until the death rates fell to more reasonable numbers of one or two a year.

I filed a Vermont Records Act request with the Vermont Department of Mental Health for the ages, places of residence and cause of death of the almost 3000 VSH patients who died during the twenty-year time period when experimentation was ongoing. My request was denied.

In a phone conversation I learned that my request was denied due to "Privacy Act" concerns. I found this to be interesting since the information I was seeking did not concern the identities of the patients. Furthermore, I was under the impression that the right to privacy ends with death.

I was very interested in learning how many VSH patients were brought into VSH from other states in the country and what the actual cause of death was for the patients. It was clear that Vermont was not going to allow me to obtain documents relating to the VSH deaths.

Numerous published accounts of the CIA drug and mind control programs detail CIA plans to conduct "terminal experiments," including BLUEBIRD, ARTICHOKE and MKULTRA. CIA maintains that it never conducted terminal experiments on American soil.

A 1954 CIA cable contained a desire for "time, places and bodies for terminal experiments."

Another CIA cable discussed, "diminishing numbers of subjects available for these tests."

According to John Marks, Ewen Cameron expressed a willingness to conduct terminal experiments at McGill University, where he was the Chairman of the Department of Psychiatry.

According to John Marks, Dr. Maitland Baldwin stated his willingness to perform terminal experiments. Baldwin was a brain surgeon at the National Institute of Health and went on to work for the CIA Technical Services Division. Baldwin was the contractor on MKULTRA Subproject 62, and was a coauthor of the McGill neurosurgeon, Wilder Penfield.

I thought about the extremely high death rates at VSH and I wondered if I had discovered the real reason CIA, the State of Vermont and the federal government were so motivated to conceal Vermont's role in MKULTRA. The cover-up was not only massive, but it was a State and federally coordinated cover-up. The behavior of federal agencies that funded VSH-UVM experiments for twenty years, yet denied that they were in possession of any documents relating to the experiments, was suspicious at best. The behavior of UVM, SAM, DOD, CIA, former Vermont Governors, United States Senators, Congressmen, Senate Committees and practically every other State and Federal official I contacted not only raises suspicions, but is indicative of a cover-up.

When I initially contacted elected state and federal officials and explained what happened to me and described the content of the VSH-UVM experiments, the responses were of concern and there was usually an expression of at least some degree of interest in helping me. Follow-up phone conversations led to the officials telling me they couldn't help. This happened over and over again. It didn't take me long to realize that the State and Federal government did not want to know about the Vermont CIA experiments and they most definitely did not want to hear about VSH patient deaths.

Terminal experiments would be the one CIA activity that would cause such a massive, coordinated state and federal cover-up to occur. I realized that because I had discovered Dr. Robert Hyde in my medical records and I went on to obtained numerous other documents that contained names, sites and procedures that I could connect back to CIA, I became the target of surveillance and harassment.

Things began to make sense. Someone was very worried about the documents and information I was obtaining about Vermont CIA experiments and with the extremely high death rates at VSH during the time when VSH-

UVM were conducting experiments using unwitting subjects, and the huge amount of documentation I gathered on CIA personnel, sites, funding sources, cover front groups and contracts, I was certain that death rates at VSH were a huge factor in the cover-up.

CIA, VSH-UVM never imagined that anyone would learn about the CIA and when I did, they never thought that anyone would believe me. Apparently they thought that if they harassed and intimidated me, I'd give up my pursuit. They were mistaken.

I thought about how close I had come on numerous occasions, to having been a number in a death statistic document. My medical records are filled with procedures that could have easily led to my death. I have no explanation for why I survived. But it appeared as if many VSH patients did not survive.

The knowledge that so many VSH patients were intentionally subjected to cruel experiments and that almost 3000 VSH patients died over the twenty years that VSH-UVM conducted experiments, changed the way I felt about my own involvement in the experimentation. I realized that my investigation was no longer driven solely by what happened to me. There is a very good chance that I knew some of the people who were experimented on and very likely permanently damaged by the experiments. It's also very possible that I knew some of those who died.

I wondered how the staff at VSH could have watched as many as 186 bodied being removed from VSH in one year and have remained silent. I wondered how numerous Vermont State officials could have read the death statistics in the Department of Mental Health Biennial for twenty years and not have had questions. I wondered how the death rates could have appeared in the 1988 book, *Empty Beds* by Marsha Kincheloe without someone expressing concern. If anyone ever did express concern or have questions, there was apparently never a follow-up or publicity. Many times over my fifteen-year investigation, I shook my head in disgust and disbelief and I still do.

In 2009, I wrote a letter to Attorney General Eric Holder in which I described the CIA experiments in VSH-UVM. I detailed the high death rates at VSH and requested that he conduct an investigation into VSH deaths during the twenty years when unwitting subjects were used in CIA experiments. No reply or acknowledgement of my concerns was received.

I wrote a similar letter to President Obama. No reply or acknowledgement was received. I wrote a letter to Secretary of Defense, Robert Gates. No reply or acknowledgement was received. I wrote to CIA Director, Leon Panetta. The letter to Panetta, mailed using Certified Mail was stolen. I was eventually able to send a letter that was received by Panetta. No reply or acknowledgement was received.

During my fifteen-year investigation, I contacted numerous state and federal officials and requested their assistance. Requests for assistance and investigation were sent to:

Senate Select Committee on Intelligence, Senator Diane Feinstein, Senator Edward Kennedy, Senator Patrick Leahy, Congressman Peter Welch, former Governor James Douglas, members of the Vermont Legislature, former UVM President Daniel Fogel, UVM College of Medicine, every member of UVM Board of Trustees, VSH, Vermont Department of Mental Health, former Commissioner of Mental Health Paul Jarris, former Commissioner of Mental Health Michael Hartman, (Hartman did speak with me on the phone but no investigation was undertaken), U.S. Department of Justice, School of Aviation Medicine, numerous branches of the Army, Air Force and Navy, Advanced Research Projects Agency, Department of Defense, United States Public Health Service, National Institute of Health, National Institute of Mental Health, Department of Health and Human Services, Food and Drug Administration, U. S. Surgeon General, Department of Energy, UVM Bailey Howe Library, Library at Brown University, Massachusetts Mental

Health Hospital (Boston Psychopathic), Butler Hospital, Rockland State Hospital, Smith, Kline and French Pharmaceuticals, CIBA and the Group For The Advancement of Psychiatry.

Senator Bernie Sanders tried to assist me on several occasions. He remains the only U.S. Senator or elected federal official to try to help. Vermont Representative, Anne Donahue and Vermont Representative, Michael Fisher also tried to assist me. Several members of the Vermont Legislature spoke with me on the phone and expressed their shock and concern at my information and about my personal experiences but there was no follow-up or action by the Vermont Legislature.

APPENDICES: THE EVIDENCE

THE SEARCH FOR DOCUMENTS

"If you want to be free, there is only one way; it is to guarantee an equally full measure of liberty to all of your neighbors. There is no other way."

Carl Shurz

Statesman, US Senator and Reformer

Request to CIA from Harold Wolff, creator and President of the Human Ecology Fund, a CIA funding front for MKULTRA:

Wolff asked the Agency for everything in its files on "threats, coercion, imprisonment, isolation, deprivation, humiliation, torture, brainwashing, black psychiatry, hypnosis and combinations of these with or without chemical agents."

From *The Search For The Manchurian Candidate*, by John Marks

When I ended my lawsuit in 2002 because of a life-threatening attack of an autoimmune disorder, it took me time to begin my investigation again. The drug I was prescribed for the autoimmune disease, Imuran, had distressing side effects, but as time passed, the active phase of the disease was quieted by the drug and I went back to my investigation.

I filed Freedom of Information requests with CIA in which I requested documents involving the use of LSD, electric shock, Metrazol, hypnosis and several other known CIA methods conducted at VSH, UVM, Degoesbriand Hospital, and Mary Fletcher Hospital during 1965-1973. I asked for documents on Dr. Robert W. Hyde, Director of Psychiatric Research at VSH. My FOIA requests were denied due to "no documents located."

I filed repeated FOIA requests with CIA in an attempt to locate documents relating to Hyde's activities in Vermont and documents relating to the participating Vermont hospitals. In the requests, I attached information to CIA about how I had been used in covert experiments without my knowledge or consent. I made it clear that my motive in seeking the documents was to be able to know what experiments I had been subjected to. I informed CIA that Hyde was cited in my medical records and that the medical records were incomplete.

Regardless of what I requested or how I worded the FOIA requests, CIA denied every request until I received what I considered to be a very interesting and surprising response from CIA:

"We have re-reviewed your request and have determined the information you are seeking relates to the CIA program known as MKULTRA...clinical records generated under MKULTRA were retained by persons or institutions that actually conducted the research."

I was surprised and intrigued by CIA's response. Were they telling me that the documents I was searching for were being held by VSH and UVM? I decided to turn my attention to VSH and UVM. I already had two books written about VSH and the information in these books was stunning.

In the book, *Empty Beds: A History of the Vermont State Hospital*, by Marsha Kincheloe, I read about a long-time VSH research and personnel exchange program with Boston Psychopathic Hospital. The Boston hospital was a well-known CIA research site for MKULTRA and Hyde was Assistant Superintendent there when LSD and other mind control experiments were conducted for the CIA.

The book listed several research grants and provided grant titles and grant numbers that I used in FOIA requests to the federal funding agencies. I saw that these research projects were funded by the National Institute of Mental Health, the National Institute of Health, the United States Public Health Service and the Department of Health, Education and Welfare. All of these federal funding agencies admitted during Senate hearings on the CIA drug and mind control programs that they wittingly funded the CIA experiments.

I filed FOIA requests with each of the federal agencies and cited VSH, UVM and the two Burlington hospitals. I requested documents relating to the use of LSD, electric shock, hypnosis, Metrazol, and sensory deprivation during the time frame of 1965-1973. I explained in each FOIA that I had reason to believe that I had been an unwitting experimental subject and I named Dr. Robert W. Hyde. Each of the federal agencies denied having any documents. I filed appeals and each appeal was denied on the basis of no documents located. I found this curious at best since these federal agencies provided the research monies to VSH-UVM.

During a follow-up phone conversation with the Public Health Service, the woman asked me why I was interested in obtaining documents on the CIA experiments in Vermont and I replied that I had information in my medical records that showed that I had been an unwitting research subject.

"The Public Health Service did brain studies that they don't want anyone to know about," the woman on the other end of the phone told me.

I turned my attention to UVM and filed a Vermont Records Act request seeking documents relating to the 1955 Air Force School of Aviation Medicine contract AF 19(604) 1093 that was cited in the Department of Energy list of participating institutions and individuals in the Report on Human Radiation Experiments. These experiments were cited as the forerunner of the CIA MKULTRA research and Robert Hyde was named as a participant. I requested documents regarding LSD, Mescaline, hypnosis, Metrazol, electric shock and sensory deprivation and documents related to Dr. Robert W. Hyde.

UVM denied the request citing no documents located. I appealed and it was denied. I wrote a follow-up letter to the President of UVM, Daniel Fogel who replied that a "diligent search" yielded no documents. I found the response to be curious at best.

I filed FOIA requests with the Department of Energy and cited the 1955 UVM-SAM contract. The Department of Energy denied my request due to no documents located. I had already obtained the 1955 contract released by the DOE during the Clinton Presidency. UVM was cited as having conducted behavior research, yet the DOE claimed it had no documents related to the UVM research. I found this to be curious at best.

I investigated the School of Aviation Medicine and learned that the former Chief of Science at the Dachau concentration camp in Nazi Germany, Hubertus Strughold was the Director of Research at the SAM when UVM conducted the research for the Air Force. Strughold is cited in numerous documents and publications on CIA drug and mind control research because his Dachau experiments in mind control were the very first drug and mind control experiments on record. Strughold's Dachau experiments resulted in the horrific torture deaths of thousands of concentration camp victims.

I shuddered at the thought that UVM conducted research with SAM when the former Nazi was the Director of Research at SAM. But I was also growing increasingly suspicious about UVM and the federal funding agencies. The FOIA denials made no sense.

I filed FOIA requests with the former School of Aviation Medicine and the Air Force seeking documents relating to the 1955 Air Force SAM contract. I provided names, dates, and the contract number. The FOIA requests were denied due to no documents located. I filed an appeal. I had portions of the 1955 contract, the contract number, names, dates and even dates and times of several trips made by SAM officials to UVM. My FOIA appeal was denied. I found this to be curious at best.

FOIA requests were filed with the Army, Navy and several Air Force bases seeking documents related to the Vermont experiments. All FOIA requests and appeals were denied due to no documents located. In the 1977 Senate Select Committee hearings on the CIA MKULTRA research, the

Army, Navy and Air Force were cited as having conducted CIA research.

I learned that the Department of Defense conducted drug and mind control experiments during the time when CIA MKULTRA was underway. I filed several FOIA requests with DOD seeking documents related to UVM-VSH and the two Burlington hospitals. I cited Dr. Robert W. Hyde, LSD and numerous mind control methods. I informed DOD that I had medical records that showed I had been used in unwitting experiments.

One FOIA request came back citing "documents located." I waited for the documents to arrive and when they didn't, I contacted DOD by phone. The FOIA officer told me on the phone that documents had been located. One document related to the names of the participating institutions. She told me that "additional documents" were also located. She asked me to write down her instructions on how to word my appeal.

I learned that someone was objecting to the release of the documents. I suspected that Vermont was the objecting party. I had begun to suspect that Vermont asked for and received protection from public disclosure regarding its activities during MKULTRA. During the 1977 Senate hearings many universities and hospitals asked for and received protection from public scrutiny. It interested me that VSH-UVM research and personnel exchange partners, Boston Psychopathic Hospital, Butler Hospital and McGill University all admitted their witting participation in the CIA MKULTRA experiments, yet Vermont was never mentioned in any testimony or in any publication as having conducted covert research.

Much to my surprise, I was informed by the DOD employee that the party objecting to the release of the documents was the Office of Secretary of Defense, Donald Rumsfeld. I began to wonder what CIA and DOD had done in Vermont institutions that would require a several decades-long cover-up. My contacts with the federal funding agencies that should have had documents relating to VSH-UVM research because they funded the Vermont research, all denied having any documentation. For the first time,

I began to think beyond my own personal involvement in the covert CIA experiments and I wondered if there was something I was overlooking.

Vermont is located within relatively easy driving distance of Montreal, Boston, New York and Washington, DC. Vermont would have been one of the very last places anyone would have imagined that the CIA was conducting experiments with its Vermont hospital and psychiatrist partners. Vermont was a good choice as a place to hide the presence and activities of CIA. The Vermont CIA experiments remained covered up despite the 1975 Rockefeller hearings and the 1977 Senate Select Committee hearings on MKULTRA. Vermont CIA experiments might very well have remained covered up except for the fact that in 1997, I found Dr. Robert W. Hyde's name in my VSH medical records.

I did not receive the documents located by DOD until Rumsfeld was replaced as Secretary of Defense by Robert Gates. I never received the "additional documents located" by DOD and the document I did receive was incomplete and told me nothing.

I continued to pepper CIA with FOIA requests and I often included letters describing some of the information I obtained that showed I had been used in drug and mind control experiments. I made it clear to CIA that I only wanted the documents and that I was not acting out of an adversarial position. I also made it exceptionally clear to CIA that I knew they were involved in the experiments conducted on me in Vermont hospitals and that I would never stop my investigation. I told them that I would eventually make the information public.

I was truthful in my communications with CIA and never tried to hide the fact that I intended to make my findings public. I even went as far as to tell them that I had no intention now or in the future of filing any type of lawsuit against CIA. I simply wanted what was rightfully mine: the truth about what CIA did to me. The truth, as I would learn, would be very difficult to find

Early in my investigation, I obtained declassified CIA documents from the National Security Archives in Washington, DC. The staff at the archives was very helpful and supportive. The first incident I had of "missing mail" involved a request to the Archives for declassified CIA documents. Another incident at the Archives involved a request I made for documents involving the CIA use of implants to control human behavior.

The CIA MKULTRA documents were stored off site at the Archives and I had to request material in advance so that the boxes in which the documents were contained could be located. When I did not receive the documents, I phoned the Archives and was told that the information I requested was "missing" from its designated box. I also learned that "certain people" known to the Archives staff had been on site after my request was received. I asked if the Archives had security cameras and although that question was not directly answered, I clearly understood who these "certain people" were believed to be.

Shortly after I began filing FOIA's with CIA and other federal agencies my mail began to vanish. Letters sent by me failed to reach their destination and were never returned to me. Letters mailed to me in response to FOIA requests never arrived. Some FOIA requests arrived opened. I learned rather quickly to follow up by phone when mail did not arrive.

I contacted a Postal Inspector in Essex Junction, Vermont and explained my problems with stolen mail. Mark Cavic listened and told me that he would look into the matter. After many months and many more incidents of stolen mail, I phoned Cavic only to learn that he had no notes on my case and had not conducted an investigation of any type. I was startled and angry.

I phoned the Postal Inspection Service in Massachusetts to find out if Cavic was actually a Postal Inspector.

The woman on the other end of the phone barked at me and said, "You called a federal agent and you better have a good reason for doing so."

I asked her if Mark Cavic from Essex Junction, Vermont was really a Postal Inspector and without hesitation she answered, "Yes."

I found it interesting that she in Massachusetts did not have to check to see if Cavic, in Vermont, was a Postal Inspector. I also found it unusual that her attitude was so hostile for no apparent reason.

My investigation had already shown me that there was evidence of the CIA experiments in Vermont. Declassified CIA documents provided me with names I could connect to VSH, including former VSH Assistant Superintendent, H. Peter LaQueur. Other names in the declassified documents matched names listed in the VSH book, *The Vermont Story: Schizophrenic Rehabilitation*.

I began to keep lists of names I obtained from CIA documents, verified funding groups, cover fronts and from noteworthy authors like John Marks, Martin Lee and Dr. Colin Ross. Cross-referencing became a key feature of my investigation and my list of names directly connected to VSH-UVM research began to grow.

I realized that I needed to be familiar with the terminology of subjects like LSD, hypnosis, the central nervous system and other areas so that I would be able to recognize information when I saw it. I gathered books on all of these subjects and tried to learn all that I could. At times I was able to obtain obscure, out of print books written on these and other key subjects and as time went along my background research paid off.

I contacted Vermont Senator Bernie Sanders' office in the early 2000's and provided him with documents and information about the Vermont CIA experiments and I asked for his help on several occasions. He sent a Congressional Liaison officer to CIA in order to try to help me obtain documents I requested under FOIA. Over the years to come, Senator Sanders and his Burlington staff were receptive to my information and tried to help me. Senator Sanders is the only United States Senator who tried to help.

My attempts to contact Senator Patrick Leahy for his help did not go well. I phoned his Burlington office several years ago and when I began to explain about the Vermont CIA experiments to his office staff, the reaction I got was dismissive. The person on the phone clearly did not want to hear the things I was saying about the Vermont CIA experiments. The all too brief phone call ended without the Senator's office offering any help.

My experience with Congressman Peter Welch was also a disappointment. The Congressman sent me a short letter that included no mention of the reason I asked for his help.

I phoned Senator Leahy's office again a few years after my initial phone call. Once again, the Senator's staff clearly did not want to hear about the CIA and he was even more dismissive than the staff was the first time I called. I hoped that the negative reaction by his staff had been a fluke, but the second phone call, convinced me that this had been no fluke. I wondered if my name had been flagged and I doubted that the staff of a United States Senator was routinely as dismissive and hostile to constituents who requested assistance.

I was still trying to learn how to cope with life as an integrated multiple and I began to be painfully aware of the losses in my life. I had been multiple for forty years and because of the hospitalizations, the brutality of those hospitalizations, separation from my family, friends, school and the loss of the normal, everyday experiences a teenager has in life, I became overwhelmed by the emerging realities of my life. The MPD had saved my life but I began to appreciate how the disorder had caused so much chaos and pain.

The lack of response that I was routinely getting from elected officials and federal agencies was a frustrating and painful experience. Maybe I had been naïve to expect that elected officials would help me and as the list of federal agencies and elected officials who refused to provide assistance grew longer, I became angry. The angrier I became, the more determined I became that I would, somehow, find the truth about the Vermont CIA experiments. The more I was lied to and dismissed out of hand, the more I dug in and continued my investigation. But the deep, pervasive sadness I felt about my government's behavior only grew as the years passed and as I continued to be dismissed and ignored by state and federal officials.

The more I learned about the CIA drug and mind control programs, the more I was able to appreciate the implications the experiments had for my life. What happened to me was not due to an accident. It wasn't because of incompetence. What happened to me was a well thought out, intentionally brutal covert CIA program of drug and mind control experiments. It didn't matter to those who chose me and who used me how old I was when it began. It didn't matter how much I suffered or how much my family suffered as a result. The bottom line was that I didn't matter. Only the objectives of the covert experiments mattered. It was a bitter realization.

I repeatedly asked myself why CIA chose Vermont for the experiments and why when other far more prestigious hospitals and universities admitted their role in MKULTRA, had Vermont's participation remained covered up? The idea that over five decades after the VSH-UVM experiments began, that Vermont's role in the covert research was still being covered up, weighed on me

The literature on the CIA drug and mind control programs describes the motive of the CIA to test drugs and mind control techniques as being driven by fears of the Soviet Union after WWII. The secret programs were begun, according to the explanation of the CIA, as a way to counter the possible use of similar tactics by the Soviets. The longer I investigated the CIA programs, the less I bought into the CIA explanation.

After WWII, American military intelligence discovered files on drug and mind control experiments conducted by the Nazis in the concentration camps. One can only imagine the horror contained in those files. Yet,

American military intelligence decided, as did the American government, to use some of the same methods contained in the Nazi files on the unwitting American public. I wondered how this was even remotely possible. Former Nazi scientists like Hubertrus Strughold were brought into the United States through Project Paperclip and given jobs working for the American intelligence community, despite in some cases, the Nazi scientists' direct involvement in torture.

MKULTRA is described in many documents as a CIA program to study how to gain control of the human mind, even against the will of the subject. The experiments involved drugs, brainwashing, covert experiments in biological and chemical agents, and the use of mental patients, prisoners, terminally ill cancer patients, children and apparently anyone CIA decided was of interest. LSD research is routinely described as having been "weapons testing."

In the 1977 Senate Select Committee hearings on the CIA MKULTRA programs, Americans were told that the details of the experiments were now known. John Marks points out in his book, *The Search for the Manchurian Candidate* that CIA personnel lied under oath. It's difficult for me to believe that the Senators were not aware of the lies.

CIA claimed it would identify and locate former MKULTRA subjects and this for the most part has never happened. Many universities and hospitals asked for and received protection from public scrutiny for their participation in the covert experiments. It was, according to testimony by United States Senators, important to protect universities and hospitals. It's painfully clear when reading the Senate Select Committee report on MKULTRA that there was no such regard for the protection of unwitting American citizens who were subjects of the covert CIA experiments. Vermont Senator Robert Stafford was a member of the 1977 Senate Select Committee hearings, as was our current Vice President, Joe Biden

In a 1979 CIA Memorandum entitled, "MKULTRA Notification of

Unwitting Subjects-Addendum to the Final Report," a concern is expressed that:

"CIA was pushed to launch a search for victims and now having found a victim possibly injured by our testing, it would look very bad if CIA ignored it or had to be pushed to investigate it...having put ourselves in the position of possibly provoked an illness, we should not now wash our hands of it and place the burden of assessing our responsibility on the heirs of the deceased."

The recommendation at the bottom of the page states, "the active portion of this investigation has been terminated."

It's obvious that CIA had no intention of trying to locate unwitting test subjects and a 1994 document entitled, "Human Experimentation, An Overview on Cold War Era Programs" shows that this has been and remains the policy of CIA.

Testimony by Frank C. Conahan, Assistant Comptroller General, National Security and International Affairs Division before the Legislation and National security Subcommittee on Government Operations, House of Representatives, reads:

"During the WWII and the Cold War era, DOD and other national security agencies conducted or sponsored extensive radiological, chemical and biological research programs. Precise information on the number of tests, experiments and participants is not available and the exact numbers may never be known...However we have identified hundreds of radiological, chemical and biological tests and experiments in which hundreds of thousands of people were used as test subjects...these tests and experiments often involved hazardous substances such as radiation... nerve agents, biological agents and lysergic acid diethylamide (LSD)."

"These tests were conducted to support weapon development programs... healthy adults, children, psychiatric patients and prison inmates were used in these tests...An unknown number of other tests and experiments were conducted under contracts with universities, hospitals and medical research facilities...From 1952 to 1975, the Army conducted a classified medical research program to develop incapacitating agents. The program involved testing nerve agents, nerve agent antidotes, psychochemicals and irritants."

Many people mistakenly believe that the CIA experiments involved only mental patients and prisoners but this was not the case. Numerous CIA and military experiments involved the use of toxins and chemical agents, some of which were used in cities all across America. Entire cities were at times exposed to potentially deadly chemicals and toxins. In 1955, CIA tested to see whether or not entire populations could be infected with biological agents. These chemicals were obtained from the Army biological warfare arsenal.

When Americans ask why the CIA drug and mind control programs, generally assumed to have only targeted "captive" populations, should be a concern to them, the answer is clear: all Americans were regarded as potential human guinea pigs. No matter who you were or where you lived, everyone was a potential target for covert biological or chemical experiments.

Frank C. Conahan continued:

"During the same period, the Army Chemical Corps contracted with various universities, state hospitals and medical foundations to research the disruptive influences that psychochemicals have on combat troops. The Air Force also conducted experiments on the effects of LSD through contracts at five universities...no effort has been made by the Air Force to determine if the participants' names are available in the universities' records."

"According to CIA officials, from 1953 to 1964, the CIA conducted a series of experiments called MKULTRA to test vulnerabilities to behavior modification drugs...LSD and other psychochemical drugs were administered to an undetermined number of people without their knowledge or consent. According to the official, the names of those involved in the tests are not available because the names were not recorded or the records were subsequently destroyed. However, some tests were done under contract and no effort has been made by CIA to determine if names are available in contractors' records."

I have never been a political person and I will never be a political person. However I am an American citizen. The things I've learned have changed me forever. I will never again be able to trust my elected officials or believe out of hand what I am told by my government. I was betrayed, as was every Vermonter and every American. Nothing could make me sadder.

I continued to file FOIA requests with federal agencies that should have had the documents I requested. I filed numerous FOIA's with FDA and had several phone conversations with FDA. The role of FDA during MKULTRA in providing exemptions to researchers for LSD testing should have produced documents but as with all the previous FOIA requests, FDA denied my FOIA requests due to no documents located.

I filed numerous FOIA requests with Army, Navy and Air Force bases that had been identified as participants in the MKULTRA experiments. All FOIA requests were denied due to no documents located.

In the mid-2000's, I was contacted by the Department of the Navy regarding a FOIA request I had made earlier. I had grown accustomed to long delays in response to my FOIA requests and at several points in my investigation I had numerous pending FOIA requests with many federal agencies. I had apparently lost track of the request to the Navy and it wasn't until many months later that I heard from them.

When I spoke with the Navy personnel on the phone, he asked me if I had any idea why a FOIA request I had made would have been found locked in a safe. I was stunned as I listened to him explain to me that my FOIA was recently discovered locked away. I had no answer for him

I wrote to every member of the UVM Board of Trustees and included information about the involvement of UVM in the covert experiments. Not one member of the Board replied to my letters. Vermont Governors are always members of UVM Board of Trustees, and I was not contacted by Governor James Douglas. I also wrote Governor Douglas on two more occasions about the CIA experiments in Vermont and he claimed not to have received one of the letters and his response to the third was not an offer to assist me.

I contacted Vermont Commissioner of Mental Health, Dr. Paul Jarris after reading a 2005 statement by him in the newspaper. "We have moved quickly to remedy past problems and have been open and transparent every time there was an opportunity to right a past wrong."

I wrote Dr. Jarris and told him about the CIA experiments and about my own personal experiences in VSH. Jarris wrote me back expressing his concern and asked me to provide him with documents, which I did. I waited for a response and none came. He left his position as Vermont Commissioner of Mental Health without ever addressing the information.

I located Dr. Jarris who was living and working in another state in the late 2000's and wrote him a letter in which I asked if leaving his position in Vermont had anything to do with my request for his help. I later learned that Jarris provided a copy of my letter to him to the State of Vermont.

I began to study the books about the VSH. The first time I read the 1961 book, *The Vermont Story*, written by Dr. Rupert Chittuck, et al, I suspected that the schizophrenic rehabilitation program described in the book, had never taken place. As I re-read the book, I began to recognize the terminology used throughout the book as terminology used by LSD researchers. I'd obtained noteworthy books on LSD like *The Use of LSD in Psychotherapy* by Harold Abramson, *Forgotten Truth* by Huston Smith and *Acid Dreams* by Martin Lee. I also obtained declassified CIA documents that described the use and actions of hallucinogenic drugs. I studied everything I could find on LSD and other hallucinogens.

I knew that CIA routinely covered up LSD research by calling the research "schizophrenia research." CIA researchers like Robert Hyde tried to create a "model psychosis" using LSD to produce schizophrenia-like conditions in experimental subjects. As I read *The Vermont Story*, I realized what I was actually reading.

The Vermont Story bibliography contains names of numerous other researchers who are noted to have influenced and/or participated in VSH schizophrenia research. The CIA declassified documents contain the names of many CIA-contracted researchers and I was able to match many of these names to the VSH research. Several of the researchers cited in the VSH book were also found to have had extensive research backgrounds in LSD, mescaline and other hallucinogenic drug testing.

One book in particular was referenced repeatedly by the authors of *The Vermont Story* as having played a significant role in VSH schizophrenic research. The 1958 book, *Schizophrenia: A Review of the Syndrome* by Leopold Bellak contains dozens of verified CIA MKULTRA researchers and known CIA methods, and gives details about the LSD research of Robert Hyde and other known CIA-contracted psychiatrists.

The book, published by Logos Press contains a very interesting name inside of the cover page: the book was "Manufactured by H. Wolff." I believe this was in fact Harold Wolff, known CIA researcher and the creator of the CIA front group, The Human Ecology Fund. Many of the researchers in the Bellak book are noted in other publications as having conducted MKULTRA research through monies provided by the Human Ecology Fund. Robert Hyde was funded in part by Human Ecology and I believe that the Bellak book was a product of the CIA Human Ecology Fund.

VSH psychiatrists noted in the Bellak book include Dr. George Brooks, Dr. Donald Eldred, and Dr. John Bockoven. The American Psychiatric Association and the American Psychological Association admitted their participation in the CIA MKULTRA programs during the 1977 Senate Investigations. The 1960 American Psychological Association President was George Albee, a Vermont psychologist, and he too is noted in the Bellak book. The American Psychological Association was cleared at TOP SECRET as the contractor on MKULTRA Subproject 107 in 1960. Under that contract, it received $15,000 for "attending meetings at foreign sites."

I had brief contact with Albee in 2009 and he denied knowing anything about the Vermont CIA experiments. I sent him information that showed that the American Psychological Association was fully aware of its involvement in CIA research and that the Association was a witting participant. As President of the Association in 1960, it is highly unlikely that Albee wasn't aware of the Association's collaboration with the CIA. Albee ended his contact with me after he received the information.

I found many examples of known CIA chemicals, procedures, sites and verified CIA researchers in Bellak's book. The book is actually a Who's Who of CIA MKULTRA. The list of names includes:

Overholser, Hoch, Hyde, Greenblatt, Hoffman, Azima, Beecher, Bender, Bennett, Denber, DeShon, Fabing, Murray, Himwich, Hoagland, Solomon, Whitehorn, Lilly, Marrazzi, Rinkel, Hebb, Houston, Osmond, Pfieffer, Rodgers, Delgado and Wittkower.

These are only a few of the numerous researchers who conducted CIA drug and mind control experiments; most of which were funded through the Human Ecology Fund.

Several researchers in the Bellak book are named in *The Vermont Story* and *Empty Beds: A History of the Vermont State Hospital*, by Marsha Kincheloe; their research on LSD and mescaline is also detailed in Bellak's book. Albert DiMascio, who conducted LSD experiments with Robert Hyde, was frequently cited in *Empty Beds* as a research partner of George Brooks, as were Paul Huston, and Herman Denber. All three researchers conducted extensive LSD and mescaline experiments. Another name of note in the Bellak book is A.M. Robinson. Robinson is cited in the *Vermont Story* as an employee of the Smith, Kline and French Mental Health Unit. Robinson began working at VSH in the late 1950's. Smith, Kline and French Pharmaceutical Company is named in declassified CIA documents as a contracted drug company for CIA and it was also under contract with VSH beginning in the mid-1950's.

Examples of procedures and experiments detailed in the Bellak book:

LSD, LAE, LD50, Bufontenine, hashish, Siamese fighting fish, wool protein, RSBT (Rhythmic Sensory Bombardment Therapy), Metrazol, model psychosis, sensory deprivation, lobotomies, Mescaline, narco-hypnosis, ATCH, Thorazine, Reserpine, Artane, BST (Brief Stimulation Therapy), implanted electrodes, Coramine, amphetamines, electro-narcosis, electro-sleep, fever therapy, hibernation therapy, histochemical studies, hormone therapy, prolonged narcosis, perpetual isolation and photoshock therapy. Also noted: pink adrenaline, narco-suggestibility, blocking agents for LSD and other hallucinogens, and radioactive isotope tracers studies with LSD.

In addition, numerous verified CIA research sites are also

referenced in Bellak as well as portions of experiments such as Robert Hyde's radioactive isotope tracer studies with LSD. I have no doubt that the Bellak book, "Manufactured by H. Wolff," was a product of the CIA front group the Human Ecology Fund.

In the CIA declassified documents I obtained from the National Security Archives, several documents show member lists of researchers who belonged to CIA front groups. The Society for Biological Psychiatry was a CIA front group and a 1962 member list includes the name of VSH former Superintendent, H. Peter LaQueur. LaQueur is also named as a member of another CIA front group, the Manfred Sakel Foundation. Other members include: Max Rinkel, Paul Hoch, Ewen Cameron, Lauretta Bender, Herman Denber, and Henry Murray. Several members of these CIA front groups are cited in *The Vermont Story* and *Empty Beds* and they include: Herman Denber, Gerald Klerman, Milton Greenblatt and Jordon Scher.

Only the 1962 Society For Biological Psychiatry and Manfred Sakel Foundation member lists are available in the declassified CIA documents. There is no way to know for sure which other VSH psychiatrists besides LaQueur would be listed as members of the two CIA front groups in other years.

I used the Vermont Records Act to obtain copies of VSH-UVM research documents beginning with the research project that *The Vermont Story: Schizophrenic Rehabilitation* was based on. The 1957 grant, MY-1752, Special Projects #180, was funded by Health, Education and Welfare and the United States Public Health Service. These federal agencies admitted their willing participation in the CIA drug and mind control programs. I also obtained the VSH-UVM project documents MY-1752-RISI that also covered the Special Project #180. Additional funding was provided by the Office of Vocational Rehabilitation.

It's noteworthy that before the influx of federal monies from agencies now known to have wittingly funded CIA experiments, VSH was a crumbling institution. In the book *Empty Beds*, former Superintendent Rupert Chittuck describes the hospital as being infested with rats and other vermin and having failing systems like plumbing and structure. When the federal research monies flooded into VSH, the hospital built the physical structure back to reasonable standards. After 1973, when the federal monies for active patient research stopped, VSH began to decline. By 2011, Tropical storm Irene flooded the hospital and damaged it beyond repair. Governor Peter Shumlin closed the aging hospital forever. I have to wonder how many lives might have been saved from the brutality of VSH if only the federal research monies had never been allotted to VSH in the 1950's. It took an act of God and a good Governor to finally close VSH forever.

It's not as if VSH hadn't come under scrutiny over the years. In 2003, the Department of Justice launched an investigation into VSH and federal funds were withdrawn from the State when the hospital was decertified. I provided DOJ with information and documentation about VSH CIA experiments and its brutal history, yet DOJ was unable or unwilling to open an investigation into VSH past research activities and blatant patient civil rights violations. Governor after Governor passed the problem along and there was no will in the Vermont Legislature to close the VSH. If it hadn't been for Tropical storm Irene, VSH would very likely still house patients.

I read the VSH-UVM research project documents, Special Project #180 and quickly realized that I was reading details of the use of unwitting VSH patients in covert drug experiments. Cited as a "Consultant" to VSH research was Dr. Milton Greenblatt, Director of Research at Boston Psychopathic Hospital. I already knew that VSH-UVM and Boston Psychopathic Hospital had a research and personnel exchange program well underway for years and I knew that Robert Hyde was conducting CIA LSD experiments at Boston Psychopathic Hospital prior to and during this time. I was also aware that Dr. George Brooks had received a Fellowship from Smith, Kline and French, in 1956, which sponsored him to spend six months on site at the Boston hospital for "special drug studies."

Dr. Milton Greenblatt, Director of Research at Boston Psychopathic Hospital conducted research with Hyde and with Albert DiMascio. A 1958 research project, "A Study in the Effect of LSD: Physiologic and Psychological Changes and their Interrelations", is cited in the psychosurgical chapter (lobotomy) of Bellak's book. In 1959, Greenblatt conducted studies in human isolation at the Wright-Patterson Air Force Base.

VSH-UVM research Special Project #180: "This investigation was supported in part, by a research and demonstration grant (No. 180) from the Office of Vocational Rehabilitation and Health, Education and Welfare, Washington, DC." The documents also cite USPHS as a funding source.

Dr. Robert Hyde's Butler research project grant, Special Project #181 includes a statement that: "This investigation was supported in part, by a research and demonstration grant (No. 181) from the Office of Vocational Rehabilitation and Health, Education and Welfare, Washington, DC."

In a 1956 Boston Psychopathic research project, the grant was a "Special Project funded by the Office of Vocational Rehabilitation and Health, Education and Welfare, Washington, DC."

In 1956, Dr. Milton Greenblatt conducted 116 lobotomies on schizophrenic patients.

The documents describe the criteria for selection of the patients for the VSH-UVM research:

"Nearly all of them had been declared financially incapable of paying anything for their own care and were committed to the hospital at state expense. They were middle-aged, poorly educated, lower class individuals. . ."

"They were seldom visited by friends or relatives. They received very few packages or letters. We feel that nearly all of these patients could reasonably be considered to be hopeless cases as far as any social recovery and establishment in homes and jobs outside the hospital are concerned."

"The majority of patients in the selected group will have received prolonged intensive drug therapy in the past without release from the hospital, thus we anticipate that relatively few among them will be discharged and lost from the group."

H.P. Albarrelli Jr. writes in his book, *A Terrible* Mistake, that the:

"Special Projects Division (SPD) was set up within the Office of The Chief, Chemical Warfare Services, to carry out particularly sensitive projects initiated by the War Research Service to oversee the crème de la crème of defensive and offensive biological warfare experiments for various federal agencies, or those contracted out to universities and private laboratories throughout the country."

"Within eight months of its creation, SPD had evolved into a massive bureaucracy...SPD maintained close liaison with the Medical, Ordnance, and Intelligence Departments of the Army and Navy, the Army, Air Force, U.S. Public Health Service, U.S. Department of Agriculture and the British and Canadian governments' biological warfare organizations."

Were the Special Projects at UVM-VSH, at Butler and at Boston Psychopathic - all research and exchange partners and all sites of CIA drug and mind control experiments – funded and contracted through the Special Projects Division as outlined by H.P. Albarelli, Jr.?

I spoke with a person, (who requested anonymity) who attended a conference held in Vermont years ago where Dr. Milton Greenblatt was the featured speaker. This person told me that Greenblatt bragged about all of the lobotomies conducted at VSH. Greenblatt's 1956 Boston Psychopathic Hospital Special Project funded the lobotomies of 116 "schizophrenic" patients. The CIA was interested in the use of lobotomies as part of their experiments on how to induce amnesia.

The VSH experimental drug referred to as SU-3822 #1 and SU-3822 #2, was described as being a "synthetic compound." The chemical agent was supplied by CIBA Pharmaceutical Company. The patients being used without their knowledge or consent were contained on the locked adult women's ward and were the most severely mentally ill VSH patients.

The primary researcher in this project was Dr. George Brooks and the project was conducted jointly by VSH-UVM. Descriptions of the patients' reactions and adverse symptoms are detailed in the project documents. Special Projects #180 included several other apparently benign research studies in "schizophrenic rehabilitation" as well. I will focus on the documents that show the use of unwitting subjects, the use of experimental drugs and experimental procedures.

From the research project, Chronic Schizophrenia, Tranquilizing Drugs and Motor Functions, USPHS grant #MY 1752, September 1957-1958:

"On the first day after the change to placebo, patients on the ward seemed somewhat tense or restless...on the second day four of the patients developed rather acute, uncomfortable reactions characterized by tension, fear, restlessness, insomnia, increased perspiration and vomiting. All patients were tense and restless. The attendant said, "It's like old times. It's bedlam."

"On the third day thirteen patients were suffering severe withdrawal reactions indistinguishable clinically from a moderate withdrawal following long term ingestion of morphine. By the fourth day, there was a total of seventeen out of twenty eight patients who were tense, restless, complaining of muscular aches and pains, breaking out in a cold sweat, sleepless, nauseated. Vomiting had become a serious problem in four patients. On the fifth day one patient became very weak and faint. The dose of the placebo was changed from three times a day to four times a day in an attempt to reassure staff."

"Following the end of the active withdrawal symptoms the behavior of the patients continued to deteriorate. During the fourth week after the change to the placebo, many patients had to be changed to what was felt to be an active chemical compound, SU-3822."

"The clinical condition of all patients continued to deteriorate. As the patients' behavior and clinical condition became intolerable the dosage was gradually raised to 100 mgs. q.i.d. At this time one patient developed a severe skin rash resembling measles. At the end of the third week of SU-3822, all patients were much worse."

"By the eleventh week of the study, two patients developed severe extra pyramidal dysfunction with all the signs of classic postencephaletic Parkinsonism. Three other patients developed severe extra pyramidal dysfunction with insomnia and marked restlessness and nine others had definite cogwheel rigidity. Seven other patients had palpable cogwheel phenomenon in the anterior muscle mass of the arm. Two patients had marked flaccid hypermobility of the elbow joint. On the sixth day following the change in medication nearly all of the patients had some signs of extra pyramidal dysfunction."

"By the eleventh day after beginning the medication, nine patients were suffering rather distressing akathesia and were described by attendants as "pacers." They were pacing back and forth like caged lions. Some attendants refused to work on the ward."

"It seems apparent that use that the substance SU-3822 is not effective...in the behavioral control of severe and chronic schizophrenics."

"Study Duration: April 7-July 17."

"Use of SU-3822#1: May 4-May 19."

:Use of SU-3822#2: May 20-June 12."

"We have been impressed by the rich variety of motor disorders that appear in patients receiving Thorazine and Reserpine, especially when used in combination. These disorders range from a general slowing of responses and impairment of fine motor abilities through cogwheel rigidity, loss of associated movements, spasmodic torticollis, choreform states, oculargyric crisis and catalepsy to full blown Parkinsonism in which patients suffer almost total muscular rigidity."

I read the statement above with particular disgust, especially when I thought about the reputation of George Brooks as a "humanitarian." I began to wonder how many of the women on the locked ward 1A had been used in this and other experiments. Almost all of the women on 1A had been kept there for many years, some for decades. I wondered if I was reading about the experiments those women had been subjected to and I wondered how damaged they had been by the experiments

It's clear when reading the research documents that VSH-UVM used active chemical substances in placebos. I suspect this is how experimental drugs were administered to me in 1970-1971.

During the same time when VSH-UVM were conducting unwitting experiments on severely mentally ill patients, hospitals throughout the country that were not conducting CIA experiments were providing compassionate and effective treatment to the mentally ill. VSH-UVM made a choice to conduct the type of research that they did. They had other options and despite their oaths as physicians, despite internationally accepted agreements like the Nuremberg Code and the Helsinki agreement, VSH-UVM chose to conduct experiments using unwitting patients.

I have no doubt whatsoever that CIA and other intelligence agencies paid for the research that was conducted at VSH. The monies that came from NIH, NIMH, USPHS and HEW during the years of the experiments kept VSH afloat for over two decades. Researchers like Hyde, Brooks, Chittuck, William Deane and others discarded widely accepted rules and regulations for medical research and created their reputations based on fiction. The true methods and treatments these doctors used are clearly described in their own research project documents. There is no excuse for what they did to countless VSH patients.

In VSH-UVM research project MY-1752-RISI: "Details of samples of blood, urine and spinal fluid will be collected for examination by the UVM Department of Pharmacology. The details of this study are given in a separate grant application."

I asked Dr. Colin Ross if it was standard procedure in tranquilizing drug research to collect samples of blood, urine and spinal fluid from patients. He replied that no it was not standard procedure in tranquilizing drug research but that samples of blood and spinal fluid might be drawn in experiments involving LSD, mescaline or other types of experimental drugs.

From MY-1752-RISI:

"A number of studies have indicated that a combination of Thorazine and Reserpine is more effective and more convenient to use especially in the treatment of chronic schizophrenia. However there is a general agreement that this combination is also more effective in producing extra pyramidal dysfunction. For these two reasons it would seem to be the ideal preparation for use in the study of relationships between changes in motor function and changes in psychological and social functions in these patients."

From MY-1752-RISI:

"Studies of the performance in lobotomized chronic schizophrenic patients have demonstrated a further impairment of motor functions immediately following the operation. This impairment coincided with an increase in the severity of the psychotic picture. Similar attempted correlations have not been reported with pharmacology."

I read the paragraph several times and came to the disturbing conclusion that VSH-UVM had intentions of trying to create chemical lobotomies.

The grant application referred to could not be located in several attempts to do so. I did however attempt to locate a VSH-UVM research project funded by USPHS: "RD-1894-P, Autonomic and Psychomotor Parameters of Rehabilitation Potential in the Mentally Disabled."

I filed Vermont Records Act requests that were denied due to no documents located. I eventually tracked this research project to the document storage facility in Middlesex. The archivist expressed surprise that research project documents would have been stored at the Middlesex facility and when I questioned if this would have been unusual, he replied that it would have been very unusual. He was even more surprised when he checked his records that the VSH-UVM research documents had been destroyed. He had no explanation.

I believe that this particular research document was stored in Middlesex and destroyed because the content would have been damaging to VSH-UVM if it had been obtained by anyone. Was this the research project that detailed the use of LSD? Or was this research project one that detailed the use of lobotomies after LSD use?

This is as far as I could go in documenting the involvement of CIA in the VSH-UVM experiments. The answers to my remaining questions are hidden behind locked doors.

BIOGRAPHIES, PUBLICATIONS AND CROSS-LINKAGES OF THE CIA RESEARCHERS

Another aspect of my research was my effort to document as many cross-linkages and connections as I could between the doctors at VSH and the network of CIA mind control doctors. I did this by collecting published papers and books, reports, grant applications and other documents.

A research grant renewal application, 02037, May 1968 - April 1972, Rupert Chittuck and Robert Hyde, USPHS grant account #869124, contains an application to use human subjects.

A December, 1966 letter to Rupert Chittuck from Eugene A. Confroy contains permission to use human subjects at VSH. Confroy was Director of Division Research Grants for USPHS and HEW. Both federal agencies were wittingly funding the CIA experiments.

I located the research documents for VSH-UVM project, "A State Hospital For Educational Therapy," Rupert Chittuck, Robert Hyde, May 1968 - April 1972, USPHS, HEW. The documents identify Hyde, John Bockoven and Dr. Richard York as being "specifically related to this project." Also named are Dr. Greenblatt and Harry Solomon.

In a section of the research documents entitled, "Work Done By Us Elsewhere," research sites named are: Boston Psychopathic Hospital; Butler Hospital; Metropolitan State Hospital; Bedford Veterans Hospital; Lowell Mental Health Center (Bockoven); Rutland Heights Rehabilitation Center (York); and John and Elaine Cummings, Lowell Mental health Center (Bockoven). Also named in the VSH-UVM documents in reference to publications "relevant to this project," were Hyde and R.H. Williams, E.L. Brown, Richard York, Milton Greenblatt, Daniel J. Levinson and Harold Pfautz.

In John Marks' documents donated to the National Security Archives, there are declassified CIA MKULTRA documents listed under Mass Mental Health and marked *New York Times*, August 2, 1977. These documents contain the names and short biographies of CIA researchers and CIA research sites:

Richard York:
Mass. General Hospital, 1953
Boston Psychopathic Hospital, 1952-57
Butler Hospital, 1957-60
Mass. Department Mental Health, 1960-63
Psychological Assessment Associates, 1962-66
Rutland Heights Rehab Ctr. 1966-68 named as a Human Ecology Fund recipient

Harold Pfautz:
Butler Hospital, 1956-1963

Harry Solomon:
Boston Psychopathic Hospital, Harvard Med, Mass.
Mental Health Center (Boston Psychopathic Hospital) 1955-1967

Max Rinkel:
Noted as working with Hyde and Solomon, 1956-1960
Published by the Josiah P. Macy Jr. Foundation, 1956
Senior Research Associate at Boston Psychopathic Hospital in 1963

The VSH research documents note that York and Bockoven personally visited VSH as "Consultants" during the research. Psychological

Assessment Associates in Washington, DC was the site of the CIA headquarters and was run by John Gittinger, Chief Psychologist for CIA.

In the bibliography of *The Vermont Story* are names cited as having contributed to and/or influenced and participated in VSH-UVM research. The book, *Empty Beds* also contains the names of researchers who conducted research with VSH or published research papers with and for VSH psychiatrists. These include:

Milton Greenblatt, Jordon Scher, D. J. Levinson, Albert DiMascio, John Cummings, Gerald Klerman, Herman Denber, Paul Huston, Eric Wittkower, E.L. Brown, and John Bockoven.

Another well-known LSD researcher, Gregory Bateson, was identified in a 1962 VSH-UVM research project document. Bateson is widely written about in books on LSD and is detailed in the Josiah P. Macy Jr. Conferences on LSD. Greenblatt, Scher, Denber, and Huston were listed as members of the Society for Biological Psychiatry in declassified CIA documents.

Other researchers cited in *The Vermont Story* include:

Paul Lemkau, D.J. Levinson, Eric Wittkower, R.H. Williams, Richard York, E.L. Brown, and Barbara Curtis.

In a VSH-UVM research project document entitled, "Problems of Opening a Rehabilitation House for Chronic Schizophrenic Patients," part of Special Project #180, by George Brooks, Harry Solomon is referenced as an influence on VSH research.

The more VSH-UVM research projects documents I was able to obtain, the more names from those documents matched the names in CIA declassified documents. Bellak's book was a goldmine for identifying CIA researchers and their relevant experiments. The number of CIA-connected names in the two VSH books, added to the relevant names in the VSH-UVM research project documents, left little doubt as to the actual research conducted by VSH-UVM.

When I obtained the VSH-UVM research project documents, "The Use of Programmed Instruction with Disturbed Students, MH-01076, George Brooks, Thomas Boag, 1963-1966," I realized I had finally located a direct research connection between CIA, VSH-UVM.

In these research documents, VSH-UVM conducted Personality Assessment System (PAS) psychological tests on child patients at VSH. The test results were sent directly to John Gittinger, 1834 Connecticut Ave, NW, Washington, DC.

In John Marks' book, *The Search for the Manchurian Candidate*, the address of CIA headquarters in Washington DC and the site of Gittinger's Personality Assessment Associates, is 1834 Connecticut Avenue, NW, Washington, DC.

I realized the significance of what I had found. In 1965, a PAS was conducted on me and by 1965, VSH had been sending test results of the PAS directly to Gittinger at CIA headquarters. The documents in the research project showed that numerous PAS's were conducted on child patients and sent to CIA headquarters.

A Progress report for MH-01076, USPHS-NIMH, and a document marked 1-R11-MH-01076 contain disturbing statements relating to the use of "programmed instruction" and a warning that sent chills up my spine:

"We expect you to use Programmed Instruction as a base for teaching and not as the ONLY means. You must use other things or else twenty years from now we will have a generation of programmed kids running around the unemployment office."

I continued to file FOIA requests with CIA and every request was denied. I attempted to have CIA fully declassify Hyde's CIA projects. Hyde died in 1976, yet CIA continues to classify most of his work for them. CIA refused either to grant my request or to deny my request, essentially keeping me in limbo. I filed a request with the Executive Secretary Interagency Security Classification Panel, (ISCAP). I learned that in order for ISCAP to make a determination on my request to have Hyde's CIA projects declassified, CIA had to make a determination and either grant or deny my request. Again, CIA refused to take any action whatsoever. My FOIA request remains in limbo.

In 2011, Dr. Colin Ross filed a FOIA request with CIA to obtain Robert Hyde's CIA subprojects. CIA would not acknowledge that Hyde worked for them, despite the fact that Dr. Ross was able to provide information that confirmed Hyde's employment by CIA, and they refused to grant his FOIA request. Dr. Robert W. Hyde's CIA research is very closely guarded by CIA.

The 1955 UVM-SAM Air Force contract which involved the UVM Department of Pharmacology during the time when former Dachau concentration camp Chief of Research, Hubertrus Strughold, was Director of Medical Research at SAM opened the door to the CIA drug and mind control experiments. The Department of Energy list of participants in the Human Radiation experiments cites UVM as conducting "behavioral studies." Robert Hyde is also noted on the list.

UVM was identified by Sidney Gottlieb as having conducted Special Interrogations. Gottleib stated that he believed that the experiments were funded by Human Ecology and/or Josiah Macy, both cover fronts for CIA. Gottleib was certainly in a position to know what he was talking about since he ran the MKULTRA drug and mind control programs.

Dr. Thomas Boag became UVM's first Chairman of the Department of Psychiatry in 1961. A July, 1961 *American Journal of Psychiatry* bulletin contains the following:

"Department of Psychiatry at the UVM College of Medicine: The office of the Dean has announced the establishment of a department of psychiatry... Chairman of the newly created department of medicine is Dr. Thomas J. Boag, Assistant to the Director of the Allan Memorial Institute and Assistant Professor at McGill. He will take up his new duties at UVM on July 1 as a full time Professor and Chairman of the Department of Psychiatry."

The Director of the Allan Memorial Institute was Dr. Ewen Cameron, contractor on MKULTRA Subproject 68. Boag would be one of the primary researchers (George Brooks was the other) in the 1963-1966 research project who sent test results of the PAS directly to John Gittinger at CIA Washington, DC headquarters.

I obtained a 2009 list of federal funding sources at UVM College of Medicine. The list includes:

NATO, National Security Agency, Department of Energy, Department of Justice, Advanced Research Projects Agency, Department of Defense, Office of Naval Research, Army Medical Research and Materiel Command, Air Force Office of Scientific Research, Interior Department, United States Department of State and NASA. The Josiah P. Macy Jr. Foundation was removed from the list prior to 2009.

I can only imagine the millions of dollars that UVM received from its federal contracts and I have no doubt that that money was a driving force during the CIA experiments at VSH-UVM.

The funding sources for VSH-UVM experiments include USPHS, NIH, NIMH, and HEW, all of which admitted their witting participation in the CIA MKULTRA programs. Cover front groups identified for VSH-UVM include:

Transcultural Psychiatry, Manfred Sakel, Society for Biological Psychiatry, Russell Sage Foundation, Group for the Advancement of Psychiatry, American Association for the Advancement of Science, and apparently the Josiah Macy Foundation and Human Ecology.

CIA sites named in VSH-UVM research project documents and identified by sources include:

McGill, Boston Psychopathic Hospital, Butler Hospital, Rutland Heights Hospital, Metropolitan State Hospital and Psychological Assessment Associates.

CIA contracted pharmaceutical companies that were contracted to VSH-UVM include:

Smith, Kline and French, CIBA and (possibly) Mead Johnson. Smith, Kline and French placed an employee, A.M. Robinson on staff at VSH in the mid-1950s. A.M. Robinson is also noted in Bellak's book.

CIBA supplied experimental drugs for the 1957-58 VSH-UVM experiments and supplied drugs to the Worcester Foundation for Experimental Biology where Hyde and Hudson Hoagland conducted MKULTRA Subproject 8.

VSH-UVM research documents and the book, *The Vermont Story* written by VSH psychiatrists include the names of CIA-contracted researchers and LSD researchers who participated in, influenced and acted in the capacity of consultants for VSH-UVM research, including:

Dr. Robert W. Hyde, Dr. Richard York, Dr. John Bockoven, Dr. Hans. Peter LaQueur, Dr. Harold Pfautz, John Gittinger, Dr. Milton Greenblatt, Herman Denber, Albert DiMascio, Paul Huston, Harry Solomon, Jordon Scher, John Cumming, D.J. Levinson, R.H. Williams, Harry Freeman, David Landy, Eric Wittkower, Philip Slater and Gregory Bateson.

Additionally, Dr. Thomas Chiu, who was employed by UVM in 1971, was a member of the CIA front, Transcultural Psychiatry. Dr. George Brooks and Dr. Thomas Boag conducted research using VSH child patients and sent the results of the PAS directly to John Gittinger at CIA headquarters. Gittinger's Psychological Assessment Associates behavioral research programs funded researchers through the Human Ecology Fund. Robert Hyde was a recipient of Human Ecology monies as well as other funding.

In the book, *A Mind For Murder* by Alston Chase, written about Unabomber Ted Kaczynski, Chase notes that Kaczynski participated in mind control experiments at Harvard, conducted by Henry Murray. Murray enlisted Hyde in order to obtain LSD that was used during the covert mind control experiments. Kaczynski cited the abusive experiments as a factor in his hatred of psychologists and psychiatrists. One of Kaczynski's intended targets in the bombings was Michigan psychologist, J.V. McConnell. Murray has been identified as conducting CIA experiments.

Gregory Bateson is widely written about in relationship to LSD. Harold Abramson, a close friend of Bateson, was a CIA researcher and MKULTRA contractor, and he conducted research with Hyde. Bateson is one of the featured participants in the LSD Conferences for the Macy Foundation. Bateson is cited multiple times in VSH-UVM research project documents.

Declassified CIA documents include membership lists in CIA front groups. Members listed in a 1962 Society for Biological Psychiatry report include:

H. Peter LaQueur, Jordon Scher, Eugene Ziskind, George N. Thompson, Huston Smith, Walter Houston Clark, and Jack Mendelson.

A 1964 Society for Biological Psychiatry membership list includes:

H. Peter LaQueur, Paul Hoch, Ewen Cameron, Max Rinkel, Lauretta Bender, Leo Alexander, Milton Greenblatt, Humphrey Osmond, Hudson Hoagland, Herman Denber, Joseph Wortis and Henry Murray.

Many of those listed in the Society for Biological Psychiatry also held membership in Manfred Sakel, including LaQueur, Rinkel, and Denber,

In a 1963 declassified CIA document, an invitation list for a M.I.T. conference on LSD shows the names of those invited to attend:

Huston Smith, Max Rinkel, Harry Freeman, Norman Gottwald, Hudson Hoagland, Erich Lindeman, Gerald Klerman, and Henry Murray.

CIA research sites and agencies that have been identified in Senate Reports, declassified CIA documents and by noted authors include:

Boston Psychopathic Hospital, Butler, McGill, Allan Memorial Institute, Georgetown Hospital, Cornell, Stanford, Harvard, Kentucky University, University of Maryland, Johns Hopkins, University of Indiana, M.I.T., Washington University in St. Louis, Missouri, Queens College, Penn State, Lexington, American Psychological Association, American Psychiatric Association, School of Aviation Medicine, Air Force, Army, Navy, Department of Energy, Department of Defense, University of Denver,

University of Illinois, Iowa State Hospital, Iona State Hospital (Michigan), University of Minnesota, Columbia, Emory University, Indiana University, Bordentown (New Jersey), Wisconsin University, University of Oklahoma, NIH, NIMH, USPHS, FDA, Naval Research, Syracuse, N.Y., Society For Biological Psychiatry, Manfred Sakel, Transcultural Psychiatry, Russell Sage Foundation, Group For the Advancement of Psychiatry, Andover-Newton Theological School, Clark University, Brown University, Brandeis University, Worcester Foundation for Experimental Biology, Manhattan State Hospital, Rutland Heights Hospital, University of Rochester, Rockefeller Foundation, Massachusetts General Hospital, Medfield State Hospital, UCLA, American Association for the Advancement of Science Missouri Institute of Psychiatry, Human Ecology Fund, Josiah P. Macy Jr. Foundation, and the Geschickter Foundation.

VSH staff researchers presented papers at numerous conferences and at hospitals across the country and published their research in noted journals. VSH-UVM research project documents list many of these presentations and publications.

References from "VSH-UVM, Rehabilitation of Chronic Schizophrenic Patients, Special Project #180" provide further evidence of the extensive cross-linkages between VSH doctors and other CIA doctors and MKULTRA sites. These include:

George Brooks, "Opening a Rehabilitation House", in Rehabilitation of the Mentally Ill, Social and Economic Aspects," edited by Milton Greenblatt and Benjamin Simon, Pub. #58 of the American Association for the Advancement of Science, Washington, DC. Indianapolis, Indiana, December 1957.

George Brooks, "Experiences with the Schizophrenics," paper presented at the Allan Memorial Institute, Montreal, Canada, January 22,

1959.

George Brooks, "Rural Community Influences and Supports in a Rehabilitation Program for State Hospital Patients," presented at Mass Mental Health (Boston Psychopathic), March 24, 25, 26, 1960.

George Brooks, Rupert Chittuck, William Deane, "The Place of the Therapeutic Community in the History and Development of a Modern State Hospital," in Denber, et al, *A Research Conference on Therapeutic Community*, Charles C. Thomas, publisher, Springfield, Illinois. Paper presented at Research Conference on Therapeutic Community, Manhattan State Hospital, NY, NY, March 13, 14, 15, 1959.

William Deane, paper presented at Mass Mental Health, March 24, 25, 26, 1960.

William Deane, The Vermont Story, presented at National Conference of the Mentally Ill, University of Wisconsin, Madison, Wisconsin. March 23, 1960.

Barbara Curtis (VSH), paper presented at the Regional Conference of the Mentally Ill, University of Wisconsin, Madison, Wisconsin. March 23, 1960.

Milton Greenblatt, Richard York, E.L. Brown, "From Custodial to Therapeutic Care in Mental Hospitals," Russell Sage Foundation, N.Y. 1955.

A.M. Robinson, "Remotivation Technique," The Mental Health Education Unit of Smith, Kline and French.

Eric Wittkower, et al, "Object Relations Therapy in Schizophrenic States," September 1957.

George Brooks, William Deane, Robert Hugel, "Some Aspects of the Subjective Experience of Schizophrenics," Dis. Nerv. Syst., 1968.

George Brooks, "A Comprehensive Approach to the Motives of Hard to Reach Patients," paper presented at the American Psychological Association Annual Meeting, Chicago, Illinois, September 2, 1960.

George Brooks, " Rehabilitation of the Mentally Ill: Social and Economical Aspects," sponsored jointly by the American Psychiatric Association and the American Association for the Advancement of Science at Indianapolis, Indiana, December 30, 1957.

Each of the sites noted above where VSH researchers presented papers were identified as CIA research sites. Boston Psychopathic (Mass Mental Health), University of Wisconsin, Allan Memorial Institute, Russell Sage Foundation, Group for the Advancement of Psychiatry, Smith, Kline and French Pharmaceutical and Manhattan State Hospital, thc American Association for the Advancement of Science and the American Psychological Association.

Carl Rodgers conducted CIA research, funded through Human Ecology at the University of Wisconsin. He was cleared at TOP SECRET as the contractor for MKULTRA Subproject 97.

In the USPHS VSH-UVM research project, "Psychomotility, Drugs and Schizophrenia," the following are listed:

George Brooks, Albert DiMascio, "Free Association to a Fantasized Psychotherapist," Arch. G. Psych. 1961.

Max Rinkel, Albert DiMascio, "Prediction of Clinical Effects of Psychopharmacologic Agents," from Drug Action Profiles in Normal Adult Human Subjects, in J. Wortis (Ed), Biological Psychiatry, 1960.

Heinz Lehmann, J. Csank, "Differential Screening of Phenotropic Agents in Man: Psychophsiologic Test Data," J. Clin.Exper.Psychopath. Rev. Psychiat. Neural, 1957.

R.B. Malmo, C. Shagrass, D.J. Belanger, A.A. Smith, "Motor Control in Psychiatric Patients Under Stress," J. Abnorm. Soc. Psychol. 1951

Ewen Cameron, R.B. Malmo, L. Levy, L. Rubenstein, "Repetition of Verbal Signals: Behavioral and Physiological Changes," *American*

Journal Psychiatry, 1959.

Heinz Lehmann, and R.B. Malmo were on staff at the Allan Memorial Institute at McGill University and conducted CIA-funded depatterning research under Dr. Ewen Cameron. Dr. Thomas Boag, UVM Chairman of the Department of Psychiatry in 1961, was Ewen Cameron's Assistant Director at Allan Memorial prior to his position at UVM. The VSH-UVM research project noted here ran from 1958 - 1962. This places two of Ewen Cameron's research partners as referenced sources in VSH-UVM projects. Boag, who went on to conduct VSH-UVM research, sent PAS results to John Gittinger.

Erwin Goffman conducted CIA research at the University of Pennsylvania and is cited in VSH-UVM Research Special Project #180 for a 1958 symposium held at the Walter Reed Army Institute of Research.

Paul Huston, frequently cited in the VSH-UVM research project documents, conducted CIA research at Iowa Psychopathic Hospital, Worcester State Hospital, and Worcester Foundation for Experimental Biology and he was Chairman of the NIMH Training Commission.

Paul Hoch conducted extensive hallucinogen research at N.Y. State Psychiatric Institute, and Manhattan State Hospital. Hoch worked under contract for the Army Chemical Corp. Hoch was N.Y. Commissioner of Mental Hygiene and conducted research at Columbia University. Hoch was the Editor of the *American Journal of Psychiatry* and the *Journal of Nervous and Mental Disease*.

Paul Lemkau conducted CIA research at Johns Hopkins as well as for the Army and NIMH.

Richard York worked out of Psychological Assessment Associates in Washington, DC with John Gittinger. York also conducted research with Hyde.

Harry Solomon conducted extensive CIA research including LSD experiments with Hyde.

Harry Freeman was Director of Research at Medfield State Hospital.

Norman Gottwald conducted research while at Andover-Newton, an identified CIA site.

Hudson Hoagland conducted extensive CIA research with Hyde, including MKULTRA Subproject 8 at the Worcester Foundation for Experimental Biology.

Max Rinkel conducted extensive CIA research including LSD research at Boston Psychopathic Hospital. Rinkel arranged to obtain one of the first shipments of LSD for Boston Psychopathic where Hyde was the very first to take the hallucinogen. Rinkel conducted extensive research with Hyde.

Gerald Klerman conducted research at and was Assistant Clinical Director at Boston Psychopathic Hospital in 1963.

Jordon Scher conducted research at Boston Psychopathic Hospital

Erich Lindeman conducted research at Mass General and is named in the Senate report on CIA drug and mind control programs. Lindeman was Chief of Psychiatric Services at Massachusetts General Hospital and Professor of Psychiatry at Harvard Medical School in 1963.

Herman Denber conducted extensive LSD and mescaline experiments. Denber is listed as a member of CIA front groups and is a frequently cited research partner of George Brooks.

Albert DiMascio conducted extensive LSD and mescaline experiments and was a frequent research partner of Brooks.

Also cited in the VSH-UVM project were:

R. Trumbill, C.H. Maag, “Annotated Bibliography and Critical Review of Drugs and Performance”, Office of Naval Research, Department of the Navy, 1958 ONR report-ACR-29. 1958.

Paul Huston, M. Singer, "Effect of Sodium Amytal and Amphetamine Sulfate on Mental Set in Schizophrenia", Arch. Neurlo. Psychi. 1945.

I looked at the Huston, M. Singer citation in the VSH-UVM research project documents with interest. I wondered if M. Singer was Margaret Singer. Margaret Singer, according to H.P. Albarelli, was a staff psychologist at Walter Reed Army Institute in 1953. Singer came in contact with Albert Biderman and she testified at the 1976 trial of Patty Hearst. Also testifying in defense of Hearst were Louis Jolyon West (cleared at TOP SECRET as a contractor on MKULTRA Subproject 43), Martin Orne (cleared at TOP SECRET as a contractor on MKULTRA Subproject 84), and Robert Lifton. Both Lifton and Singer interviewed US Korean War pilots who had been captured by the North Koreans and been coerced into making confessions of germ warfare. Robert J. Lifton authored books on "thought reform," which is a synonym for mind control.

Albert Biderman was funded by CIA and Human Ecology and he assisted John Gittinger, Harold Wolff and Lawrence Hinkle in organizing the Human Ecology Fund.

In 2001, I was surprised to learn that a co-author of Singer's and a psychologist noted in books on CIA mind control, Richard Ofshe, was an expert witness in a Vermont trial where coercion was alleged. I immediately recognized Ofshe's name, although I doubt that too many other Vermonter's did.

I include the strong possibility that the M. Singer who is cited with Huston in the VSH-UVM research project documents, is Margaret Singer. It's noteworthy that VSH-UVM research project documents cite Walter Reed Army Institute in the Special Project #180 citations.

Dr. Robert W. Hyde's research in LSD included several researchers noted in VSH-UVM research project documents:

Robert Hyde, Max Rinkel, H.J. DeShon, Harry Solomon, " Experimental Schizophrenia-like Symptoms," American Journal Psychiatry, 1952.

Robert Hyde, Max Rinkel, Harry Solomon, "Experimental Psychiatry III. A Chemical Concept of Psychosis," Diseases of Nervous System, 1954.

Robert Hyde, Max Rinkel, Hudson Hoagland, "Experimental Psychiatry II: Chemical and Physiochemical Observations in Experimental Psychosis," American Journal Psychiatry, 1955.

Robert Hyde, Max Rinkel, Harry Solomon, "Experimental Psychiatry IV: Hallucinations, Tools in Experimental Psychiatry," Diseases of the Nervous System, 1955.

Robert Hyde, S. Salvatore, "Progression of Effects of Lysergic Acid," A.M.A., Archives Neurological Psychiatry, 1956.

Robert Hyde, Milton Greenblatt, Albert DiMascio, "A Study of the Effects of LSD: Physiologic and Psychological Changes and their Interrelations," American Journal Psychiatry, 1958.

Additional studies by other researchers noted in VSH-UVM research project documents include:

Robert Hyde, Milton Greenblatt, David Landy, John Bockoven, "Rehabilitation of Mentally Ill, Impact of a Project upon a Hospital," American Journal of Psychiatry, 1958.

Max Rinkel, Gerald Klerman, Albert DiMascio, Milton Greenblatt, J. Brown, "Psycho-Physiologic Evaluation of Phenyltoxamine. A New Phrenotropic agent: A Comparative Study with Reserpine and Placebo" - 1958.

It is clear when reading the contents of the VSH-UVM research documents that the research personnel involved in the experiments at VSH were directly involved in and aware of known CIA groups and activities. Almost every site VSH psychiatrists presented their research papers at was a known CIA-funded research site. The authors cited in the VSH-UVM research project documents are overwhelmingly identified as CIA researchers. VSH researchers, Brooks, Deane and others were very clearly presenting the results of their CIA-funded research to their fellow CIA-funded researchers. VSH psychiatrists were extensively published in medical journals edited by CIA researchers.

The direct connection of VSH-UVM to the CIA drug and mind control programs is, by the sheer volume of the connections, simply astonishing. Despite the 1977 Senate hearings on CIA drug and mind control programs, where the "facts" about the covert research supposedly came to light, Vermont's massive role in the CIA research remained and remains covered up.

A close examination of VSH-UVM research project documents shows that not only did VSH-UVM conduct research using unwitting human subjects, but that their research associates were overwhelmingly CIA-connected researchers. The out-of-state sites where VSH psychiatrists attended conferences, (frequently sponsored by agencies and groups that were funding CIA research) were almost exclusively sites where CIA research was being conducted. VSH research was published frequently by medical journals whose editors were conducting CIA research and the extensive number of CIA researchers cited in VSH-UVM research project documents and in the book, *The Vermont Story* leads to a disturbing conclusion.

VSH-UVM research conducted at VSH over a twenty-year period when CIA monies, funneled through cover front groups and federal agencies that admitted wittingly funding CIA experiments, appears to have been funded by CIA, conducted by CIA and published by CIA researchers. Before the influx of CIA funds, VSH was literally falling down. When CIA halted MKULTRA, VSH stopped conducting active patient research and the hospital began a slow death. The only reason VSH "thrived" during the 1950's, 1960's and early 1970's was directly because of the CIA.

Why was VSH-UVM shielded during the 1977 Senate hearings? Why was Vermont's role in the CIA drug and mind control programs kept covered up? Why was Vermont's role so much more important to keep covered up than was Harvard, McGill, Johns Hopkins, Cornell, Brown University, Columbia University or Stanford? What happened in VSH-UVM that requires a decades-long cover-up by state and federal officials, and state and federal agencies?

How is it possible, given the huge volume of direct connections to CIA, that Vermont Governors during the 50's, 60's and early 70's were not aware of the CIA experiments? How is it possible that Vermont's Legislature was not aware? How is it possible that the 1977 Senate Select Committee on Intelligence didn't know about Vermont's massive role in the CIA programs? In my opinion, it isn't possible and if they knew about it, they turned their backs on every single mental patient who was used and abused in the VSH-UVM research and they continue to turn their backs, even today.

I believe the primary reason that the Vermont CIA experiments remain covered up is because almost 3000 VSH patients died during the research. The actual number of deaths is not known. I believe that VSH-UVM conducted terminal experiments for CIA and that this is the reason for the cover-up and the reason why I have been harassed for investigating the CIA role in Vermont.

What did Vermont look like in the early 1960's?

1960: Commissioner of Mental Health, Rupert Chittuck

1960: Superintendent of the Vermont State Hospital, Rupert

Chittuck

1960: Assistant Superintendent VSH, H. Peter LaQueur

1960: President of American Psychological Association, George Albee

1960: Governor of Vermont, Robert Stafford

1960: VSH patient deaths, 115

1961: Chairman UVM Department Psychiatry, Thomas Boag. In1960, Boag was Assistant to Director Ewen Cameron at the Allan Memorial Institute

1961: VSH patient deaths, 124

1961-63: President of the American Psychiatric Association, Vermonter, Walter Barton

1962: Vermont Governor, F. Ray Keyser Jr.

1962: Assistant Superintendent VSH, H. Peter LaQueur, member Society for Biological Psychiatry and Manfred Sakel

1962: VSH patient deaths: 116

Author Alston Chase in his book, *Mind For Murder*, explains how CIA used universities, professors, psychiatrists, psychologists and federal funding agencies to cover the drug and mind control experiments conducted on unwitting American citizens:

"CIA had a wide range of associations with universities, colleges, research groups, think tanks, technical schools, secretarial schools and even high schools throughout the country and abroad. The relationships defy simple description."

"Hundreds of college professors had been given special clearances by the Agency's Office of Security to perform a wide variety of tasks for different CIA components...CIA employed individual professors and at times the entire university departments or research institutes for its research and development projects."

"Psychologists within this network...supported secret research with their private funds (Ford, Rockefeller, Russell Sage foundations), thus insuring that this research would remain "off budget" and would never be exposed to congressional oversight."

Chase explains how CIA:

"...relied on federal funding agencies such as the National Institute of Mental Health and the National Science Foundation to support favored projects...it made grants through entirely bogus foundations set up for this purpose."

"The CIA probably used at least 50 foundations in an involved method of funneling funds to certain organizations. Under a method of transfer known as "triple pass," the usual procedure was for CIA to convey funds to "dummy" foundations it had established to act as fronts for its activities. The "dummy" foundations then made grants to legitimate foundations. These foundations, which also handled other funds, then made grants to certain CIA-designated organizations, using the funds from the "dummy" foundations."

The VSH-UVM research project documents show that within the scope of Special Projects #180, there were seven or eight projects within the same grant. For the most part, seven of the eight projects were bland and involved statistical information. It was the eighth project that showed the use of unwitting subjects and experimental drugs.

I suspect that VSH-UVM used "cover projects" such as the ones described above.

My fifteen-year investigation into CIA drug and mind control programs in VSH-UVM began with the name of Dr. Robert W. Hyde in my medical records and the 1961 VSH book, *The Vermont Story*, by Rupert

Chittuck, George Brooks, William Deane and Francis Irons.

William Deane graduated from Andover-Newton Theological School in 1944 and obtained his Ph.D. from Washington University in St. Louis, Missouri. Both institutions were identified as CIA sites. George Brooks completed a six-month post-graduate course at Metropolitan State Hospital in Waltham, Massachusetts, a CIA site. Brooks worked out of the Army General Dispensary in New York City and was stationed during 1944-45 at Nichols General Hospital in Louisville, Kentucky.

H.P. Albarelli writes in his book, *A Terrible Mistake: The Murder of Frank Olson and the CIA's Secret Cold War Experiments*, that Dr. Amedeo Marrazzi, Director of the Clinical Research Division, Army Chemical and Biological Corps, conducted CIA-funded research at the St. Louis State Hospital and the Missouri Institute of Psychiatry, part of the State Hospital, and at the University of Minnesota.

Albarelli writes that the Rockland State Hospital was conducting CIA-Army experiments and that:

"Rockland State Hospital was a notoriously cruel facility that had been shockingly but accurately portrayed in the 1948 award-winning film The Snake Pit, starring Olivia de Havilland. Dr. Paul Hoch decided that Rockland needed a public relations "overhaul.""

Concerning testimony given in 1975 by former employees of Marrazzi and the Missouri Institute, Albarelli writes, "Former employees of the Institute testified in 1975 that the experiments used patients who were homeless and had no relatives in the area."

Marrazzi's criterion for choosing experimental subjects sounds familiar. VSH-UVM's criteria, as stated in their research project documents, were similar.

In VSH-UVM research project documents, USPHS NIMH, MH-

01076 and USPHS No. 1-R11-MH-01076, it is stated that:

"We have been interested in the successful use of (programmed instruction) with emotionally disturbed children at Rockland State Hospital under the supervision of Dr. Gordon Barclay...Dr. Barclay reports indicate we should add this."

The VSH-UVM research relationship with Rockland State Hospital included sending biographical and clinical patient updates using the Rockland Project computer data system. This system included sending the PAS of children at VSH directly to John Gittinger at CIA headquarters in Washington, DC. The Rockland Project is currently a subject about which state and federal officials, the federal funding agencies that supplied the monies to the project, VSH, UVM and Rockland State Hospital all share a collective amnesia.

SIMILARITIES BETWEEN VERMONT DOCUMENTS AND THE CIA-LSD LITERATURE

As part of my investigation, I looked for similarities in the vocabulary, language and attitudes between VSH-UVM documents and published books and papers about LSD. I found many. Specifically, I cross-referenced passages from *The Vermont Story* with publications about LSD. The results were startling:

From the book *Acid Dreams*, by Martin Lee and Bruce Shlain:

"Heisenberg's uncertainty principle stated that the observer influenced the movement of particles observed. LSD research suggests the uncertainty principle was operative in psychology as well, in that the results were conditioned by the investigator's preconceptions."

From the book, *The Vermont Story*, by Chittuck, et al:

"Our approach is also highly progressive and is in the advanced tradition of the natural sciences as reflected by Neils Bohrs and the Heisenberg principle of interdetermanency, (the uncertainty principle)."

From UVM-VSH Special Project #180:

"Our approach is highly progressive and is in the advanced tradition of the natural sciences as reflected by Neils Bohrs and the Heisenberg principle...the uncertainty principle."

From the book, *Acid Dreams*:

"State of consciousness (on LSD) psychedelic therapy familiarity could only be obtained by taking the drug...often times those who underwent psychedelic therapy...reported a whole sale revamping of value systems."

From the book, *The Vermont Story*:

"In some cases this has meant a frank avowal of values...we have asked, "How did I influence this result?"

From the book *Acid Dreams*:

"During the apotheosis of the LSD high self concept may be diminished to the point of depersonalization...LSD apprehension, fear mounting to panic, fear of death and feelings of depersonalization."

From the book, *The Vermont Story*:

"The impending dissolution of the personality which accompanies the experience of fragmentation of the ego is accompanied by a deep seated sense of panic or overwhelming fear."

From the book, *Forgotten Truth* by Huston Smith:

"Death, rebirth...concerned with things other than self...identify with the suffering of others,"

From the book, *The Search For the Manchurian Candidate* by John Marks:

"I didn't want to leave it."

From the book, *The Vermont Story*, VSH patient quotes:

"I didn't understand how people felt before;" " I didn't want to go through it again but I wouldn't want to give it up;" " I became more sympathetic toward people."

From the book, *Acid Dreams*:

"LSD trip hallucinations...fear mounting to panic...intense irritability, suspiciousness, perplexity...feelings of depersonalization...floating in and out of space...between this life and the next."

From the book, *The Vermont Story*:

"Patients seemed confused and had some impairment or distortion of recent or remote memory...they were suspicious, temperamental, unpredictable...they had a very constricted sense of time, space and other people."

From the book *The Use of LSD in Psychotherapy* by Harold Abramson, quote from a patient on LSD:

"I have died and now I have been reborn."

From *The Vermont Story*: Quotes of patients:

"I woke up." " I was risen;" " I came alive again."

VSH doctors wrote in *The Vermont Story*:

"Patients gave detailed descriptions of the strange, unusual and bizarre feelings...hard to explain...it was like being in a nightmare all day and all night, all of the time...nothing seemed real to me...I didn't realize how strange things seemed...I don't have words."

VSH doctors went on to say:

"It frightened patients to talk about it...that it arouses echoes in them of the horror and panic experienced at the time...patients expressed relief from those feelings and said it was a "horrible experience.""

VSH summed it up by saying:

"It seems to us that this information supports the view that something really has happened in the direction of recovery. Some change has taken place in their psychic functioning."

Hyde's MKULTRA Subproject 66 notes that in LSD research:

"...different observers use different methods of assessment closely related to the observers' values."

The book *Acid Dreams* by Martin Lee explains how LSD researchers' values were influenced after experimenting with LSD:

"State of consciousness on LSD psychedelic therapy, to succeed had to be well acquainted with the psychedelic terrain...this familiarity could only be obtained by taking the drug...often times those who underwent psychedelic therapy...reported a wholesale revamping of value systems."

From UVM-VSH Special Project# 180:

“In some case this had meant a frank avowal of values...How did I influence this result? What values did I hold and how did they operate to produce that which has been obtained?”

Hyde’s CIA-LSD MKULTRA Subproject 8:

“Little is known of how adequately or how closely therapist’s self-expectations about their roles as therapists are met in the actual therapeutic interview.”

From Hyde’s MKULTRA Subproject 8 documents:

“...social interaction after LSD...sociological and social psychological measurements such as quality-quantity of verbal production in different structured social situations such as problem solving in group discussion and occupational task situations.”

Hyde writes that the subject’s ability to describe the subjective experience during LSD has been limited to words like “ weird,” “strange,” etc. and that it was important to get better descriptions of the experience.

Several noteworthy books written about LSD by authors Martin Lee, John Marks, Huston Smith and Harold Abramson contain descriptions by subjects under the influence of LSD. These descriptions include:

"Concern with things other than self...death, rebirth... identify with the suffering of others...I have died and been reborn...I didn’t want to leave it...”

From UVM-VSH Special Project #180, quotes by patients include:

"I didn't understand how people felt before...I didn't want to go through it again but I wouldn't want to give it up...I woke up...I came to... I was risen...I came alive again...It's hard to explain. It was something like being in a nightmare...nothing seemed real to me." " Patients were able to indicate that they had a very strange or unusual experience..." "I didn't realize how strange things seemed... It's very hard to explain... I don't have words for it."

Statements by UVM-VSH doctors include:

"Many stated spontaneously that it frightened them to talk about it, that it aroused echoes in them of horror and panic they experienced at the time. They expressed a great relief from those feelings...I have so much more sympathy for others...The concern and feelings which patients show for each other after release seems to validate such statements...49% of patients said the drugs...had been an important factor in their recovery."

"The question was asked, "Was there a turning point when things started to clear up for you?" Eighty-two percent named a specific incident or a specific day...when things cleared up for them. Fifty percent said it was related to...drugs."

From Hyde's CIA MKULTRA Subproject 66, 1957-1958:

"Prospectus - 1. Prediction of subject's reaction to drugs in various situations. 2. Placing different personalities in different structured situations. 3. Making large groups available to Externalizer by using the total culture of the hospital. 4. Making solitude available to the Internalizer. 5. Force isolation on subject. 6. Force group participation."

The references to "Externalizer" and "Internalizer" are direct links to John Gittinger's Personality Assessment System (PAS). Gittinger system used the terms "Externalizer" and "Internalizer" in his PAS as a way to calculate whether the subject was more introverted or more extroverted. Hyde used Gittinger's PAS extensively in his LSD research and UVM-VSH used Gittinger's PAS beginning in 1958.

There is little doubt that VSH patients were subjected to LSD, based on the content of the UVM-VSH documents and based on the fact that UVM was experimenting with LSD and Mescaline, according to Albarelli. UVM-VSH documents note numerous times that occupational therapy, industrial therapy, and a "re-education in social values" were prominent in the research. Hyde's CIA documents repeatedly refer to his LSD experiments for CIA and the interest in "social situations" and "the social attributes of the subject...social interaction and social adjustment."

Hyde's MKULTRA Subproject 10 notes include a statement that:

"...interpersonal interactions defining social personality...are observed in relationship to LSD as well as his interest in...observing individual's reactions to specified social situations."

From *The Use of LSD in Psychotherapy* by MKULTRA contractor, Harold Abramson:

"Studying the social interactions of individuals under drugs can help in the identification of properties of social systems. We can see a great usefulness in drugs like LSD and others in creating a kind of experimental social science."

UVM-VSH 1962 project, RD-1062-P-M references "social integration," the "cultural personality configuration," the "re-socialization of patients and the social functioning" of patients. This research project is noted to have begun in 1955. This particular project initially carried the designation in May, 1962 of NACVR but was changed in June, 1962 to RD-1062-P-M. VR was likely Vocational Rehabilitation. The "N" and the" AC" are interesting in their implications for the funding source for this project.

The Navy used the designation letter N in its research. The Army Chemical Corps used the designation AC. Were the Navy and the Army funding UVM-VSH research in 1962?

Dr. Harris Isbell, a prominent CIA-LSD researcher, was cleared at TOP SECRET as a contractor on MKULTRA Subproject 73. He conducted his research under the Office of Naval Research (ONR) in 1962; according to H.P. Albarelli Jr., "for apparent security reasons...the ONR funding ended and was picked up by another CIA front."

Hyde's research publications during this time frame include:

"The Rehabilitation of the Mentally Ill: Impact of a Project upon the Hospital Culture," Coauthors on this 1968 paper were Hyde, Greenblatt, Bockoven and Landy.

"The Effects of LSD on Group Interaction," Hyde, Slater, Morimoto, 1963. "Patient Government: A New Form of Therapy," Hyde and Solomon, 1951.

"Experimental Schizophrenia-like Symptoms," Hyde, Rinkel, DeShon and Solomon, 1952.

Bellak notes in his 1958 book, *Schizophrenia: A Review of the Syndrome* that:

"Hyde and Solomon at Boston Psychopathic Hospital discuss a

group therapy project...the program took the form of patient government which permitted the patients to participate in hospital administration and contribute to their own personal care and comfort...they developed a sense of personal responsibility which contributed to their own recovery and feelings of freedom and a desire to be of service to others...however in order for such a program to be effective, the hospital administration must be ready to democratically share authority."

From UVM-VSH Special Project #180:

"It is difficult to see how the full therapeutic potential can be mustered unless administration permits a large amount of autononomous thinking and acting on the part of the staff...we can discuss the effective use of ancillary personnel from a somewhat different perspective which calls attention to the essential differences between a total institution and the democratic society. The gap between the culture in a total institution and a democratic society can only be filled by changes in the total institution or democratic society."

"Group activities are designed to encourage group cooperation... they are graded to direct the interests of patients first toward each other, then toward the entire hospital and finally, the community...we feel fortunate to have returned to the refreshing positivism of moral treatment."

"Are there marked differences between the type of democratization of the mental hospital represented by our policy of graduation and piece-meal assumption of responsibilities by patient communities and the more and less as patients. . ."

"A patient government which does not have real power is not a government."

UVM-VSH documents refer to the beginning of their research

efforts in 1955 with “a reorganization of the present project in 1957.”

Noted in the bibliography of the project:

John Bockoven, “Moral Treatment in American Psychiatry,” 1956.

Also noted:

“Moral Treatment and the Mental Hospital,” Lucy Ozarin, 1954. Lucy Ozarin was a research partner of Robert Hyde, as was Bockoven.

It would appear that UVM-VSH were utilizing Hyde’s CIA playbook over and over again. UVM-VSH adopted the same methods and procedures being employed by Hyde and other CIA researchers like Bockoven, Greenblatt, Solomon and Rinkel.

From Hyde’s MKULTRA Subproject 8:

“It is the responsibility of the examiner to successfully be an annoyer until the subject can no longer tolerate the frustration experience. Since this is a motor task, discharge of tension through over activity could be observed.”

From UVM-VSH *Psychomotility, Drugs and Schizophrenic Rehabilitation*:

“Positive reinforcement tends to raise the level of performance for simple motor tasks but is less effective for more complex tasks.”

From UVM-VSH Special Project #180:

“DiMascio and Rinkel have applied a battery of psychomotor

tests as part of an effort to predict the effectiveness of psychopharmologic agents."

From Hyde's MKULTRA Subproject 10 Prospectus:

"In the past three years of research with the drug LSD-25, we have developed reliable methods of analyzing social situations and interactions. Our progress in assessing personality types is useful in diagnosis and prediction. These methods are based on a multi-discipline assessment of personality in dynamic social adjustment under normal circumstances and under stress, i.e. drug effect, irrespective of the attributes of any specific drug."

"The briefest phrase to characterize our main area of study is "social personality." A laboratory of experimental social psychiatry has been established in such a way that various types of personality and many situations may be subjected to critical study. For example, its methods can be applied to any specific problem such as the effects of LSD or other drugs like alcohol, on the improvement of interpersonal relations."

"Trying out the utility of these tests and our special interview and questionnaire methods developed in the course of our studies for predicting specifiable change in social behavior following the ingestion of various drugs, particularly LSD and alcohol."

From UVM-VSH Special Project #180:

"Indeed most of the methods of social science have been utilized... questionnaires and schedules have been administered to patients and formal interviews with patients and staff have been frequent."

From UVM-VSH Special Project #180:

"One of the implicit moral imperatives of the project has been to fit the method to the situation. If sometimes the method seemed to lead us to the outer peripheries of scientific respectability, as normally defined, we have not been alarmed."

"Participant observation...becomes a method by which we bridge the gap between speculation and observed fact is made and the method by which an observed fact can be speculated upon and further developed... findings resulting from participant observation may be expressed qualitatively rather than quantitatively but that the demands on the observer are very great in the sense that he is called upon to enter the social field in the fullest possible way, taking into account of all that goes on while giving himself to the ensuing activities in a natural and spontaneous fashion."

From *The Use of LSD In Psychotherapy*:

"The problem is complicated because we are not studying the drug itself, but, rather, a partnership of the therapist and the assistant, both working simultaneously, the drug in this case, being the assistant. Ordinarily, the interaction of the therapist with the drug itself is only modified by a subtle skepticism or a tempered enthusiasm for a new compound. With LSD, a novel situation obtains, because both the conscious and the unconscious attitudes of the therapist and patient as well as the community as a whole, toward the production of a psychotic process in the patient as part of therapy, may and usually do contaminate the therapeutic process in unusual ways. The therapist himself suffers more than the usual amount of scrutiny."

From *Acid Dreams*:

"Scientific objectivity - Heisenberg's uncertainty principle stated that the observer influenced movement of particles observed. LSD research suggested that the uncertainty principle was operative in psychology...in that the results were conditioned by the investigator's preconceptions..."

From UVM-VSH Special Project #180:

"The usual canons of scientific objectivity necessary to the use of scientific methodology have to be reconsidered. We have approached each situation with both a research and therapy orientation. In some cases this has meant a frank avowal of values. In other cases we have not been aware of what values we did hold but in making a retrospective analysis of a situation we have asked, "How did I influence this result? What values did I hold and how did these operate to produce that which was obtained?" In either case we have recognized the existence of a value system and rather than attempting to rid ourselves of it, we have attempted to analyze it...our approach is also highly progressive and is in the advanced tradition of the natural sciences as reflected by Neils Bohrs and the Heisenberg principle... the uncertainty principle."

Hyde's MKULTRA Subproject 10 notes an interest in:

"...interpersonal interactions of subjects...and defining social personalities..."

From Hyde's MKULTRA Subproject 66 notes, Hyde's research interests included:

"training non-professional observers," "environmental events and agents...and predicting reactions to specified social situations in subject's environment."

From UVM-VSH Special Project #180:

"Non-medical staff can have considerable latitude in dealing with patients...the latitude should be so great as to include autonomy in all areas other than the medical phase of patient care...this kind of freedom aids the effective emergence of therapeutic trends and makes realistic the attempt to satisfy needs of the familial order...it is difficult to see how the full therapeutic potential can be mustered unless administration permits a large amount of autonomous thinking and acting on the part of the staff..."

From *The Use of LSD in Psychotherapy*: Gregory Bateson is quoted as saying:

" My interest in LSD began when Dr. Abramson gave me LSD two years ago...One of my interests is in something which I call "schizophrenia" in particular the formal patterns, the formal characteristics of experience of members of families containing schizophrenics. We have been trying to relate the characteristic distortions of schizophrenic behavior to formal characteristics of experience within these families, as a function of how these families are organized. Whether or not these two approaches, experiences with the drug and experiences with families are in any way...related"

The bibliography of UVM-VSH research project RD-1062-P-M contains the citation, Gregory Bateson, "Group Dynamics of Schizophrenia," 1960.

From UVM-VSH Special Project #180:

"In order to establish the fact that patients do have therapeutic relationships with each other we need to know if friendships actually developed among patients. In this case the observational method was implemented by the use of sociometrics, quantitative analysis of who speaks to whom and who sat next to whom at meetings...a checklist was filled out by attendants on ward interaction...Indeed most of the methods of social science have been utilized...questionnaires and formal interviews with patients and staff have been frequent."

From UVM-VSH RD-1062-P-M:

"Do successful patients solve problems of the home while hospitalized by either establishing new and positive relationships with family members or by rejecting or being rejected by them? We are also concerned with the question of changes in family relationships between patients and families and if such changes or their absence associate with post hospital success."

"Bateson has described the double bind family pattern of the schizophrenic and has in fact suggested that schizophrenia is a disease of communication which most affects the weakest member of the family but is at the same time pervasive in all family transactions."

From *The Use of LSD in Psychotherapy:*

Sandison: "The hospital environment is a very complex thing, but it as a whole, may determine success or failure."

Eisner: "By environment I understand you mean the hospital in general? Do you also mean, specifically, the person or persons who are with the individual under treatment...whether or not the therapist has had much experience with LSD; what the expectations of the therapist are? Do you call this environment?"

Sandison: "Include the environment. The particular environment I was thinking about was the whole administrative, structural hospital. Whether LSD will be given individually or in a group, in what kind of room, whether the data will be recorded...these are administrative aspects."

Whittlesey: "Can you describe the setting a bit?"

Malitz: "Yes. These are hospitalized patients in a psychiatric hospital on a ward devoted exclusively to psychiatric research techniques."

Bateson: "Do these techniques include lobotomy?"

Malitz: "Yes."

Bateson: "This is part of the situation then, let's not forget it."

Malitz: "Not all of them, just some of them."

Murphy: "No, it's part of the environment."

Bateson: "Yes, an essential part of the environment in which the experiment (LSD) was conducted."

John Marks writes about Hyde's research group that, "The quality of a person's reaction (LSD) was determined by the person's basic personality structure or SET and the environment (SETTING) in which the subject took LSD."

From *Acid Dreams*:

"Practitioners of LSD therapy were cognizant of the complex interaction between the SET and the SETTING."

From UVM-VSH Special Project #180:

"A new type of data...research-researcher is an integral part of how things turn out, which is on an order best described as a penetration of the ethos rather than as a description or an analysis of behavior from a position apart...Because the researcher appreciates the role he plays in the social situation he becomes aware of the subjects of research in a different way. Patients become not merely people to be studied but they become participants in the research. Their statements about how they feel, what schizophrenia is like, what reactions they produce in the researcher, what they say by way of suggestions for programming and so on, are all taken seriously and given a validity on par with any other information a researcher might obtain through his own intellectual and methodological efforts."

From Hyde's CIA MKULTRA Subproject 66:

"Training of non-professional observers...to determine observations employed to predict reactions to situations other than the administration of LSD...Such situations include the rehabilitation of hospitalized patients (mental)."

The similarities between the LSD literature and the VSH-UVM documents confirm that VSH researchers were familiar with the LSD literature, and must have used LSD on unwitting patients at VSH, including myself.

DOCUMENTS

DR. HYDE DOCUMENTS

SECRET
(When Filled In)

ACCOUNTING BY INDIVIDUAL FOR ADVANCE

NOTE: Follow Instructions on Reverse

SUBMITTED BY: MKULTRA Sub 63

PERIOD OF ACCOUNTING: FROM 1 January 1962 TO 31 December 1962

VOUCHER NO. (Finance use only)

RECEIPTS			
1. CASH ON HAND BEGINNING OF PERIOD			$
1a.			
2. RECEIPT NUMBER	DATE	DESCRIPTION	
	30 Dec. 1961	MKULTRA Sub 63 Invoice 14 MKCOTTON	5,580.00
		TOTAL TO ACCOUNT FOR	$5,580.00

DISBURSEMENTS			
3. VOUCHER NUMBER	DATE	DESCRIPTION	AMOUNT
			$
		See Attached Certification	
3a.		Total Expenses	5,580.00
4. REFUNDED HEREWITH		CASH / CHECK / MONEY ORDER	
5. CASH ON HAND END OF PERIOD			
		TOTAL ACCOUNTED FOR	$5,580.00

I CERTIFY FUNDS ARE AVAILABLE

OBLIGATION REFERENCE NO.: 2320 — CHARGE ALLOTMENT NO.: MI25-1390-3902

DATE: 26 AUG 1964 — SIGNATURE OF AUTHORIZING OFFICER

APPROVED — DATE: 25 AUG 1964 — SIGNATURE OF APPROVING OFFICER: Sidney Gottlieb, DC/TSD

CERTIFIED FOR PAYMENT OR CREDIT — DATE — SIGNATURE OF CERTIFYING OFFICER

I certify that the expenditures listed hereon and on any attachments were incurred for official purposes of a confidential nature, that payment or credit therefor has not been received, and that this accounting is true and correct.

SIGNATURE OF PAYEE: John W. Gittinger

SPACE BELOW FOR EXCLUSIVE USE OF FINANCE DIVISION

PREPARED BY — REVIEWED BY — VOUCHER NO. 7-12

23-39 DESCRIPTION - ALL OTHER ACCOUNTS / DESCRIPTION - A/P ITEMS 13-34 / DESCRIPTION - ADVANCE ACCOUNTS 13-24	34-39 PAYABLE VOU. NO.	40-42 EXPEND CODE	45-46 PAY PER. LIQ. CODE	47-52 OBLIG REF. NO. ADVANCE ACCT. NO. EMP. NO.	53 FI YR	54-57 GENERAL LEDGER ACCT. NO.	59-67 ALLOT. LEDGER ACCT. NO. 62-67 CK. NO. X VOU. NO.	68-70 DUE DATE OBJECT CL	
									check
									Crypt MKcotton

FORM 6-57 282 USE PREVIOUS EDITIONS. (1)

SECRET

63-5

~~SECRET~~

7 December 1961

MEMORANDUM FOR: THE RECORD

SUBJECT : Transfer of Project MKULTRA, Subproject No. 63 to MKCOTTON H

1. The research of [redacted] which has been funded to date through Subproject No. 63, is currently being integrated into the total research effort of the Human Ecology Fund (MKCOTTON). C B B H

2. The balance of the funds for Subproject No. 63 will be sent to the Human Ecology Fund for disbursal to [redacted] Accounting for these funds shall accord to practices established for the Fund. With the transfer of the remaining funds, Subproject No. 63 shall be considered closed. B C B

[redacted] A
Chief
TSD/Research Branch

~~SECRET~~

A-2
8/95

SECTION I

DEPARTMENT OF HEALTH, EDUCATION, AND WELFARE
PUBLIC HEALTH SERVICE

APPLICATION FOR GRANT

(Check one) ☐ MENTAL HEALTH PROJECT GRANT
☐ MENTAL HEALTH HOSPITAL IMPROVEMENT GRANT

LEAVE BLANK (For PHS Office Use Only)

TYPE	PROGRAM	NUMBER
REVIEW GROUP		FORMERLY
COUNCIL (Month, Year)		DATE RECEIVED
APPLICANT CODE		O CODE

TO BE COMPLETED BY PROGRAM DIRECTOR (Items 1 through 9 and 17A)

1. ABBREVIATED TITLE OF PROPOSAL (Do not exceed 53 typewriter spaces)
A STATE HOSPITAL CENTER FOR EDUCATIONAL THERAPY

2. TYPE OF APPLICATION (Check one)
☐ NEW PROJECT
☐ REVISION OR PHS APPLICATION NO. ______
☒ RENEWAL OF PHS GRANT NO. 02037
☐ SUPPLEMENT TO PHS GRANT NO. ______

3. DATES OF ENTIRE PROPOSED PROJECT PERIOD (This application)
FROM: May 1, 1968 THROUGH: April 30, 1972

4. TOTAL AMOUNT REQUESTED FOR PERIOD IN ITEM 3: $403,353.

5. AMOUNT REQUESTED FOR FIRST 12-MONTH PERIOD: $93,583.

6A. NAME OF PROGRAM DIRECTOR (Last, First, Initial)
Chittick, Rupert A.
Hyde, Robert W., M/D., Co-Director

B. DEGREE: M.D.
C. SOCIAL SECURITY NO.: 009-26-1620
D. TELEPHONE DATA: Area Code 802 Telephone No. 244-7331

E. TITLE OF POSITION: Superintendent

F. DEPARTMENT, SERVICE, LABORATORY OR EQUIVALENT (See Instructions): Mental Health

G. MAJOR SUBDIVISION (See Instructions)

H. MAILING ADDRESS OF PROGRAM DIRECTOR (Street, City, State, Zip Code)
Vermont State Hospital
Waterbury, Vermont 05676

7A. IDENTIFY ORGANIZATIONAL COMPONENT RESPONSIBLE FOR CONDUCT OF SCIENTIFIC ASPECTS OF PROJECT
Vermont State Hospital

B. DEPARTMENT: Mental Health

8. ADDRESS WHERE PROJECT WILL BE CONDUCTED (If same as Item 6H, check box) ☒

9. ARE FEDERAL FACILITIES TO BE USED FOR THIS PROJECT?
☒ NO ☐ YES ______ % OF TIME

TO BE COMPLETED BY RESPONSIBLE ADMINISTRATIVE AUTHORITY (Items 10 through 15 and 17B)

10. APPLICANT ORGANIZATION (Name and Address-Street, City, State, Zip Code) (See Instructions)
Vermont State Hospital
Waterbury, Vermont 05676

11. NAME, TITLE AND ADDRESS OF OFFICIAL TO WHOM CHECKS SHOULD BE MAILED
Peter J. Hincks, Treasurer
State of Vermont
Montpelier, Vermont 05602

12. TYPE OF ORGANIZATION (Check applicable item) ☐ INDIVIDUAL
PUBLIC INSTITUTION: ☐ FEDERAL ☒ STATE ☐ LOCAL ☐ OTHER
PRIVATE INSTITUTION: ☐ NONPROFIT, ☐ PROFIT

13. NAME AND TITLE OF OFFICIAL SIGNING FOR APPLICANT ORGANIZATION
R. A. Chittick, M.D.
Superintendent

14. PHS ACCOUNT NUMBER (Enter if known): 869124

15. ESTABLISHED INDIRECT COST RAT (See Instructions) ______

16. TERMS AND CONDITIONS. The undersigned accept, as to any grant awarded, the obligation to comply with Public Health Se vice Research Project Grant Regulations in effect at the time of the award (42 CFR, Part 52) and the terms and conditions in t Grants for Research Projects Policy Statement. The undersigned further agree to comply with Title VI of the Civil Rights Act 1964 (P.L. 88-352), and the Regulation issued pursuant thereto and state that the formally filed Assurance of Compliance w such Regulation (Form HEW-441) applies to this project. The undersigned also certify that they have no commitments or oblig tions, including those with respect to inventions, inconsistent with compliance to the above.

17. SIGNATURES (Use ink. "Per" signatures not acceptable)

		DATE
A. SIGNATURE OF PERSON NAMED IN ITEM 6A		
B. SIGNATURE OF PERSON NAMED IN ITEM 13		

PAGE 1

Form Approved
Budget Bureau No. 68-R 61

DRAFT- A
26 May 1954

MEMORANDUM FOR THE RECORD

SUBJECT: Project MKULTRA, Subproject 10

1. Subproject 10 is being set up as a means to continue the present work in the general field of L.S.D. at the [redacted] B
B [redacted] from 15 June 1954 until 15 September 1955.

2. This project will include a continuation of a study of the biochemical, neurophysiological, sociological, and clinical psychiatric aspects of L.S.D., and also a study of L.S.D. antagonists and drugs related to L.S.D., such as L.A.E. A detailed proposal is attached. The principle investigators will continue to
C be [redacted] and [redacted] all of C
B [redacted]

3. Original Subproject 10 for the sum of $32,000.00 was initiated for the production of certain rare organic chemicals. The committed money was never actually spent. It is the proposal of TSS/CD to add an additional $10,744.00 to the original sum of Subproject 10 making a total of $42,744.00 to underwrite the present proposal which is attached. [redacted] will B serve as a cut-out and cover for this project and will furnish the above funds to the [redacted] as a philanthropic B grant for medical research. A service charge of $1,644.00 (4% of the estimated cost) is to be paid to [redacted] for B this service.

4. Thus the total charges for this project will not exceed $42,744.00 for the period ending 15 September 1955.

C
5. [redacted] and [redacted] B-C
B [redacted] are cleared through TOP SECRET and are aware of the true purpose of the project.

Sidney Gottlieb
SIDNEY GOTTLIEB
Chief
Chemical Division, TSS

Downgraded to CONFIDENTIAL
by authority of 187475
date JUN 1977

EXEMPTED BY

HOSPITAL DOCUMENTS

February 17, 1971

Mrs. George Wetmore
38 Maple Street
Brandon, Vermont

Dear Mrs. Wetmore:

I am sorry for the long delay in answering your letter of November 29 regarding your daughter, Karen, who is at the Vermont State Hospital. As you are aware, many different episodes have occurred in the management of Karen's case since last October. This problem has been thoroughly investigated and has been discussed frequently by Dr. Curlin, Dr. Hyde, Dr. Laqueur, Dr. Havas, and Dr. Treial.

All the aspects of the case have been thoroughly investigated by the Department. The particular time that you mention in your letter was especially difficult and there are very detailed notes from that period. As long as there was a suspicion that Karen had hepatitis, it was necessary to try to prevent her from infecting others. Her behavior was very difficult and at times she represented a real danger to herself or others. She was never, of course, left for three days and nights unattended in a separate room as all patients are taken out at frequent intervals for care and exercise and an opportunity to use the toilet.

I do hope that if we can all work together, we will eventually be able to help Karen out of this very distressing situation so that she may go and make a life for herself.

Very truly yours,

Jonathan P. A. Leopold, M.D.,
Commissioner
Department of Mental Health

JPAL/GWB/vrg

MEDICAL CENTER HOSPITAL OF VERMONT
ELECTROENCEPHALOGRAM REPORT

DATE June 28, 1971 ROOM OR OUT. PT. Pav. 4
NAME Karen Wetmore HOSP. NO. 5421763
ADDRESS Vermont ST. HOsp. AGE 19 SEX F
TOWN STATE Waterbury, Vt. DOB 52
PHYSICIAN Dr. Poser

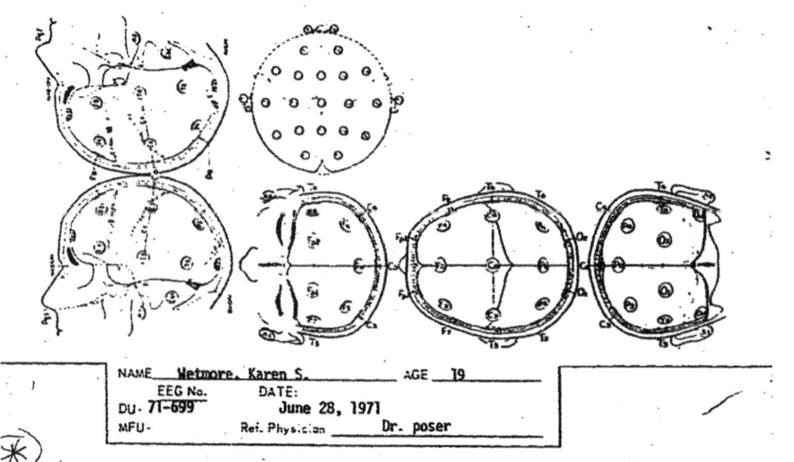

NAME Wetmore, Karen S. AGE 19
EEG No. DU- 71-699 DATE: June 28, 1971
MFU- Ref. Physician Dr. poser

This is a 19-year-old girl with episodes of violent behavior, depression, and a question of temporal lobe seizures. The present record was a length record with Metrazol activation.

EEG Description: In the resting state this record consisted predominantly of low voltage fast, but occasional irregular alpha activity at 8-10 Hz was discernible as in previous recordings. This patient was extremely anxious and had frequent intermittent muscle artifact due to gritting of the jaws, movements or talking.

An intravenous injection was started of 5 % dextrose in water. Metrazol was slowly injected according to a modification of the method of Torres. one half cc. (50 mg.) of metrazol was given approximately every 30 seconds (on occasion, 45 seconds elapsed) with intravenous Valium and phenobarbital on hand for immediate injection. Following approximately 10-12 cc. of Metrazol (a total of 1,000 to 1200 mg.), some slight change in the record occurred in the direction of slowing with theta activity becoming more prominent, particularly in central regions. The patient had mounting apprehension and following a total of 1400 mg. of Metrazol she became upset with crying. The injections were continued during which there occurred increasing amounts of muscle artifact with the patient becoming more and more upset and more prominent low voltage to moderate voltage fast activity in all head regions with interposed muscle artifact. Following 17 cc. of Metrazol (1700 mg.) superimposed on the muscle artifact there did occur a high voltage, irregular slow and sharp wave which could have been artifactual or a real discharge. At that point 2.5 mg. of Valium was given intravenously. The record continued to be dominated mostly by muscle artifact, however, one minute later during a relatively quiet period, the Metrazol injection was continued up to a total of 1800 mg. At that time the record became uninterpretable because of diffuse muscle artifact. The

Physician's Signature ______

MEDICAL CENTER HOSPITAL OF VERMONT

ELECTROENCEPHALOGRAM REPORT

DATE June 28, 1971 . OR OUT PT. Pav.4

NAME Karen Wetmore HOSP NO

ADDRESS AGE SEX

TOWN, STATE DOB

PHYSICIAN

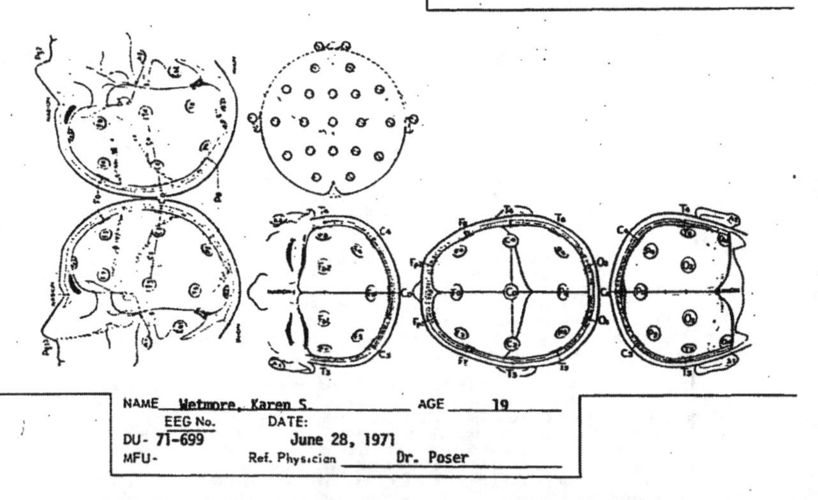

NAME Wetmore, Karen S. AGE 19

EEG No. DATE:

DU- 71-699 June 28, 1971

MFU- Ref. Physician Dr. Poser

patient was obviously very clinically upset, however, no epileptiform discharges were seen. 200 mg. of phenobarb were injected IV shortly thereafter.

Immediately following the Metrazol injection the patient was questioned in her emotionally upset state regarding feelings and sensations. My notes indicated that she said the following: "I never felt this way before". "You gave me the medicine and it made me do this. My legs feel all funny. I am seeing different people in different colors. My back aches. I never felt this way before. You mad me do it. (Cough). It made me cough. I am so sick inside; not mentally, but physically. My head hurts, my back hurts, I have to cough. I am seeing things that arent there. My ears are ringing." The patient rapdily quieted down following the IV administration of phenbbarbital.

EEG Interpretation: This patient exhibited an extremely high tolerance to Metrazol, 1800 mg. did not precipitate any discharges. This fact may well be due to the phenobarb which she had recently been on and, indeed, 100 mg. of phenobarbital was given in the early morning on which this record was run. No physical signs of seizure activity were observed during or immediately after the injection. The patient's subjective sensations are recorded above and at the time seemed to represent more anxiety than the hallucinations of seizure activity. In any event, no EEG abnormality was seen concommittant with these sensations, although the record was quite artifactual because of muscle potentials during that time. In conclusion, the Metrazol activation fails to activate a temporal lobe discharge, and suggests a very high threshold to Metrazol, possibly related to previous medication:

Pav.4
Dr. Poser
EEG/H

Physician's Signature Dictated but not proofread by:
Buntington Mavor, M.D

Page DD-3

VERMONT STATE HOSPITAL

No. 17998 Name KAREN WETMORE

TESTED: DECEMBER 21 & 22, 1965 BIRTHDATE: , 1952

PSYCHOLOGICAL REPORT (CON'T.)

THE RORSCHACH RESULTS SUPPORT THE PICTURE GIVEN ABOVE OF AN INDIVIDUAL WHO IS STRONGLY INTROVERSIVE RATHER THAN EXTRATENSIVE AND WHO IS UNLIKELY TO ENGAGE IN A GREAT DEAL OF OVERT REACTION TO ENVIRONMENTAL STIMULI EVEN AS SHE IS STIMULATED SOMEWHAT MORE THAN NORMALLY BY SUCH STIMULI. IN SHORT WE GET SOMETHING OF THE REPRESSIVE PICTURE FOUND IN HYSTERIA. SOME OF THE RORSCHACH CONCEPTS WERE OF QUESTIONABLE QUALITY, AND AGAIN WE SEEM TO HAVE SUPPORT OF THE PICTURE DESCRIBED ABOVE OF AN INDIVIDUAL WHO MAY BECOME SOMEWHAT UNCONVENTIONAL, SOMETIMES EVEN BIZARRE, UNLESS SHE HAS ACCEPTABLE EXTERNAL GUIDANCE AND DISCIPLINE. ONE ALSO FINDS EVIDENCE OF ANXIETY AND TENSION. THESE IN TURN MAY CAUSE PECULIAR BEHAVIOR AT TIMES.

HOWEVER, THE RORSCHACH DOES NOT IMPRESS ME AS INDICATING A PSYCHOSIS, THOUGH THE PATIENT MAY SHOW SCHIZOID TRAITS. IN MY OPINION THE PRESENT RORSCHACH RESULTS SUGGEST MORE A NEUROTIC INDIVIDUAL WHO MAY SHOW SYMPTOMS SUCH AS MIGHT BE FOUND IN ANXIETY HYSTERIA. AT TIMES SHE MAY BECOME DEPRESSED AND EVEN ENGAGE IN IMPULSIVE SUICIDAL GESTURES. HOWEVER, THERE SEEMS TO BE ENOUGH OF THE HYSTERICAL AND DISSOCIATIVE TO CAUSE HER TO HAVE ONLY A CONFUSED, ALMOST AMNESIC REACTION TO SUCH EPISODES.

THE RORSCHACH RESULTS ALSO SUGGEST THAT DURING THE PATIENT'S EARLY YEARS SHE SUFFERED FROM EGO MALNUTRITION AND ALSO THAT SHE WAS SOMETHING OF A BASE OF CONTENTION BETWEEN HER PARENTS. OR POSSIBLY SHE EXPERIENCED THE CONFLICT, DISCUSSED EARLIER, BETWEEN WHAT SHE WANTED TO BE AND WHAT OTHERS TRIED TO MAKE HER BECOME. IN VIEW OF ALL THAT HAS BEEN SAID IT IS INTERESTING THAT THE HUMAN IDENTIFICATION CARD WAS THE CARD LIKED LEAST "BECAUSE I JUST DON'T LIKE IT." THE HELPLESSNESS AND DEPENDENCY MENTIONED EARLIER SEEMS TO BE IN THE RORSCHACH PICTURE TOO.

THE RORSCHACH ALSO SUGGEST THAT THE PATIENT HAS NEVER BEEN ABLE TO HAVE THE RELATIONSHIP WITH HER FATHER THAT SHE'D LIKE TO HAVE AND THAT SHE WISHES SHE WERE A BOY RATHER THAN A GIRL. THIS MAY BE ONE REFLECTION OF AN UNRESOLVED ELECTRA COMPLEX. IF THIS BE SO, THEN THE PATIENT'S GUILT FEELINGS MAY WELL BE AGGRAVATED BY THIS.

THESE TEST RESULTS ALSO INDICATE A DESIRE TO BE LOVED AND ACCEPTED, TO BE CONSIDERED INTELLIGENT, AND BEAUTIFUL. IF THIS SEEMS TO CONTRADICT WHAT HAS BEEN SAID ABOUT WANTING TO BE A BOY, THEN LET THIS BE CONSIDERED AS FURTHER EVIDENCE OF THE PATIENT'S CONFUSION AND AMBIVALENCE.

THE BENDER REVEALS STRONG AMBIVALENCE AND DUALITY OF ROLE. CERTAINLY THE BENDER RESULTS SHOW A GREAT DEAL OF DIFFICULTY IN INTERPERSONAL RELATIONSHIPS. SOMETIMES HER REACTION IS THAT OF WITHDRAWAL; AT OTHER TIMES SHE SEEKS TO HAVE CLOSER RELATIONSHIPS, BUT SHE SEEKS RATHER CLUMSILY. THE REASONS FOR THIS SHOULD BE CLEAR BY THIS TIME. THE BENDER RESULTS ARE ALSO REMARKABLE FOR THE INDICATIONS OF REGRESSION AND REGRESSIVE ACTIVITY WHICH THE PATIENT MAY DISPLAY AT TIMES IN HER CONTINUING QUEST FOR LOVE, ACCEPTANCE, AND A DEPENDENCY RELATION-

WILLIAM H. SORRELL
ATTORNEY GENERAL
SUSANNE YOUNG
DEPUTY ATTORNEY GENERAL
WILLIAM E. GRIFFIN
CHIEF ASST. ATTORNEY
GENERAL

TEL: (802) 828-2163
FAX: (802) 828-2468

http://www.atg.state.vt.us

STATE OF VERMONT
OFFICE OF THE ATTORNEY GENERAL
LEGAL DIVISION
26 TERRACE STREET
REDSTONE BLDG.
MONTPELIER, VT
05609-1101

October 16, 2013

Karen Wetmore

VT

Re: Public Records Request, received October 9, 2013

Dear Ms. Wetmore:

The records you requested in your letter, dated October 7, 2013, are not available because they were discarded pursuant to a public records retention schedule, effective March 3, 2010, on file with the State Archives & Records Administration.

Under the records retention schedule, contracts are retained for three years past the expiration date of the contract. Generally, financial files (invoices, payment information, etc.) are kept for five years beyond the end of the fiscal year they were relevant to.

Since the records you requested are about 50 years old, they were discarded pursuant to the record schedule approved by the State Archivist. *See* 1 V.S.A. § 317a.

Sincerely,

Philip Back
Assistant Attorney General
Department of Mental Health

91st PSALM

He who dwells in the shadow of the Most High
will rest in the shadow of the Almighty.
I will say of the Lord, “He is my refuge and my fortress,
My God, in whom I trust.”
Surely He will save you from the fowler’s snare
and from the deadly pestilence.
He will cover you with His feathers
And under His wings you will find refuge
You will not fear the terror of the night
nor the arrow that flies by day,
nor the pestilence that stalks at mid-day.
A thousand may fall at your side,
ten thousand at your right hand,
but it will not come near you.
You will only observe with your eyes
and see the punishment of the wicked.
If you make the Most High your dwelling,
even the Lord, who is my refuge,
then no harm will befall you,
no disaster will come near your tent.
For He will command his angels concerning you,
To guard you in all your ways;
They will lift you up in their hands,
so that you will not strike your foot against a stone.
You will tread upon the lion and the serpent
“Because he loves me,” says the Lord, “ I will rescue him;
“I will protect him, for he acknowledges my name.
“He will call upon me and I will answer him.”

I will be with him in trouble,"
I will deliver him and honor him,
with long life I will satisfy him,
And show him my salvation."

REFERENCES

Vermont State Hospital and University of Vermont College of Medicine research project documents:

1. MY - 1752, Special Projects No. 180, HEW, Vocational Rehabilitation, 1957-1958.
2. MY- 02037, 1965-67.
3. MY-1752-RISI, 1958.
4. RD - 1894-P, destroyed at Vermont Public Records Division, Middlesex, VT.
5. MH - 01076, 1963-66.
6. MH - 01752-06, 1963.
7. 02037 - Application grant renewal, 1968.
8. OM - 372, 1958-1962.
9. No.1-1-R11-MH-01076, 1963.
10. RD - 1062-PM, NACVR, 1962.
11. RD - 1062-P-65, 1957.
12. AF (604)1093, UVM-SAM, 1955.
13. MH -17350-01, 1969.

Additional Material:

14. ACHRE, Advisory Committee on Human Radiation Experiments, 1994.
15. *Rutland Herald*, September 4, 2005, Jarris statement.
16. *Rutland Herald-Barre-Times Argus Associated Press*, November 30, 2008, “Evidence Suggests CIA Experiments at State Hospital”, by Louis Porter.
17. *Rutland Herald*, August 4, 1977, Judge Henry Black obituary.

18. *Rutland Herald*, August 4, 1977, "CIA Experiments Confirmed: Turner Says None Going Now," Nicholas Horrock.
19. United States Senate Select Committee on Intelligence and Subcommittee on Health and Scientific Research of the Committee on Human Resources. *Project MKULTRA: The CIA's Program of Research in Behavioral Modification.* 95th Congress, First Session, Washington, DC: GPO, 1977.
20. CIA MORI DOCID: 295498.
21. Memorandum for Director CIA, MKULTRA Notification of Unwitting Subjects, Addendum to the Final Report, 9 October, 1979. Testimony of Frank C. Conahan, Assistant Comptroller General, National Security and International Affairs Division. "Human Experimentation: An Overview of Cold War Era Programs."
22. *American Journal of Psychiatry*, July, 1961: UVM Chairman Department Psychiatry, Dr. Thomas Boag.
23. H.P. Albarelli, Jr. *A Terrible Mistake: The Murder of Frank Olson and the CIA Cold War Experiments.* Walterville, OR: Trineday, 2009.
24. Harold Abramson. *The Use of LSD in Psychotherapy.* New York: Madison Printing Co., 1960.
25. Alston Chase. *A Mind For Murder.* New York: WW Norton, 2003.
26. Rupert Chittuck, George Brooks, William Deane, & Francis Irons. *The Vermont Story: Rehabilitation of Chronic Schizophrenics.* Burlington, VT: Queen City Press, 1961.
27. Leopold Bellak. *Schizophrenia: A Review of the Syndrome.* New York: Logos Press, 1958.
28. Marsha Kincheloe & Herbert Hunt. *Empty Beds: A History of the Vermont State Hospital.* Barre, VT: Marsha Kincheloe, 1988.

29. Martin Lee & Bruce Shlain. *Acid Dreams*. New York: WW Norton, 1979.
30. John Marks. *The Search for the Manchurian Candidate*. New York: WW Norton, 1979.
31. The National Security Archives, John Marks Donation. CIA Behavioral Experiments. Washington, DC.
32. Colin A. Ross. *The C.I.A. Doctors: Human Rights Violations by Psychiatrists*. Richardson, TX: Manitou Communications, 2006.
33. Huston Smith. *Forgotten Truth: The Primordial Tradition*. New York: Harper and Row, 1976.
34. Harvey Weinstein. *A Father, A Son and the CIA*. Toronto: James Lorimer and Co, 1988.
35. Blink Films, London, England. *The Real Bourne Identity*. Smithsonian Channel, May, 2010.
36. *Counterpoint Newspaper*, Vermont Psychiatric Survivors, article, "The Untold Vermont Story," by Karen Wetmore, December, 2011.
37. Medical Records: Mary Fletcher Hospital, September 1965 - October 1965.
38. Medical Records: Vermont State Hospital. October 1965-66.
39. Medical Records: Rutland Hospital. November, 1970.
40. Medical Records: Vermont State Hospital, 1970 - 1972.
41. Medical Records: Degoesbriand Neurology Unit. Medical Center Hospital of Vermont. June, 1971 – July, 1971.
42. Medical Records: Baird 6, Medical Center Hospital of Vermont. July 1971-October 1971.
43. Medical Records: Vermont State Hospital. October 1971 - September. 1972.
44. Rutland Court documents contained in VSH Medical records.

45. Letter from Jonathan Leopold, Vermont Commissioner of Mental Health to Dorothy Wetmore, February, 1971.
46. Rockland Project, ISD-MSIS - Patient Biographical and Clinical Update Data. December 30, 1970; February, 1971; April, 1971.
47. CIA Behavior Control Experiments, John Marks Collection, National Security Archives, Washington, DC. MKULTRA Subprojects, 8, 10, 10A, 63, 66 (Hyde); Mass Mental Health, Society for Biological Psychiatry, Manfred Sakel Fund membership lists; PROJECT OFTEN, MORI ID 146136, Use of Metrazol for Interrogations, Negation of LSD.
48. Wetmore vs. State of Vermont, et al. November 1998 - May 2002.
49. Additional documents including Vermont Department of Mental Health Biennial Reports, 1962-1970 and a 1963 declassified CIA document: An invitation list issued by M.I.T. for a conference on LSD.
50. Robert Hyde's more fully declassified CIA MKULTRA Subprojects 8, 10, 63 and 66.
51. Letter from Phil Fass to Alan George (Karen Wetmore) 1999.

Interviews, Correspondence and Other Sources

52. Telephone Communications, Former Staff from1965, Mary Fletcher Hospital Psychiatric unit.
53. Former Staff, from 1971, Baird 6, Medical Center Hospital of Vermont.
54. Governor Phil Hoff, 2009.
55. Staff Vermont Public Records Division, Middlesex, Vermont.
56. Dr. Frederick Curlin, 1998.
57. Jane Youngbaer, 2009, 2011.
58. Janice Pitch, Staff, National Security Archives.

59. Senator Bernie Sanders' Burlington Office, Gretchen Bailey.
60. Senator Patrick Leahy, Burlington Office.
61. Senator Diane Feinstein Office, Washington, DC.
62. FBI Office, Rutland, Vermont.
63. FBI Office, Albany, New York.
64. NIMH, NIH, USPHS, HHS, DOJ, DOE, FDA, DOD, Brooks Air Force Base, UVM Office of General Counsel, Thomas Meccurio.
65. Vermont Commissioner Mental Health, Michael Hartman.
66. Central Intelligence Agency, 2000-2009.
67. Department of Defense.
68. Social Security Administration, St. Louis, Missouri.
69. Rockland State Hospital, Orangeburg, New York.
70. Postal Inspector Mark Cavic, Essex Junction, Vermont.
71. Postal Inspection Agency, Boston, Massachusetts.
72. Postmaster, Rutland, Vermont.
73. Fairpoint Communications, Verizon, NYNEX.
74. Department of the Navy.
75. Vermont Attorney General Office, staff, May 2008.
76. Vermont Department Mental Health.
77. Vermont Department Health.
78. Vermont State Hospital.
79. George Albee.
80. Vermont Records Act Request, October 7, 2013.
81. Reply from Vermont Records Act Request, October 16, 2013.
82. FOIA Request to CIA, October 24, 2013.
83. CIA response to FOIA, November 15, 2013.
84. Vermont State Archives and Records Administration, Series VSH - 003, VSH-0011-2, Director of Research, Dr. Robert W. Hyde, 1940-1975, VSH-0011-3, Director of Research, Dr. Robert W. Hyde, 1943-1975.